Anthems of Resistance

Ali Husain Mir and Raza Mir grew up in Hyderabad on a steady diet of progressive Urdu poetry. They divide their time between India and the US and earn their living as university professors.

OTHER INDIAINK TITLES

Anjana Basu	*Black Tongue*
Anjana Basu	*Chinku and the Wolfboy*
Anjum Hasan	*Neti, Neti*
Anuradha Majumdar	*Infinity Paper: A mysterious quest, an unforgettable adventure*
A.N.D. Haksar	*Madhav & Kama: A Love Story from Ancient India*
Boman Desai	*Servant, Master, Mistress*
Chitra Banerjee Divakaruni	*Shadowland*
Claudine Le Tourneur d'lson	*Hira Mandi*
C.P. Surendran	*An Iron Harvest*
Haider Warraich	*The Auras of the Jinn*
I. Allan Sealy	*The Everest Hotel*
I. Allan Sealy	*Trotternama*
Indrajit Hazra	*The Garden of Earthly Delights*
Jaspreet Singh	*17 Tomatoes: Tales from Kashmir*
Jawahara Saidullah	*The Burden of Foreknowledge*
John MacLithon	*Hindutva, Sex & Adventure*
Kalpana Swaminathan	*The Page 3 Murders*
Kalpana Swaminathan	*The Gardener's Song*
Kamalini Sengupta	*The Top of the Raintree*
Madhavan Kutty	*The Village Before Time*
Pankaj Mishra	*The Romantics*
Paro Anand	*Pure Sequence*
Rakesh Satyal	*Blue Boy*
Ranjit Lal	*Bambi Chops and Wags*
Ranjit Lal	*The Life &Times of Altu-Faltu*
Ranjit Lal	*The Small Tigers of Shergarh*
Ranjit Lal	*The Simians of South Block and Yumyum Piglets*
Sanjay Bahadur	*The Sound of Water*
Sanjay Bahadur	*Hul: Cry Rebel!*
Selina Sen	*A Mirror Greens in Spring*
Shandana Minhas	*Tunnel Vision*
Sharmistha Mohanty	*New Life*
Shree Ghatage	*Brahma's Dream*
Sudhir Thapliyal	*Crossing the Road*
Sumedha Verma Ojha	*Urnabhih*
Susan Visvanathan	*Nelycinda and Other Stories*
Susan Visvanathan	*The Visiting Moon*
Susan Visvanathan	*The Seine at Noon*
Tanushree Podder	*Escape from Harem*

FORTHCOMING TITLES

Lavanya Shanbaoug	*An Imperial Friend*
Tanushree Podder	*On the Double*

a celebration of
Progressive Urdu Poetry

Anthems of Resistance

Raza Mir
Ali Husain Mir

 *IndiaInk*

First published in 2006
Third impression 2014

IndiaInk
An imprint of
Roli Books Pvt. Ltd.
M-75, Greater Kailash-II Market
New Delhi 110 048
Phones: ++91 (011) 4068 2000, Fax: ++91 (011) 2921 7185
E-mail: info@rolibooks.com; Website: www.rolibooks.com
Also at
Bengaluru, Chennai, Kolkata & Mumbai

Cover design: Sneha Pamneja
Layout: Narendra Shahi
Calligraphy of Urdu verses: Azeem Saheb and Faheem Saheb

ISBN: 978-81-86939-26-0

Typeset in Century Schoolbook by Roli Books Pvt. Ltd.
and printed at Repro India Ltd., Mumbai.

CONTENTS

ACKNOWLEDGEMENTS

It has been a wonderful life, thanks to strokes of fortunes, inherited privileges, deliberate choices and chance encounters. Not to mention a loving family, extraordinary companions, strong comrades, amazing friends. If one is known by the company one keeps, then I am in good shape.

I hope that those who have touched my life in meaningful ways know how much I treasure their friendship and love. Still, since this might well be the only book I ever write, I want to acknowledge some of them in these pages.

My mother read me progressive Urdu poetry when I was very young, setting me off on a path of discovery and delight. My father's speech was peppered with wisdoms encapsulated in Urdu couplets that helped shape my instincts and my politics in remarkable ways. My sister, Syeda, fills my life with laughter, and I routinely dial her number when I need a mood boost (or instant medical advice). My brother is not merely my co-author; he is my alter ego, my doppelganger, my conscience, and my lifeline. Without them, there would be no me, let alone this book.

A blank IOU to Saadia Toor, who knows how much her sharp mind, her honed political understanding, her vast knowledge of the Progressive Movement in Urdu literature, and her ready willingness to go through drafts of this work have contributed to this volume. She should really be listed as a co-author. Thanks Toorie, for this and a lot more besides.

To those old friends from YOCs who provided the impetus to so many early intellectual voyages, *ehsaan mere dil pe tumhaara hai dosto*. Thanks to K.T. Sandip, Ashhar Farhan, Amirullah Khan, Rashid Abdul Rahman, Radhika Murthy, Rajendra Prasad, Sarita Rani, Muqtedar Khan, Preeti Parekh, Narsing Rao, Ahsan Abid and many others, whose curious minds and articulate tongues made those hundreds of verbose Saturday evenings at the Secunderabad YMCA so much more interesting than watching the weekly Hindi movie on Doordarshan.

To my companions at the University of Massachusetts without whom those graduate school years would have been so much the poorer. Diana Wong, Raju Sivasankaran, Bobby Banerjee, Aparna Sindhoor, Wayne Millette, Jayanta Dey, Vamsicharan Vakulabharanam, Kuldhir Bhati, Rajiv Kashyap, and especially Maya Yajnik were the safekeepers of my sanity and the source of my strength.

To my comrades at CSFH, who provided me with purpose during a period of the pessimism of the intellect and offered me reason to make space for an optimism of the will. I owe a lot to Raja Harish Swamy, Ra Ravishankar, Girish Agarwal, Shalini Gera, Usha Zacharias, Kamayani Swamy, Brendan Laroque, Biju Mathew, Angana Chatterji, Ashwini Rao, Mubeen Bolar, Anantkrishna Maringanti, Jayant Eranki, Ravi Rajan and others who fight the good fight.

The members of the YSS collective and others in the

'South Asian' diaspora in NYC – my political *humsafars*, my fellow party-ers, my acquired family – have taught me a lot about solidarity and commitment, and offered an endless, and often unconditional reservoir of love. If I ever find myself in a tight spot, I cannot think of a better group to have in my corner. Prerana Reddy, Ashwini Rao, Prachi Patankar, Rupal Oza, Tejasvi Nagaraja, Anjali Kamat, Ragini Shah, Sonali Sathaye, Arvind Grover, Ayaz Ahmad, Miabi Chatterjee, Amita Swadhin, Saba Waheed, Dawn Philip, Fareen Ramji, Marian Yalini Thambinayakan, Debanuj Dasgupta, Jason Da Silva, Svati Shah, Shomial Ahmad, Raju Rajan, Surabhi Kukke, Virali Gokaldas, Sam Quiah, Sonny Suchdev, Biju Mathew, Aleyamma Mathew, Linta Verghese, Naeem Mohaiemen, Leena Khan, Sekhar Ramakrishnan, Saadia Toor, Sue Susman, Aniruddha Das, Smita Narula, Balaji, Jawad Metni ... I am lucky to have found them.

My friends in India continue to make each of my frequent returns a homecoming. My love and thanks to Ashhar Farhan, Elahe Hiptoola, Aalok Wadhwa, Saleema Rizvi, Reetika Khera, Arudra Burra, Amirullah Khan, Azam Khan, Asiya Khan, Humera Ahmed, Soma Wadhwa, Bhashwati Sengupta, Sandhya Venkataraman and Shivani Choudhry.

My gratitude to those activist-friends who share the vision of the poets of this book, who work each day to bring about a socially just world, and whose contributions give me hope and heart: Aruna Roy, Nikhil De, Sowmya Kidambi, Preeti Sampat, Shankar Singh, Bhanwar Meghwanshi, Lal Singh, Chunni Singh, Dauba, Brahmachari, Shabnam Hashmi, Javed Anand, Anand Patwardhan, Teesta Setalvad, Rakesh Sharma, Anurag Singh and hundreds of others.

To those who have sustained me in ways too numerous to mention, a whole lot of love: Vijay Prashad, Sangeeta Kamat,

Amitava Kumar, Lisa Armstrong, Simona Sawhney, Christi Merrill, Chris Chekkuri, Srikanth Manjunath, Deepak Chandrasekhariah, Ahmad Karim, Shabnam Tejani, Nirupama Ravi, R. Radhakrishnan, Kerstin Schmidt, Kristy Bright, Shay McAllister, Sox Sperry, Kavita Pallav, Bhairavi Desai, Dalia Basiouny, Nagesh Kukunoor, Kamila Shamsie ...

To some very special people in my life who hopefully know how much they have meant to me over the years: Kamala Visweswaran, Syed Akbar Hyder, Ashwini Rao, Sangeeta Rao, Rupal Oza, and the incomparable Satish Kolluri.

To Sreekanth 'Loony' Bollam for an intensely loyal friendship, for shared exploits that could fill a book all on their own.

To those who made our annual 'road show' at the University of Wisconsin such a deep pleasure and showered us with their generous *wah-wahs*, my gratitude; especially to Tayyab Mahmud, C.M. Naim, Mohammad Umar Memon, Carla Petievich, Geeta Patel, David Lelyveld, Chris Lee, Frances Pritchett, Phil Lutgendorf, Ravina Agarwal, Mohsin and Farhat Haq, and the wonderful Agha Shahid Ali.

To Elahe Hiptoola for always being there, especially when I have needed her most, for the 'smiling countenance' receptions at the Hyderabad airport, for a hundred favours, big and small.

To Biju Mathew, my safety net, my political and moral compass, and my life-support system.

To Javed Akhtar and Shabana Azmi for reading the manuscript and for their support.

To Abbas and Youhanna for providing food that sustained the soul during the cold winters of the northeast. To my Ecuadorian neighbours downstairs, especially Ivan and his mother, for those stairwell conversations and for so frequently sharing their meals with me.

To Renuka Chatterjee and Nandita Bhardwaj of Roli Books for being wonderful, insightful, and patient editors. It has been a pleasure working with them.

To my large extended family whose unconditional love is a source of great strength: Mamu, Haji, Tari, Nadir, 'Mir' Mohammad, Apu, Fatti, Soghra, Narjis, Alloon, Ali Zaheer, Shabbir, Hyder, Hasan, Jawadi, Sakina, Mujju, Narjis, Sabiha, Ghazanfar, Aelia, Ali, Jawadi, Joohi, Mami, Ather 'Bhaijan', Tanveer, Masooma, Nishi, Zafar, Shazmeen, Chots, Ali Bhai, Asma, Najma. And to Hasan 'Imam', the Biradaraan, Hyder Babu.

To Mo, for his gentle energy, for his unflappable temperament, for entering our lives. To Farah, for her quiet strength, for her loving compassion, for making sure that I have a safe haven here.

Salaams to my comrades at FOIL, YSS, Ghadar, SAMAR, Awaaz, the Brecht Forum, CSFH, MKSS, the New York Taxi Workers' Alliance and others in the large community of activists and collectives who help keep me anchored and remind me that there are things greater than one's own self that are worth stuggling for.

Voh subha kabhi to aayegi.

– Ali Husain Mir

I begin by expressing my humble gratitude to the communities of Left activists in India and the US who have nurtured my politics, my ethics, and hopefully, my lyrics. Thank you comrades, for the space to laugh and cry in a world where relatedness is a tough find.

I piggyback on Ali Mir's great list of friends and relatives, and would add thanks on his behalf and mine, to I.K. Shukla,

S.M. Shahed (Mamu!) and Sultan Lateef for painstaking feedback on earlier drafts. Props too, to dear friend Tayyab Mahmud for introducing us to Habib Jalib, and to K.T. Sandip, who once forwarded me Majaz's 'Raat Aur Rel', and sent my mind on a treasure hunt that finds place in this book. Farah Hasan provided tireless assistance with turns of phrase, translations and was gentle with her comments on style. Amirullah Khan, Anu Paul, Mohammed Umar Memon, Amitava Kumar and Sundeep Dougal helped in placing earlier versions of some of the ideas in this book in the public domain. Inspiration and encouragement for this endeavour came from varied sources: we remember the late Agha Shahid Ali as an early enthusiast, and were greatly encouraged by Asif Raza, Anwar Moazzam and Jeelani Bano.

In the 'words-are-inadequate' department, *aaj ek harf ko phir dhhoondta phirta hai khayaal,* to adequately thank Zakia Sultana, our mother who read Sahir to us before we knew the Urdu script, our father Taqi Ali who treasured Josh Malihabadi more than his ancestors, our sister Syeda whose entire speech is a song unto itself, and Safdar and Sahir, who are too young to know that they have already inherited a legacy. A lot of love to that co-author as well. Finally, my *intesaab* to my wife Farah (Mem) in anticipation of a life that will be a true symbol of shared dreams and hopes. For love is the greatest form of solidarity. *Zindagi dhoop, tum ghana saaya.*

– *Raza Mir*

A NOTE ON TRANSLATION AND TRANSLITERATION

The issue of what is gained and lost in translation has been elaborately discussed in a number of places. Rather than add further to that discourse, all we want to say is that while our translation choices have been contingent and personal (aren't they always?), we have tended to err on the side of being literal rather than poetic.

A number of transliteration schemes have been developed by Urdu academics, some of them highly precise and consistent. However, they tend to be somewhat intimidating to the eye. To maintain the 'popular' flavour of the book, we have chosen to go with an informal style. For instance, a standard transliteration scheme would write this line from a Hindi film song thus: *Har fikr kō d*^{h}*ûēN mēN uṛātā čalā gayā*. We have instead transcribed it as *Har fikr ko dhueñ meiñ uḏaata chala gaya.*

We have made the following formal stylistic choices for the transliterations:

1 The nasal 'n' has been transliterated as 'ñ'. This is important because the full 'n' sound is longer than its nasal

equivalent. For example, the word for blood has to be pronounced sometimes as *khoon* (with the full 'n' sound at the end) and at others as *khooñ* (with the nasal 'n' at the end). Substituting one for the other interferes with the rhythm of the poem. We have, however, used a simple '*n*' even if the sound is nasal in the cases where it is followed by a hard consonant, since the word will invite the reader to pronounce it accurately. So the word for colour is written as *rang*, not as *rañg*.

2. The words for 'I' and 'in' have been transliterated as '*maiñ*' and '*meiñ*'.
3. 'aa' has been used to indicate the long vowel, except when the word ends with it, in which case we expect that the reader will naturally tend to draw out the sound.
4. The guttural 'kh' and 'gh' have been underlined. If 'kh' and 'gh' are not underlined in the transliterations, the 'h' sound has to be aspirated. This helps the reader differentiate between, say, *khaana* (to eat) and *khaana* (house, dwelling, room, compartment, drawer), between *ghani* (thick, dense) and *ghani* (wealthy, rich, opulent).
5. The hard 't' and 'd' sounds have been underlined to help differentiate between words like *dar* (door) and *dar* (fear), *taal* (musical measure) and *taal* (delay, evade).

A note to our fellow Hyderabadis: while we have, in the interests of the larger readership, reluctantly transliterated the two different letters of the Urdu script as *kh* and *q*, feel free to pronounce them alike, for:

Qaaf aur khai meiñ hai kya farq, hameñ kya maaloom
Hum zabaañ apni chalaane ko zabaañ kahte haiñ

PREFACE

Uṯho aur uṯh ke inhiñ qaafiloñ meiñ mil jaao
Jo manziloñ ko haiñ gard-e safar banaaye hue

Arise, and join those moving caravans
That have left several destinations in their wake

Our father's voice would boom in the small room where we slept, while we, less interested in joining caravans than in getting a little more time in bed, would try in vain to ignore it. It was his ritualistic way of waking us up every school morning. Even though the couplet was usually an unwelcome intrusion into our slumber, it planted itself firmly in our psyche, along with scores of others that routinely adorned daily conversations in our home and community. The oral tradition of Urdu poetry was an essential part of the structure of feeling of old-city Hyderabad. People unselfconsciously emphasized a point or illustrated a mood by drawing upon a couplet here and a quatrain there, to say ordinary things in extraordinary ways.

Our parents had an impressive command over a massive repertoire of classical and contemporary poetry and would harvest it periodically. Both of them had grown up during the heady days of the independence struggle, at a time when the Urdu poets of the Progressive Writers' Movement strode majestically on the stage of cultural production in the country. Josh Malihabadi, Sahir Ludhianvi, Israr-ul-Haq Majaz, Kaifi Azmi, Ali Sardar Jafri, Faiz Ahmad Faiz, Majrooh Sultanpuri, and Makhdoom Mohiuddin were household names and we learnt to appreciate the spirit of their powerful verses. Their poetry – critical, insightful, angry, passionate – helped inculcate in us a sense of social justice, mediated our understanding of reality, and offered us a framework to interpret social and political conditions.

A Faiz poem 'Lahu Ka Suraagh' (Trace of Blood) thus came to mind when an obscure statistic about 11 September 2001 caught our attention. The United Nations Food and Agriculture Organization estimated that on the same tragic day when the towers came crashing down in our adopted city of New York, around 35,615 children starved to death across the world. This everyday, routine tragedy quietly bypassed the world's consciousness. No editorials were written denouncing it, no flags flew at half-mast, no impassioned speeches were made, no war was declared on poverty and hunger. Faiz's poem compellingly drew our attention to this 'banality of evil' through the following lines:

Kahiñ nahiñ hai kahiñ bhi nahiñ lahu ka suraagh
Na dast-o naakhun-e qaatil, na aasteeñ pe nishaañ
Na surkhi-e lab-e khanjar, na rang-e nok-e sinaañ
Na khaak par koi dhabba, na baam par koi daagh
Kahiñ nahiñ hai kahiñ bhi nahiñ lahu ka suraagh

Na sarf-e khidmat-e shaahaañ ke khooñ-baha dete
Na deeñ ki nazr ke bayaana-e jaza dete

Na razmgaah meiñ barsa ke mo'atabar hota
Kisi alam pe raqam hoke mushtahar hota

Pukaarta raha be-aasra yateem lahu
Kisi to bahr-e sama'at na waqt tha na dimaagh
Na mudda'i na shahaadat hisaab paak hua
Ye khoon-e khaak-nasheenaañ tha rizq-e khaak hua

Nowhere, nowhere at all, is any trace of the Blood
Not on the murderer's hands, fingernails or sleeve
No blood reddens the tongue of the blade nor brighten the tip of the spear
No blood marks the soil or stains the rooftop
Nowhere, nowhere at all, is any trace of the Blood

This blood wasn't shed in the services of kings that it could receive recompense
Nor was it sacrificed at the altar of religion that it could be rewarded
Neither did it spill on in the battlefield that it could be honoured
Or memorialized on a battle standard

It cried out, this helpless, orphaned Blood
But none had the ability to listen, nor the time, nor the patience
No plaintiff stepped forward, no one bore witness and so the account was closed
While the blood of the dirt-dwellers seeped silently into the dirt

Faiz's verses indict all those who stand silent, indifferent to everyday human suffering. His call to action is expressed even more explicitly in 'Aaj Baazaar Meiñ Pa-bajaolaañ Chalo':

Chashm-e nam jaan-e shoreeda kaafi nahiñ
Tohmat-e ishq-e posheeda kaafi nahiñ
Aaj baazaar meiñ pa-bajaolaañ chalo

Not enough to shed tears, to suffer anguish
Not enough to nurse love in secret
Today, walk in the public square fettered in chains

This demand to declare one's politics explicitly and publicly was made at a time when Urdu poetry offered a significant space for the articulation of resistance against explotative systems – a space that seems to have shrunk considerably in our times. Today, Urdu itself occupies a precarious position in India, and while it continues to be spoken by a large number of people, it is largely exoticized as an aesthetic commodity, vilified as the language of the Other, or relegated to the realm of nostalgia. And in Pakistan, while not in any danger as a language, its progressive literary movement is a shadow of its former self, the victim of post-colonial politics at the national and international level. The voice of the progressive Urdu poets that resonated during the anti-colonial struggle, that sought to hold the newly formed state to its promise of an egalitarian and just society, and that attempted to forge a solidarity with peoples' movements across the world, is a faint memory. Sahir is now remembered mainly as a film lyricist. Faiz continues to have an iconic status, but only insofar as he has been assimilated into the tradition of the classical poets. A handful of other voices remain, some stronger than others. However, the passion and anger of Josh, Majaz, Kaifi, Makhdoom, Jafri and others who explicitly wrote about exploitation and oppression, about justice and equality, and about resistance and struggle is largely forgotten.

This book grows out of a desire to reverse this 'willful loss of memory' and to reclaim the legacy of the progressive poets in an age when their words, insights, and politics continue to be relevant. As the subtitle of the book – 'A Celebration of Progressive Urdu Poetry' – makes clear, ours is not a dispassionate, 'objective' account. It is an attempt to retrieve the spirit of resistance that once roamed so freely in the landscape of Urdu literature during the progressive writers' movement.

In that sense, this book is more than a recounting of a bygone age; it is our own political project. It is not just a history of the past, it is a history of the present, and hopefully, a history of the future as well.

Mataa-e lauh-o qalam chhin gayi to kya gham hai

Ke khoon-e dil meiñ duboli haiñ ungliyaañ maiñ ne

Zabaañ pe mohr lagi hai to kya, ke rakh di hai

Har ek halqa-e zanjeer meiñ zabaañ maiñ ne

So what if my pen has been snatched away from me

I have dipped my fingers in the blood of my heart

So what if my mouth has been sealed; I have turned

Every link of my chain into a speaking tongue

– Faiz Ahmad Faiz

1

OVER CHINESE FOOD

The Progressive Writers' Association[1]

Bhadka raheñ haiñ aag lab-e naghmagar se hum
Khaamosh kya rahenge zamaane ke dar se hum
Le de ke apne paas faqat ek nazar to hai
Kyoñ dekheñ zindagi ko kisi ki nazar se hum
Maana ke is zameeñ ko na gulzaar kar sake
Kuch khaar kam to kar diye, guzre jidhar se hum

Here we go, stoking fire through song-laden lips
The fear of the world can never staunch the flow of our words
In all, we have just one view, our own
Why should we see the world through someone else's eyes?
It is true, we did not turn the world into a garden
But at least we lessened some thorns from the paths we travelled

– Sahir Ludhianvi

On the evening of 24 November 1934, the atmosphere at London's Nanking Hotel must have been electric. A group of young Indian intellectuals were engaged in an intense discussion over a draft document that had been circulated by the convenor of the meeting, Sajjad Zaheer. The document was audacious in its scope, for it sought to articulate a manifesto for the future of Indian literature.

Some of the faces in the meeting were to become familiar personalities. Jyotirmaya Ghosh would rise to prominence as a key figure in Bengali literature. Mulk Raj Anand had already begun to gain global prominence as an English novelist. Mohammad Din Tasir was to go on to become the founder of the magazine *Nairang-i-Khayaal* in Lahore. The British writer Ralph Fox was attending in the capacity of an adviser. The fog of history has blurred the names of other attendees, but the institution that was emerging through this meeting was destined to majestically straddle the traditions of Indian literature in general and Urdu poetry in particular for a long time.

The fact that this meeting was being held in London was no accident. Rather, it was a curious outcome of the history of the colonial experience of India. Many among the gathering were students in England, who had been sent by their affluent parents to develop professional skills in areas such as law and medicine. Yet, their experiences with colonial servitude back home were fresh in their minds, and this smouldering energy was readily spurred by the emerging anti-fascist and socialist currents all over Europe. The formation of the United Front in France, the protest against the persecution of writers like Georgi Dimitrov, and the workers' rebellion in Austria in the early 1930s[2], had galvanized the attendees of the Nanking meeting. In their minds, the literary manifesto that was being discussed would serve to lay the framework for the emergence of a new, emancipated identity.

This gathering had its genesis in an interesting episode that had taken place in 1932 with the publication of a book in India called *Angaare* (Embers), a set of ten short stories written by Sajjad Zaheer, Rashid Jahan, Mahmuduzzafar and Ahmed Ali, which had attacked a whole range of sacred cows.

The stories dealt with prevailing familial and sexual mores, the decadence and hypocrisy of social and religious life in contemporary India, and took more than one potshot at religious orthodoxy, attacking it with what Ahmed Ali later referred to as 'the absence of circumspection'. Within months of its publication, the book generated an uproar within Muslim circles, and was condemned by a variety of organizations as being 'obscene' and 'blasphemous'. The All India Shia Conference, for example, passed a resolution in 1933 sharply condemning 'the heart-rending and filthy pamphlet called *Angaare* ... which has wounded the feelings of the entire Muslim community by ridiculing God and his prophets and which is extremely objectionable from the standpoint of both religion and morality.' Responding to this outcry, the Police Department of the United Provinces promulgated an order on 15 March 1933 declaring 'forfeited to his Majesty every copy of (the book) ... on the grounds that the said book contains matter the publication of which is punishable under Section 295A of the Indian Penal Code.'

The *Angaare* authors were unrepentant. Writing in the 5 April 1933 issue of *The Leader*, an Allahabad-based newspaper, Mahmuduzzafar's article 'Shall We Submit to Gagging?' declared:

> The writers of this book do not wish to make an apology for it. They leave it to float or sink of itself. They only wish to defend the right of launching it and all other vessels like it ... They have chosen (to critique) the particular field of Islam not because they bear any 'special' malice towards it, but because, being born into that particular society, they felt better qualified to speak for that alone ... Our practical purpose is the formation immediately of a league of progressive authors, which should bring forth similar

> collections from time to time, both in English and the various vernaculars of our country.

Undettered by the widespread criticism, Sajjad Zaheer, the leader of the Angaare group had set about trying to use the field of literature as a battering ram to break down the orthodox and conservative fortifications of Indian society. The Nanking Hotel gathering was a significant step in that direction.

By the end of the meeting, the attendees had resolved to formalize their group as an institution, which would be called the All India Progressive Writers' Association (henceforth, the PWA). The PWA was to be based in India, and Sajjad Zaheer volunteered to give it institutional shape in the subcontinent. By the middle of 1935, the final manifesto of the PWA was ready. Zaheer returned to India with the document and circulated it among prominent Indian literary figures. The manifesto found an immediate champion in Premchand, one of the most highly respected figures in Hindustani literature, who published its Hindi translation in the October 1935 issue of his journal *Hans* (Swan). Subsequently, the English version of the manifesto was published in the February 1936 issue of London's *Left Review.* The text of the manifesto was as follows:

> Radical changes are taking place in Indian society. Fixed ideas and old beliefs, social and political institutions are being challenged. Out of the present turmoil and conflict a new society is emerging. The spirit of reaction however, though moribund and doomed to ultimate decay, is still operative and is making desperate efforts to prolong itself.
>
> It is the duty of Indian writers to give expression to the changes taking place in Indian life and to assist in the

spirit of progress in the country. Indian literature, since the breakdown of classical literature, has had the fatal tendency to escape from the actualities of life. It has tried to find a refuge from reality in spiritualism and idealism. The result has been that it has produced a rigid formalism and a banal and perverse ideology.

Witness the mystical devotional obsession of our literature, its furtive and sentimental attitude towards sex, its emotional exhibitionism and its almost total lack of rationality. Such literature was produced particularly during the past two centuries, one of the most unfortunate periods of our history, a period of disintegrating feudalism and of acute misery and degradation for the Indian people as a whole.

It is the object of our association to rescue literature and other arts from the priestly, academic and decadent classes in whose hands they have degenerated so long; to bring the arts into the closest touch with the people; and to make them the vital organs which will register the actualities of life, as well as lead us to the future.

While claiming to be the inheritors of the best traditions of Indian civilization, we shall criticize ruthlessly, in its political, economic and cultural aspects, the spirit of reaction in our country and we shall foster through interpretive and creative work (with both native and foreign resources) everything that will lead our country to the new life for which it is striving. We believe that the new literature of India must deal with the basic problems of our existence today – the problems of hunger and poverty, social backwardness and political subjugation, so that it may help us to understand these problems and through such understanding help us to act.

With the above aims in view, the following resolutions have been adopted:

1. The establishment of organizations of writers to correspond to the various linguistic zones of India; the co-ordinations of these organizations by holding conferences, publishing of magazines, pamphlets, etc.
2. To cooperate with those literary organizations whose aims do not conflict with the basic aims of the association.
3. To produce and translate literature of a progressive nature and of a high technical standard; to fight cultural reaction; and in this way, to further the cause of Indian freedom and social regeneration.
4. To strive for the acceptance of a common language (Hindustani) and a common script (Indo-Roman) for India.
5. To protect the interests of authors; to help authors who require and deserve assistance for the publication of their works.
6. To fight for the right of free expression of thought and opinion.

The manifesto was unabashedly modernist and anti-religious in its tenor, and utilized a left-liberal vocabulary that was popular at that time. It sought to play an integrative role in the Indian literary landscape through the acceptance of a common language and script. It made a case for building international solidarities. Importantly, it emphasized realism, with its insistence that literature be used as a tool to display the 'actualities of life'. Finally, despite the stridency of its tone, it sought to leave the door open for coalitions with other literary groups 'whose aims do not conflict with the basic aims of the association'. The manifesto was an astute political document, and a highly ambitious one that sought to position the PWA as the harbinger of revolutionary changes in the literary landscape of India.

The publication of this manifesto had a huge impact, especially in Urdu literary circles. The ideas it espoused were, however, not entirely new. Just a year earlier, a young literary critic named Akhtar Husain Raipuri had published an essay called 'Adab aur Zindagi' (Literature and Life), in which he had attempted to analyse the entire corpus of Urdu literature, and had denounced all works of fiction and poetry that did not directly link themselves to the material conditions of the society in which they were produced. Raipuri's essay in some measure made the manifesto easier to sell to Urdu literary figures, just as Premchand's support (and subsequent endorsements by the Hindi poets Sumitranandan Pant, Maithilisharan Gupt and Suryakant Tripathi 'Nirala'[3]) succeeded in broadening the horizon of the PWA's influence.

Stalwarts of Indian literature like Mohammad Iqbal and Rabindranath Tagore also provided legitimacy to the PWA through their approval, and eventually Urdu poets like Hasrat Mohani, Josh Malihabadi, and Firaq Gorakhpuri also joined it, as did the Telugu poet Sri Sri, the Gujarati poet Umashankar Joshi, the Punjabi writer Gurbaksh Singh and the Marathi writer Anna Bhau Sathe. The PWA's anti-colonialist reputation was enhanced and its credentials endorsed by the fact that the British government expressed its deep suspicion of the group. On 7 September 1936, the Home Secretary of India sent a private circular[4] to relevant authorities, which read:

> I am directed to address you in connection with an organisation known as the Progressive Writers' Association ... The proclaimed aims of the association are comparatively innocent and suggest that it concerns itself solely with the organisation of journalists and writers and the promotion of interest in literature of a progressive nature. The inspiration however comes from ...

> organisations and individuals who are ... advocating policies akin to those of the communists ... I am desired to suggest therefore, that suitable opportunities may be taken to convey, preferably in conversations, friendly warnings about this association to journalists, educationists and others who may be attracted by its ostensible programmes.

It appeared that the PWA had perceptively tapped into the groundswell of a great upheaval in Indian society. The first all-India meeting of the PWA was held at Lucknow in 1936, and was presided over by Premchand, whose inaugural address *Sahitya Ka Uddeshya* (The Purpose of Literature) remains one of the most important documents of the movement[5]. The manifesto of the association was reworked to make it more inclusive of those whose politics were not avowedly socialist. Further the demand for a common language and script for Indian literature was dropped, reflecting the political realities of the country's multilingual structure.

The Hindi version of the manifesto also attempted to articulate a definition of 'Progressive' which could accommodate a wide spectrum of views and attract as many people as possible, and included the following additional paragraph:

> All those things which take us toward confusion, dissension, and blind imitation are conservative; also, all that which engenders in us a critical capacity, which induces us to test our dear traditions on the touchstone of our reason and perception, which makes us healthy and produces among us the strength of unity and integration, that is what we call Progressive.

From its very inception, the PWA had a group of committed socialists at its core but its larger membership was not limited to writers of any particular political persuasion. In fact, it was consciously opened out to include all writers who shared the manifesto's basic commitments. The PWA thus functioned as an umbrella under which progressive writers of all stripes could find a place. The PWA understood its mission to be that of constructing a 'united front' of writers against imperialism and reactionary social tendencies, and for a life-affirming art. For the longest time then, *taraqqi-pasandi* or 'progressivism' in Urdu literature was justifiably identified with the PWA. Never before had writers across India been mobilized around a single platform so effectively, and in no previous movement[6] had a literary school so redefined the terms of its creative output and its engagement with its society and times.

***

While the inaugural meeting of the PWA was a huge success and included representative literary figures from many language groups, the longevity of the association and its legacy is primarily linked with Urdu literature, and particularly with Urdu poetry. Progressive poetry in Urdu already had a long tradition of progressivism and an inherited iconoclasm. The Progressives[7] were eager to push this in newer directions while retaining the link with their past. An editorial penned by Sibte Hasan, Ali Sardar Jafri and Israr-ul-Haq Majaz for the inaugural issue of *Naya Adab* (New Literature) claimed that 'Progressive literature does not break off relations with old literature; it embodies the best traditions of the old and constructs new edifices on the foundations of these traditions. In fact, progressive literature is the most trustworthy guardian and heir of ancient literature.'

The progressive poets sought to keep the link with tradition alive, while forging fresh paths. Faiz illustrates this mood by deploying a Ghalib couplet in his poem 'Khatm Hui Baarish-e Sang' (The Rain of Stones Ends), adding himself and the other poets of his generation to the lineage of those in whose hands Urdu poetry had flourished:

Koo-e jaanaañ meiñ khula mere lahu ka parcham
Dekhiye dete haiñ kis-kis ko sada mere baad
'Kaun hota hai hareef-e mai-e mard-afgan-e ishq
Hai mukarrar lab-e saaqi pe sala mere baad'

The bloodied flag of my love unfurls on the street of my beloved
Let us see who follows in my footsteps
'Who will now drink the hemlock of love
The question lingers on the wine bearer's lips after I have gone'

The Progressive Movement in Urdu poetry also thrived because it spoke to its time, its history and its politics. The anti-imperialist struggle, the Second World War, the trauma of Partition, the Telangana uprising, and the failure of the new nation to deliver on its promise of a better life for all citizens, all allowed these poets to speak in a voice that resonated with the aspirations of the people. As Sahir writes:

Chalo ke aaj sabhi paayemaal roohoñ se
Kaheñ ke apne har ek zakhm ko zabaañ kar deñ
Hamaara raaz hamaara nahiñ, sabhi ka hai
Chalo ke saare zamaane ko raazdaañ kar deñ

Come let us ask all oppressed souls
To give voice to their wounds
Our secret is not merely ours
Let's share it with the entire world

The progressive Urdu poets, partly by accident and partly by choice, also staked a substantial claim in the realm of popular culture, particularly in the arena of Hindi films. Several poets of the association such as Sahir Ludhianvi, Kaifi Azmi, and Majrooh Sultanpuri (and to a lesser extent, Ali Sardar Jafri and Jan Nisar Akhtar) made a name for themselves writing lyrics for films, thus occupying a prominent place in the public space. While many factors, some detailed in the rest of this book, combined to produce the ascendancy of the progressive sentiment in Urdu poetry, the incontrovertible fact, shared even by the strongest detractors of the Progressives, is that the PWA became, in Aijaz Ahmad's words the 'strongest and proximate shaping force' in Urdu literature from its very inception and very soon became ideologically hegemonic 'to the extent that it defined the parameters of the broad social agenda and cultural consensus among the generality of Urdu writers, including those who were not members of the association; those who did not subscribe to the broad consensus were relegated to the fringes of the writing-community.'[8] This hegemony, Ahmad reminds us, obviously 'did not materialize out of thin air', being 'in its own time, part and parcel of the national movement'.

After Independence: The All India Progressive Writers' Association

The PWA, whose dominance had been established during the freedom struggle and its radicalizing compact, soon found itself under attack after the formation of the independent state. By the early 1950s, the cultural consensus that the PWA had generated had begun to wither away. There were a number of factors that contributed to this decline. The biggest of these, of course, was the partition of the nation. The promised independence arrived, but its *surḵẖi* (redness) was not that of the awaited socialist 'red dawn' but came from the blood of the victims of the violence that accompanied the division of the country. And hardly had the new government found its feet when it launched a brutally repressive attack against the peasant movement of Telangana, which had held out such a high hope to the socialist aspirations of the PWA poets. Referring to the state violence that crushed the movement, Krishen Chander wrote: 'After Telangana, our dreams were singed, our hope was dead within our breasts, this was our darkest hour. Our frustration and desperation led to finger-pointing, internal fighting, literary purges, and the disintegration of our movement.'

The Progressives also had to come to terms with the growing communalization of the polity, an issue that became increasingly urgent after the Partition of the country along religious lines. An unfortunate corollary was the communalization of Urdu itself in India. Urdu suffered a debilitating blow when it became identified as the language of Pakistan, and by specious extension, the language of Muslims, resulting in, among other things, a loss of state patronage, particularly in the north, leading a bitter Sahir to comment on the centenary celebration of Ghalib's birth:

Jin shahroñ meiñ goonji thi G͟halib ki nava barsoñ
Un shahroñ meiñ aaj Urdu be-naam-o nashaañ t͟hahri
Aazaadi-e kaamil ka ailaan hua jis din
Ma'atoob zabaañ t͟hahri, g͟haddaar zabaañ t͟hahri

Jis ahd-e siyaasat ne ye zinda zabaañ kuchli
Us ahd-e siyaasat ko marhoomoñ ka g͟ham kyooñ hai
G͟halib jise kahte haiñ Urdu hi ka shaayar tha
Urdu pe sitam dha kar, G͟halib pe karam kyoñ hai

The same cities where once Ghalib's voice resounded
Have now disavowed Urdu, made it homeless

The day that announced the arrival of freedom
Also declared Urdu a cursed and treacherous language

The same government that once crushed a living tongue
Now wishes to mourn and honour the dead
The man you call Ghalib was a poet of Urdu
Why praise Ghalib after suppressing his language?

The process of communalization did not entirely bypass the PWA either. In his book, *Taraqqi Pasand Adab* (Progressive Literature), Ali Sardar Jafri, one of the chief ideologues of the association admits that by 1949, extremism and narrow-mindedness of a sort had entered the movement: 'The Partition and the communal riots so impaired the conditions that some progressive writers moved away from progressivism, some became partisans of communalism and fell in the pit of decadence.'

Eventually, the All India PWA did not find itself equal to the task of dealing with the changing times and the association became a shadow of its former self. It is, however, unfair to seek the reasons for this decline within the association alone. The period of the 1930s and beyond was characterized by the resistance of dominated subjectivities to the ravages of oppressive and exploitative colonialism. The mass movements engendered by the anti-colonial struggle created the conditions under which the analytical categories of socialism along with their attendant binaries – oppressor/oppressed, exploiter/exploited, capital/labour, capitalist/worker – found ready and broad acceptance.

But the exuberance of the victory of independence, dampened to a considerable degree by the horrors of Partition, slowly turned into disillusionment with the nation-state, which was increasingly seen as a puppet of monopoly capital and as a system that replicated earlier modes of exploitation, merely replacing foreign elites with local ones. Over a period of time, this disillusionment made way for resignation under the steady onslaught of transformed politics, opportunistic leadership, and the growth and consolidation of global capital.

In this context, the decline of the PWA can be seen not so much as a defeat of the Progressives as the withering away of an ideological formation accompanied by a 'willed loss of memory'. The hope of a revolutionary transformation, kept alive for a while, faded with each blow to socialist movements in India and elsewhere, culminating with the break-up of the Soviet Union. Writing on the day the Soviet flag was replaced by the individual flags of the various republics, Ali Sardar Jafri penned a dirge, which while mourning the current moment, seemed to be an obituary of the PWA itself.

Alvida ai surkh parcham, surkh parcham alvida
Ai nishaan-e azm-e mazloomaan-e aalam alvida
Deeda-e purnam ne kal dil se kaha tha marhaba
Aaj lekin kah rahi hai chashm-e purnam alvida
Razmgaah-e khair-o shar meiñ yaad aayegi teri
Haañ maiñ ab aur lashkar-e Iblees-e Aazam alvida
Ai furaat-e tishnakaamaan-e jihaad-e zindagi
Khulzum-e tishnaalabi ki mauj-e barham alvida

Farewell O Red Flag, Red Flag farewell
Farewell, O symbol of the dynasty of the oppressed
Till yesterday, my brimming eyes cheered you on
Today, these eyes filled with tears, bid you farewell
You will be missed in the battles between good and evil
Today I find myself alone in the fight against the Great Satan, farewell
O, the river that slaked the thirst of the martyrs in the struggle of life
O, eager waves that fed the parched ones, farewell

After Independence: The All Pakistan Progressive Writers' Association

Independence brought about several changes in the cultural and political landscape of the nations of India and Pakistan, many of which had significant implications for the Progressives. For one, the Partition divided the Urdu literary community into two, even if it did not rupture its shared secular character[9]. Although this community was reconstituted to the degree possible given the constraints of the new political context – writers from both sides continued to publish in each other's magazines and take part in important intellectual debates – there were fresh political challenges and new ideological divides to be dealt with.

Soon after Independence, the progressive writers of Pakistan set about producing explicit critiques of the new, and in their mind neocolonial, state, which were published in several newspapers and periodicals under the umbrella of Progressive Papers Limited (PPL), a holding company that was set up by Mian Iftikharuddin, a staunch socialist. The establishment, in turn, launched an assault on the Left through a multi-pronged strategy: discrediting the socialist vision by using the Cold War propaganda, presenting the Progressives as Fifth columnists and enemies of the Pakistani nation-state and consolidating the ideological front against them within the literary cultural sphere. These measures were backed by the coercive power of the state which was increasingly directed against progressive publications and members of the association. Meetings were regularly disrupted, publications proscribed and activists imprisoned. One of the most egregious of these repressive measures was the arrest and trial of Faiz Ahmad Faiz and Sajjad Zaheer (who had been deputed by the CPI to help with the movement in Pakistan) in the Rawalpindi Conspiracy Case in 1951. Faiz and Zaheer, along with some senior army officers such as Major Ishaq, were charged with conspiring to overthrow the government and spent several years in prison. These actions laid the foundation for the ultimate banning of the Communist Party of Pakistan (CPP) and its various fronts in 1954.

The progressive critique of the Muslim League government and the class interests it represented began almost as soon as Pakistan was formally established. The line taken by the Pakistani Left was strident in tone and aggressive in its demands[10]. With the ascendancy of the new Ranadive doctrine within the CPI, the old 'united front' policy of class collaboration against imperialism was abandoned in favour of an explicitly anti-capitalist line[11]. Since the CPP was not established till the Second Communist Party of India Congress in 1948, the Progressive Writers' Association was the only organized platform for ideological work available to Pakistani leftists and thus acquired great significance.

Although the All Pakistani Progressive Writers' Association (APPWA) did not technically exist until its formal establishment during the 1949 conference, individual branches of the association had started functioning immediately after the Partition in both Lahore and Karachi, while newer branches continued to be established in other towns and cities of the new state. The PPL provided an institutional platform for the Pakistani Left, particularly for its progressive writers. The staff list of PPL newspapers and periodicals read like a membership list of the PWA. Faiz Ahmad Faiz was the editor-in-chief, Mazhar Ali Khan was appointed as the editor of the *Pakistan Times,* Ahmad Nadeem Qasmi edited *Imroze*, while *Lail-o-Nihaar* was Sibte Hasan's domain. The crucial role played by PPL as a platform for the Pakistani Left, especially after the ban on the CPP and the APPWA, is evident from the fact that one of General Ayub Khan's first acts after the October 1958 coup was to take over the company and establish its publications into organs of the *sarkari* (official) voice.

The Ranadive line found expression in the rhetoric and tactics of the progressive writers even before APPWA was formally consolidated into one all-Pakistan association in November 1949. The progressive critique of the Pakistani state, and its call for a literature of a socialist revolution became more and more explicit, especially in the articles published in the major progressive magazines of this period – *Savera, Naqush, Sang-e Meel* and *Adab-e Latif.* The more radical members of the APPWA – Safdar Mir, Sibte Hasan, Hajra Masroor, Ahmad Nadeem Qasmi, Abdullah Malik, Arif Abdul Mateen, Zaheer Kashmiri, Mumtaz Hussain, Khadija Mastoor, among others – came to be known as the 'Savera group'.

The new 'take no prisoners' stance of the Communist Party was a significant departure from the earlier strategy of the United Front, which was now seen as a form of collaboration. While this move has been often read by critics as the reason for the 'isolation' of the communists in Pakistan and for the ban placed on the APPWA, the Pakistani Progressives took what they believed was the only possible principled stance within the new neocolonial context. The fact that they ultimately could not hold out against the state power, at least in the organizational context, should not be understood as a 'failure' on their part. Given the domestic and international political re-alignments which followed Independence, it is worth noting that the Progressives were the only ones who consistently articulated a significant critique of the elitist establishment.

Although the loss of organizational and institutional platforms was clearly a severe blow to the Left, it is incorrect to assume that the ban marks the 'death' of the Progressive Movement in Pakistani literature. This has clearly not been the case, as several generations of Pakistani writers and poets have demonstrated, from Habib Jalib and Ahmad Faraz in the 1960s and 1970s to the feminist poets such as Kishwar Naheed and Fehmida Riyaz in the 1980s and later. Besides, arguments about the 'decline' of the Progressive Movement in Pakistan are tenable only if one looks in the wrong places. By all accounts, progressive poetry in Pakistan is alive and well – it's just not where people expect it to be (or only there). For example, the progressive voice in Pakistan is increasingly to be found in non-Urdu literary spaces such as Sindhi, Punjabi and Hindko. Just as importantly, the progressive voice in Urdu literature can no longer be identified with one literary group or faction. Although socialism may no longer be the frame of reference, the progressive sentiment infuses, informs, and some would say, dominates a significant part of Urdu literary production in Pakistan even today. This is the legacy of a generation of writers, who against all odds, stood up to the state and the establishment, often paying a heavy personal price in the process.

In December 1980 the Karachi Press Club, directly flouting the orders of the Zia-ul-Haq government, organized a gathering under the stewardship of Sibte Hasan to felicitate Habib Jalib. Jalib had a long-standing and hard-earned reputation as a firebrand who had opposed military dictatorships for years. After all, this was the same courageous poet whose verses had defined the anger of the people at Ayub Khan's constitution in 1962. Jalib's words, simple and ringing, had framed the dissent against dictatorship in Pakistan thus:

Deep jis ka mahallaat hi meiñ jale
Chand logoñ ki khushiyoñ ko le kar chale
Voh jo saaye meiñ har maslehat ke pale
Aise dastoor ko, subh-e benoor ko
Maiñ nahiñ maanta! Maiñ nahiñ jaanta!

A lamp that sheds light only on palaces
That caters to the whims of a chosen few
That flourishes in the shadow of compromise
This system, this light-starved morning
I do not accept!

Jalib who was imprisoned several times, including during the Zia regime, had only recently been released from jail. Far from being tempered by his punishment, the Avaami Shaayar (Poet of the People) began with a characteristically hard-hitting *nazm* that attacked the dictator through a clever but obvious parody that played on the word *zia* (Light), contrasting it with *zulmat* (Darkness):

Zulmat ko 'Zia', sarsar ko saba, bande ko khuda kya likhna? Kya likhna?
Patthar ko gohar, deewaar ko dar, jugnu ko diya kya likhna? Kya likhna?
Ek hashr bapa hai ghar ghar meiñ, dum ghut-ta hai gumbad-e be-dar meiñ
Ek shaqs ke haathoñ muddat se rusva hai vatan duniya bhar meiñ
Ai deedavaro, is zillat ko, qismat ka likha kya likhna?Kya likhna?

Why refer to Darkness as Light, write of a rustle as if it is the wind,
Or of a man as if he is God? Why?
Why call a stone a diamond, a door a wall
Why write that a firefly is a lamp? Why?
A cry of grief rises in every house, we are smothered in this airless tomb
One man's actions have shamed our country all over the world
We who can see, why should we consider this humiliation
Is but our written fate? Why?

All that remains of that December 1980 meeting is a scratchy audiotape, but the recording still resounds with the voice of resistance and the determination of struggle. Jalib's characteristic sarcasm is on ample display in his poem skewering the rulers of Pakistan and their subservience to the new imperialist order:

Firangi ka jo maiñ darbaan hota
To jeena kis qadar aasaan hota
Mere bachche bhi Amreeka meiñ padte
Maiñ har garmi meiñ Inglistaan hota
Meri English bala ki chust hoti
Bala se jo na Urdudaan hota
Jhuka ke sar ko ho jaata jo Sir *maiñ*
To leader *bhi azeem-ush shaan hota*
Zameeneñ meri har soobe meiñ hoti
Maiñ wallaah sadr-e Pakistaan hota

Had I too been a courtier of the imperialists
Life would have been a piece of cake
My children too would have studied in America
And every summer would have been spent in England
My English would be devilishly clever
Had I not been a lowly Urdu waala
Had I bowed my head for a knighthood
I too would have been called an exalted leader
I would have owned lands in every region
By God! I could have been the President of Pakistan!

Another poet who has kept the progressive sentiment blazing is Ahmad Faraz, who despite being imprisoned and exiled during Zia's regime continued to compose poems about the importance of freedom, dignity and struggle. Using the aesthetic popularized by the earlier Progressives, Faraz writes:

Raat ke jaañ-guzaar zulmat meiñ
Azm ki mash'aleñ jalaae hue
Dil meiñ lekar baghaavatoñ ke sharaar
Vahshatoñ ke muheeb saaye meiñ
Sar-bakaf, jaañ-balab, nigaah-ba-qasr

Surkh-o khoonee alam uthhaaye hue
Badh rahe haiñ junooñ ke aalam meiñ
Chand naadaan, chand deevaane

In the murderous darkness
Having lit the torches of their determination
Carrying the sparks of rebellion in their hearts
In the intimidating shadows of danger
Heads high, lives on their lips, and eyes on the palace
Carrying red, bloodstained banners
They march with frenzy
Those foolish ones, those mad ones

Despite the opposition they faced from the establishment, the Progressives made a deep impact on the people of Pakistan, particularly its workers and peasants. When the APPWA held its first All Pakistan Conference in Lahore in 1949, it faced significant harassment by the state and its allies within the 'civil society'. Goons and stooges led by Sarosh Kashmiri (the editor of the weekly *Chataan,* and a diehard opponent of the progressive writers) tried to disrupt the proceedings. Hameed Akhtar recalls that, unfortunately for the hirelings, the gathering was attended by a large number of peasants carrying their traditional lathis. Since the gatecrashers were not prepared for this opposition, they were easily routed. The conference ended with the speakers and the guests escorted down the Mall Road accompanied by their impromptu guards!

Bol, Ke Lab Aazaad Hain Tere

The PWA went through a life cycle of birth, rapid growth, and eventual decline and an examination of this process reveals a lot about Urdu and its engagement with issues of nationalism, class, religion and social justice. The association's insistence on a progressive social sensibility was so powerful that it created a near-consensus in the field of Urdu literary production for several decades, dominating the literary agenda of its times despite the obstacles it faced. The Progressives fashioned a new poetic tradition, turning the conventional metaphors of *shama-parwaana* (flame-moth), *firaaq-visaal* (separation-union) and *husn-ishq* (beauty-love) on their heads in the service of a new aesthetic of social change. Instead of writing ghazals about pining lovers, they penned popular poems to celebrate progress and modernity. Instead of elegies to Majnoon and Farhad, they composed dirges about martyred revolutionaries like Patrice Lumumba and Martin Luther King. The rival in love *(raqeeb)* was recast not as a hated figure but as a fellow combatant in a revolutionary cause. The playful iconoclasm of the godless was transformed into a no-holds barred attack on the orthodoxy and conservatism of religious practices.

The only serious literary (and ultimately political, since the absence of politics is a kind of politics in itself) opposition to it was the literary tendency known as *jadidiyat* (a more or less direct and self-conscious translation of 'modernism' – as an aesthetic and formal/stylistic movement/preoccupation). The Jadidiyat Movement in Urdu literature that came to the fore after independence was represented by the Halqa-e Arbaab-e Zauq – the Association of the Aesthetes – which was established in opposition to the PWA's demand that writers use their works to fulfil a social responsibility. Notwithstanding this difference, there was a considerable overlap between the PWA and the Halqa, both in terms of membership and ideology, especially on the issues of nationalism and secularism.

Even though the Progressive Writers' Association eventually collapsed, the Progressive Movement it fostered and the ideals it espoused dominated literary production for most of the century and remain popular to this day. The Progressives actively engaged in the process of creating a community of writers and poets which saw itself not merely as a group that produced art for art's sake but as one that engaged with the issues of the times in order to make an intervention in the cause of egalitarianism and justice. It was a community that was not based on an inherited or imposed identity, but one that was founded on the basis of ideologies and praxis, one that believed in the possibility of a just society, and one that consistently and courageously spoke truth to power; sentiments that find voice in Faiz's poem 'Bol' (Speak):

Bol ke lab aazaad haiñ tere
Bol zabaañ ab tak teri hai
Tera sutvaañ jism hai tera
Bol ke jaañ ab tak teri hai

Dekh ke aahangar ki dukaañ meiñ
Tund haiñ sholay, surkh hai aahan
Khulne lage qufloñ ke dahaane
Phaila har ek zanjeer ka daaman

Bol ye thoda waqt bahut hai
Jism-o zabaañ ki maut se pehle
Bol ke sach zinda hai ab tak
Bol jo kuch kahna hai, kah le

Speak, for your lips are still free
Speak, for your tongue is still yours
Your body, though frail, is still yours
Speak, for your life is still yours

Look, in the blacksmith's workshop
The flames are hot, the steel is red
The mouths of the locks are beginning to open
The links of chains are coming undone

Speak, for the little time you have is enough

متاعِ لوح و قلم چھن گئی تو کیا غم ہے
کہ خونِ دل میں ڈبو لی ہیں اُنگلیاں میں نے
زباں پہ مُہر لگی ہے تو کیا کہ رکھ دی ہے
ہر ایک حلقۂ زنجیر میں زباں میں نے

بھڑکا رہے ہیں آگ لبِ نغمہ گر سے ہم
خاموش کیا رہیں گے زمانے کے ڈر سے ہم
لے دے کے اپنے پاس فقط اِک نظر تو ہے
کیوں دیکھیں زندگی کو کسی کی نظر سے ہم
مانا کہ اِس جہاں کو نہ گلزار کر سکے
کچھ خار کم تو کر دیتے گُزرے جدھر سے ہم

دِیپ جس کا محلّات ہی میں جلے
چند لوگوں کی خوشیوں کو لے کر چلے
وہ جو سائے میں ہر مصلحت کے پلے
ایسے دستور کو صُبحِ بے نُور کو
مَیں نہیں مانتا مَیں نہیں جانتا

2

URDU POETRY AND THE PROGRESSIVE AESTHETIC

Before your body and tongue die
Speak, for truth still lives
Speak up, say that which you must!

Fan jo naadaar tak nahiñ pahuncha
Apne meyaar tak nahiñ pahuncha

The art that doesn't reach the poor
Has not achieved its potential

– Sahir Ludhianvi

The issue of 'people's art' has occupied scholars, thinkers, philosophers and activists of the Left for over a hundred years[12]. A variety of questions have been raised in this connection: What constitutes people's art? What is the role of art in provoking social change? At what level of simplicity or complexity must art be pitched to the people? If new society is born out of the old, is new culture too born out of the old? Are elements of a proletarian culture and civilization already present in the bourgeois epoch? If so, what does this imply for those who are engaged in organizing the working class? Is there a need for cultural organizations of the proletariat along with economic and political ones? What should art-as-doctrine look like?

These were some of the questions that engaged the artists of the Progressive Writers' Association (PWA), which in its 1935 manifesto had promised to 'rescue literature and other arts from the priestly, academic and decadent classes in whose hands they have degenerated so long; to bring the arts into the closest touch with the people ... (to) deal with the basic problems of our existence today – the problems of hunger and poverty, social backwardness and political subjugation, so that it may help us to understand these problems and through such understanding help us to act.'

The PWA borrowed heavily from a discourse that had been playing itself out in the Left at least since the early twentieth century. The 1932 resolution of the Soviet Communist Party that created the Union of Soviet Writers and promoted the doctrine of Socialist Realism only sharpened the debate. The PWA took its cues from theorists such as Georgi Plekhanov (who insisted that the belief in art for art's sake arises only when artists are out of harmony with their social environment), Maxim Gorky (whose contention was that 'the rotten soul of the bourgeoisie' failed to understand that cultural development should result in progress for all of humanity and, therefore, produced literature that promotes 'cheats and thieves as heroes'), Vladimir Mayakovski (whose position was that art should be addressed to the masses, the workers and the peasants, and ought not to be directed at the few economic and social elites), Mao Tse-Tung (who thought that the artist should learn from the people and not the other way around), and a variety of others like Bertolt Brecht, Walter Benjamin and Lu Xun.

The early approach of the writers who produced *Angaare* (a collection of short stories published in 1932 that spurred the formation of the PWA) seemed to take a leaf out of the 1912 manifesto written by Victor Khlebnikov titled *A Slap in the Face of Public Taste* which recommended that those who were complacent about the past and the present needed to be shocked into acknowledging new socio-political realities. *Angaare* did precisely that, particularly through Sajjad Zaheer's story 'Jannat ki Bashaarat' (A Vision of Heaven), a story that ridiculed the religious orthodoxy in a rather shocking fashion.

As the PWA gained momentum, the question of what constituted progressive literature was raised periodically and debated vigorously. The first major controversy within the movement surfaced around 1939 when Ahmed Ali, one of the contributors to *Angaare* and the then-editor of the English-language progressive journal *New Indian Literature* contended that there was a growing tension between what he termed the 'creative section' and the 'political section' of the movement. The latter, he claimed, were pressurizing him to refuse to publish work which was not significant from the point of view of the workers and peasants. Soon after, and probably as a consequence of this rift, Ahmed Ali dropped out of the PWA, and the journal ceased publication. The debate continued over the next several years with the so-called 'political section' taking control over the movement. Much of the writing following this was of the 'didactic' kind and literary production was dominated by work that was explicitly socialist in its politics.

This mode of cultural production faced a significant amount of resistance and more than a little ridicule from various factions of Urdu literature[13]. In response to this criticism, Abdul Aleem wrote a series of essays titled *Some Misunderstandings about Progressive Literature* in which, among other things, he argued that, in contemporary writing, content should take precedence over form. Preoccupation with form, he contended, was the hallmark of individualism and negated the very basis of progressive literature.

The passion for content led the Progressives to challenge existing literary norms in multiple ways. Even the venerable ghazal came in for its share of flak and was referred to as a medium of reactionary thought and an instrument that reflected an era of *jaagirdaari* and *ayyaashi* (feudalism and debauchery). Akhtar Ansar Dehlvi, Mumtaz Hussain and Inteshar Hussain all wrote scathing critiques of the ghazal arguing that despite its beauty and depth, '*Ghazal apni zahniyat ki vajah se jazbaati lamhoñ aur aarizi kaifiyatoñ ki tarjumaani ban kar rah jaati hai* (Because of its temperament, the ghazal remains a mere translation of emotional moments and transient conditions)'. The ghazal, according to these interlocutors, could not deal with the life of the common people or the new culture and that its *tang-daamani,* or narrowness, made it an unsuitable mode of expression for progressive thought.

This critique, incidentally, was more than a bit odd since most, if not all, of the progressive Urdu poets chose to write ghazals at some point or the other in their literary lives. Majrooh Sultanpuri, in particular, never really sacrificed the form at the altar of content, choosing instead to rework this genre in order to pen rather radical verses in the ghazal tradition:

Ab ahl-e dard ye jeene ka ehtemaam kareñ
Use bhula ke gham-e zindagi ka naam kareñ

Sikhaayeñ dast-e talab ko adaa-e bebaaki
Payaam-e zer-e labi ko salaa-e aam kareñ

Ghulaam rah chuke, todeñ ye band-e ruswaai
Kuch apne baazu-e mehnat ka ehteraam kareñ

Let the lovers prepare to face the world
Forget their beloveds, focus on the sorrows of life

Teach the supplicating hand to be bold
Turn that which has been whispered into a public cry

Slaves no more, break the fetters of dishonour
Learn to respect the hands that labour

This dramatically different ghazal included the startling *makhta* (signature couplet), that was derided by many purists and got Majrooh a dressing down from Rashid Ahmed Siddiqui for straying too far from convention:

Meri nigaah meiñ hai arz-e Moscow, Majrooh
Voh sar zameeñ ke sitaare jise salaam kareñ

I behold the land of Moscow, Majrooh
Look, the stars too salute it

The PWA managed to hold the line for the most part against what it thought was reactionary verse and relentlessly pushed the cause of using art as a tool for invoking social and material conditions and effecting transformative politics.

The ambivalence of some of the writers of this period did find periodic voice, but for the most part, the PWA remained the hegemonic force behind cultural production in this period of Urdu literature. While many of its stalwarts were card-carrying members of the Communist Party, the PWA was launched with a cast of characters that included communists such as Sajjad Zaheer, Gandhians such as Premchand and a whole host of others who occupied various positions on the ideological spectrum. What kept these diverse groups together was a shared sense of solidarity in the struggle against the British occupiers.

The social conditions following Independence were devastating for the PWA. The Partition divided the nation and its writers into two. The cleavage was particularly traumatic for the PWA since its strength lay in Urdu, Punjabi and Bengali; all of them linguistic communities that found themselves on different sides of the new borders. Soon after Independence, the newly formed states of India and Pakistan began to exercise their repressive power against their own citizens. Ahmed Rahi writes:

Maayoosi meiñ umr kaṯi thi, aas ne angḏaayi si li thi
Socha tha qismat badlegi, lekin hum ne dhoka khaaya

Our lives were spent in despair; hope had begun to stir in our hearts
We thought our destiny would change, but alas, we were deceived

As Ali Sardar Jafri put it, the 'romanticism' engendered by the revolutionary fervour of the independence struggle gave way to 'realism'. As a response to the changing times, the PWA, spurred by the election of the radical B.T. Ranadive (over the moderate P.C. Joshi) to the position of the General Secretary of the Communist Party of India (CPI), came out with its most explicitly leftist manifesto in 1949 at the Bhivandi conference (not coincidentally, a similar manifesto was produced by the newly formed Pakistan PWA at the same time). In an attempt to create ideological clarity for a movement that was threatening to lose its bearing, the manifesto took an uncompromisingly socialist stand.

Ali Sardar Jafri followed up with an editorial in *Naya Adab* and an essay titled 'Taraqqi Pasand Shairi ke Baaz Masaa'el' (Some Issues Facing Progressive Poetry). Major periodicals of the time such as *Shahraaz, Mahaaz* and *Tahreek* published this essay, thus signalling to their contributors that these were the new guidelines of the times. Among other things, Jafri's essay sought to offer a formula of sorts for writing progressive literature. Some of its suggestions were:

1) The themes of progressive poetry should be based on *gham-e duaraañ* or the (material) sorrows of the world, not *gham-e jaanaañ* or *gham-e zaat* (the sorrows of the heart or the self). *Infiraadi ehsaas/tajrube* (personal feelings/ experiences) were the signs of reactionary thoughts *(ruj'at pasandi ki alaamat).*
2) Poets ought to focus on issues of freedom, revolution and international struggles against oppressive conditions and regimes.
3) Those who labelled progressive poetry as propaganda and, therefore, considered it inferior were supporters of the status quo and of the capitalist order and should be opposed.
4) Progressive poetry ought to be explicit. Poets should not use metaphors and similes *(iste'aara* and *tashbeeh*) to refer to oppression, injustice and brutality, but name these conditions directly.
5) Poets should write verses of optimism (*rajaiyat*) and eschew sorrow and lament (*gham, udaasi, afsurdagi*).
6) Poets who ignored the masses and their struggles were guilty of abandoning their calling.

In response to Jafri's call, poets such as Wamiq Jaunpuri, Niyaaz Haidar, Arif Abdul Ameen, Khatir Ghaznavi, Ahmed

Riyaz, Sulaiman Areeb and others wrote verses about workers' struggles in China, Japan, Burma, Malay, Indonesia, Korea, Egypt, Turkey, Iran and Tunisia. Critics charge that the poetry of this time was bland and programmatic. A collection of poems produced during this period titled *Shikast-e Zindaan* (Prison's Defeat) edited by Ghulam Rabbani Taabaañ got a snide remark from Josh Malihabadi, himself a diehard progressive:

Aafreeñ bar Ghulaam Rabbaani
Kya nikaala hai mendakoñ ka juloos

Congratulations to Ghulam Rabbani
For giving us this procession of frogs

The 1949 manifesto was intended to draw a line of ideological clarity, but the enthusiasm with which the leaders of the PWA went after those who appeared to cross it damaged its own cause. The process of chastising the poets and writers who were seen as guilty of abandoning their ideology had started before the new manifesto, but intensified soon after. The public disavowal of Ismat Chughtai, Saadat Hasan Manto, N.M. Rashid and Miraji for their writings on sex and sexuality is well known. Rajender Singh Bedi was taken to task for not focusing on political themes in his writing. Even Faiz came under attack, mostly for his 'ambiguity' and was even accused (clearly, a ludicrous charge) of being a Muslim League sympathizer. There were, of course, some in the PWA who did become enamoured with the Muslim League. Ibrahim Jalees and Nazir Hyderabadi joined the Majlis Ittehadul Muslimeen (Association for the Unity of Muslims) and formed the Anjuman-e Muslim Musannifeen (Association of Muslim Writers). Across the border, M.D. Taseer, Mumtaz Shirin, Samad Shaheen and others took up the Muslim League cause with vigour. Solidarity based on issues of social justice was sacrificed with surprising ease at the altar of identity politics based on religious affiliations.

In India, conditions for the Left got worse and the ruthless crushing of the Telangana Movement proved to be a huge blow to the aspirations of those who were struggling for class equality. A worried Indian PWA issued a new manifesto in 1953 which abandoned the leftist tone of 1949 in favour of a soft, liberal line that championed humanism and nationalism while carefully avoiding any statement about class politics. In many ways, the new manifesto signalled the beginning of the end of the phase of the domination of the PWA in Urdu literature. While the poets continued to write their fiery verse, the PWA became a shadow of its former self.

What does one then make of this period in the history of Urdu literature? How does one, from the vantage of hindsight, make sense of the movement and its approach towards cultural production?

The critiques of the PWA are not exactly in short supply. Despite the fact that it produced the finest Urdu poets of the twentieth century, the association has been accused of abandoning the glorious traditions of the Urdu classical poets, of producing inferior poetry, and of didacticism, unsubtlety and polemicism. We wish to, however, suggest that these charges can stick only if we read the progressive writers in a decontextualized manner. In an attempt to retrieve their contribution to literature and history (and if we may borrow a phrase, to rescue them from the condescension of history), we offer our take on the progressive aesthetic.

***

One can make a reasonable claim that the period of the PWA

was hardly the first attempt to use Urdu as a vehicle for social reform. The Lahore mushaira (poetic gatherings) of 1874 is but one example, where Colonel Holroyd, the Director of Public Instruction asked Urdu poets to write poetry modelled on western examples, even suggesting the theme of the next poetic gathering (the rainy season; a suggestion that was thankfully ignored!). Further, Altaf Husain Hali in his landmark work, *Muqaddamah-e Sher-o-Shairi,* had proposed a systematic theory of literary criticism, didactic in tone and utilitarian in its base, suggesting that Urdu expand its vocabulary of metaphors (go beyond the *sham'a-parvaana* routine), stop writing about the wonders of wine, eschew reproaches to orthodoxy and express a variety of sentiments other than love (such as sorrow and social problems) while writing about love itself in contexts other than the erotic or the mystical (by, for example, including themes around the love of one's country).

In some ways, the PWA experiment can be seen as building upon this history, though the progressive writers went far beyond Hali's utilitarianism. The Progressives insisted on looking at poetry through the lens of the politics of radical social transformation. However, they did not throw the baby out with the bath-water, constantly arguing that the purpose of their writing was to build on the legacy of the past.

An editorial penned by Sibte Hasan, Ali Sardar Jafri and Israr-ul-Haq Majaz for the inaugural issue of *Naya Adab* (April 1939) sought to explain the notion of progressive literature in the following fashion:

> It is wrong to say that the term progressive literature denotes protest and hatred of all old things. Progressive literature sees all things in their proper perspective and historical background; this very fact is the touchstone of literary achievement. Progressive literature does not break

> off relations with old literature; it embodies the best traditions of the old and constructs new edifices on the foundations of these traditions. In fact, progressive literature is the most trustworthy guardian and heir of ancient literature ... In our view, progressive literature is that which keeps in view the realities of life; it should be a reflection of these realities; it should investigate them and should be the guide to a new and better life.[14]

In this attempt to imagine this new and better life the PWA set out to create a corpus of work that had a new politics, which in turn demanded a different aesthetic. In the following sections, we try and identify a few defining features of this aesthetic.

New Wine, Old Bottles: The Reworking of Themes

Urdu poetry had always demonstrated a strong streak of humanism. Khusrau, Wali, Mir, Sauda and others spoke compellingly of the human condition and the need for a humane and just society. Ghalib, and later Iqbal, added new edges to their poetic output by infusing their verse with social commentary. But mainstream Urdu poetry, for the most part, remained preoccupied with love, romance and death. *Sham'a-parvaana* (flame-moth), *bulbul-sayyaad* (nightingale-hunter), *saaghar-jaam-meena* (goblet-wine-flask), and *gul-bahaar-khizaan* (rose-spring-autumn) remained its dominant themes.

It took the iconoclasm of the PWA poets to shatter this mould. In Majaz's verse, for example, the moon, hitherto a metaphor for the desired beloved, was identified with objects of scorn and hatred.

> *Ek mahal ki aad se nikla voh peela maahtaab*
> *Jaise mullaah ka amaama, jaise baniye ki kitaab*

> From behind the palace rose the yellow moon
> Looking like the mullah's turban, like the moneylender's ledger

In the hands of the PWA poets, the metaphors of Urdu poetry were altered as never before. The rose still bloomed in the spring, the cup of wine was still passed around, the moth was still scorched by the flame, the bulbul still sang songs of love, and the lovers still paced the street of their beloveds who dispensed favour to all but the wretched protagonists. But as N.M. Rashid says about Faiz (although it could apply to several others), this poetry 'enables the timeworn cliches of the Persian and Urdu ghazal to acquire a renewed sensitivity and to be recharged with meaning, so that the solitary suffering of the disappointed romantic lover is transformed into the suffering of humanity at large.'

Or, as Faiz himself writes: 'One cannot isolate oneself from the rest of the world and be oblivious to the environment. Isolation, even if it is possible, is an unprofitable act because an individual ... is a very limited and ordinary being. The measure of one's depth is only to be found in one's emotional (and psychological) relationship with the human community, particularly those relationships that involve the sharing of pain and suffering. The sorrows of loving and the sorrows of living are different forms of the same expression.'

In his presidential address to the first meeting of the PWA, Premchand, announced: *Hameñ husn ke meyaar badalne honge* (We will have to transform the standards of beauty). The PWA poets took this to heart and set about altering the aesthetic of the literature and the very standards of literary merit. Beauty for them had to be sought not just in the face of the beloved, but in the body of the toiling worker. Accordingly, Makhdoom

Mohiuddin, addressing the Telangana woman working in the field, wrote:

Dekhne aate haiñ taare, shab meiñ sun kar tera naam
Jalve subh-o shaam ke hote haiñ tujh se hum-kalaam
Dekh fitrat kar rahi hai, tujh ko jhuk-jhuk kar salaam

The stars rise at night upon hearing your name
The beauty of morning and evening speak out to you
Behold, the bounties of nature pay you homage

Majrooh, using the vehicle of the ghazal to articulate fresh thoughts and seeking to transform the spaces where one seeks beauty, composed the following:

Maiñ ke ek mehnat-kash, maiñ ke teeragi dushman
Subh-e nau ibaarat hai, mere muskuraane se
Sur<u>kh</u> inquilaab aaya, daur-e aaftaab aaya
Muntazir thi ye aankheñ jis ki ek zamaane se
Ab zameen gaayegi, hal ke saaz par na<u>gh</u>me
Vaadiyoñ meiñ naachenge har taraf taraane se
Manchale bunenge ab rang-o boo ke pairaahan
Ab sañvar ke niklega, husn kaar<u>kh</u>aane se

I am a worker, I am the enemy of darkness
My smile is what brings about the new morning
The red revolution arrives, that day of brightness dawns
Which these eyes have been awaiting for so long
Now the earth will sing songs to the beat of the plough
Anthems will dance in the valleys
The carefree will weave garments of colour and fragrance
And beauty shall emerge, adorned, from within the factory walls

Calling a Spade a Spade: The Poetry of Bluntness

Classical Urdu poetry is suffused with a certain kind of subtlety. Smilies and metaphors are its calling cards. Words stand in for whole sets of narratives and emotions. It is left to the erudite reader to draw the connections and make assumptions about the poet's intent. While the progressive poets hardly abandoned this armoury, their verses were characterized by a certain bluntness of expression.

On the theme of religion, for instance, the Progressives took the standard reproaches to orthodoxy to a different level. So while Mir is rather gentle in stating his apostasy thus:

Mir ke deen-o mazhab ko, ab poochhte kya ho, un ne to
Qashqa khaincha dair meiñ baiṯha, kab ka tark Islam kiya

Why do you now ask Mir about his faith; for he
Sits in the temple, ash on his forehead, having long forsaken Islam

a poet like Sahir writes:

Aqaa'ed vahm hai mazhab khayaal-e khaam hai saaqi
Azal se aql-e insaan basta-e auhaam hai saaqi

Faith is but superstition, religion but a crude system
Human intellect has been held captive by these since eternity

On the theme of sorrows other than love, a staple sentiment of Urdu poetry, Ghalib says:

Teri wafa se kya ho, talaafi ke dahr meiñ
Tere siva bhi hum pe bahut se sitam hue

Your fidelity notwithstanding, this world of recompense
Has subjected me to oppressions other than your love

Faiz, on the other hand, is more forthright:

Aur bhi dukh haiñ zamaane meiñ mohabbat ke siva
Raahateñ aur bhi haiñ vasl ki raahat ke siva
Mujh se pahli si mohabbat, meri mahboob na maang

There are sorrows in this world other than the sorrow of your love

Comforts other than the comfort of lovers' union
Don't ask me for that old love any more

Another aspect of this directness can be seen in the relative simplicity of expression and language that was favoured by the progressive poets. Their writings were not hermeneutic puzzles whose meanings had to be teased out and debated. Unlike the ghazals of Ghalib that still vex his translators, the poetry of the Progressives can hardly be accused of being unclear about what it wishes to say. Sahir writes:

Ye duniya do rangi hai
Ek taraf se resham oḏe, ek taraf se nangi hai

Ek taraf andhi daulat ki paagal aish parasti
Ek taraf jismoñ ki qeemat roti se bhi sasti
Ek taraf hai Sonaagaachi, ek taraf Chaurangi hai
Ye duniya do rangi hai

This world is double-faced
One side covered with silk, the other naked

On the one hand, the hedonism of blind wealth
On the other, bodies sold cheaper than bread
On the one hand lies Sonagachi, on the other Chowringee[15]
This world is double-faced

The poetry of the progressive writers also insistently engaged with contemporary issues and commented on them. There was little room in their work for the mystical, the esoteric, the recondite or the abstract. The Bengal famine, the anti-imperialist struggles, the disaster of Partition, the injustices of war and the American intervention in Vietnam were all dealt with, not merely as lamentations in the manner of *shahr-ashoob* or *marsiyas* (dirges), but as events that deserved explicit attention and action.

The Poetry of Incitement, the Poetry of Anger

The new breed of revolutionary Urdu poets *(Urdu ke jadeed inquilaabi shaayar,* as Sajjad Zaheer called them) took their label seriously and sought to make their poems reverberate with a novel passion. Theirs was a poetry of incitement; its anger against oppressors was palpable. Josh had ended his poem, 'East India Company ke Farzandoñ Se' (To the Sons of the East India Company) with the lines:

Ek kahaani waqt likhega naye mazmoon ki
Jis ki surkhi ko zaroorat hai tumhaare khoon ki

Time is about to write a story with a new theme
Whose redness will need to partake of your blood

In a similar vein, Majaz offers a bloody prognosis to the British occupiers in his poem 'Inquilaab' (Revolution):

Khatm ho jaane ko hai sarmaayadaari ka nizaam
Rang laane ko kai mazdooroñ ka josh-e inteqaam
Khoon ki boo le ke jangal se havaaeñ aayengi
Khooñ hi khooñ hoga nigaaheñ jis taraf ko jaayengi
Jhopddiyoñ meiñ, mahal meiñ khooñ, shabistaanoñ meiñ khooñ
Dasht meiñ khooñ, vaadiyoñ meiñ khooñ, bayaabaanoñ meiñ khooñ
...
Aur is rang-e shafaq meiñ ba-hazaaraañ aab-o taab
Jagmagaayega vatan ki hurriyat ka aaftaab

The rule of capitalism is about to end
The passion of the workers' revenge is coming to a boil
Winds bearing the scent of blood will soon blow from the forests
Blood shall soon be flowing everywhere
Blood in the huts, the palaces, the night chambers
Blood in the desert, in the valley, in the desolation
...
And on that horizon, amidst a thousand tumults
Shall rise the sun of our land's freedom

Apart from the sanguine imagery, it is interesting to note the equation of the rule of the British with capitalism and the simultaneous foregrounding of labourers as the vanguards of the freedom struggle.

The anger against the capitalists who oppress the workers is evident in a large number of poems written by the Progressives, as in Viqar Ambalavi's 'Inteqaam' (Revenge):

Khaaeñ bhi mazdoor ka, mazdoor par ghurraaeñ bhi
Din ko mehnat bhi karaaeñ, raat ko rulvaaeñ bhi
Bhook se mazdoor ke bachche bhi bilkeñ maaeñ bhi
Tuf hai saramaaya parastoñ par kahiñ mit jaaeñ bhi
Inteqaam, ai inteqaam, ai inteqaam, ai inteqaam

Not satisfied with appropriating the workers' share, you growl at them too
Not enough that you make them slave during the day,
you make them weep at night too
Not only do the workers' children wail with hunger, their mothers cry too
Damn you, O capitalism-lovers, may you perish
Revenge, revenge, revenge, revenge

Kaifi Azmi, bemoaning the fate of the willing workers who fail to find employment, speaks in their voice urging them to realize that their only hope lies in rebellion and revolution:

Kahaañ tak ye bil-jabr mar mar ke jeena
Badalne laga hai amal ka qareena
Lahu meiñ hai khaulan, jabeeñ par paseena
Dhadakti hai nasbeñ, sulagta hai seena
Garaj ai baghaavat ke tayyaar hooñ maiñ

How long will I live this oppressed death-like existence
The times are about to change
My blood boils, my brow is sweaty
My pulse pounds, my chest is fiery
Roar O Revolution, for I am ready

Changing the World: The Possibilities of Transformation

Perhaps the most significant feature of the progressive aesthetic is that while the progressive writers concurred with the classical poets that human suffering was a universal condition, they vehemently insisted that this was not a permanent state of affairs, but one that could be transformed through action. As Sahir writes:

In kaali sadiyoñ ke sar se jab raat ka aanchal dhalke-ga
Jab dukh ke baadal pighlenge, jab sukh ka saaghar chhalke-ga
Jab ambar jhoom ke naachega, jab dharti naghme gaayegi
Voh subha kabhi to aayegi

That morning, when the veil of night will slip away from the head of these dark centuries
When the clouds of suffering melt, when the wine-glass of happiness sparkles
When the sky dances joyously and the earth sings songs of delight
Surely, that morning will dawn some day

There was an understanding that human suffering was based on material conditions of deprivation and that struggle would change the state of the world for the betterment of all. Therefore, Sahir adds the following:

Voh subha hameeñ se aayegi

We are the ones who will bring about that morning

And as Faiz announces in his memorable poem:

Hum dekhenge
Laazim hai ke hum bhi dekhenge, hum dekhenge
Voh din ke jis ka vaada hai
Jo lauh-e azal pe likha hai
Hum dekhenge

We will witness it

It cannot be but that we too will witness it
That day which has been promised to us
That which has been inscribed on the parchment of life
We too will witness it

The explicit objective of these poets, if we may appropriate another saying, was not merely one of interpreting the world, but of changing it. Sahir concludes his *do-rangi* poem with the following lines:

Ek sangam par laani hogi dukh aur sukh ki dhaara
Naye sire se karna hoga daulat ka baṯvaara
Jab tak oonch aur neech hai baaqi, har soorat be-ḏhangi hai
Ye duniya do-rangi hai

The separate streams of joy and sorrow will have to be brought into a confluence
Wealth will have to be redistributed in a new fashion
For as long as there are the privileged and the dispossessed, there can only be disorder
In this two-toned world

And in the two-toned world, one had to take sides. To sit on the fence was not an option. The Progressives echoed Gorky's famous questions: 'On whose sides are you, masters of culture? Are you with the handiworkers of culture, and for the creation of new forms of life; or are you against them, and for the perpetuation of a caste of irresponsible marauders, a caste which has decayed from the head downwards?'

So, Faiz writes:

Chashm-e nam jaan-e shoreeda kaafi nahiñ
Tohmat-e ishq-e posheeda kaafi nahiñ
Aaj baazaar meiñ pa-bajaolaañ chalo

Not enough to shed tears, to suffer anguish
Not enough to nurse love in secret
Today, walk in the public square fettered in chains

And in their pursuit of justice, the Progressives sought to make common cause with struggles all over the world. The notion of solidarity extended well beyond the narrow confines of religion, community, or nation. For the first time in its history, Urdu poetry developed an international sensibility. While Iqbal had broached the notion of a transnational community, his was one that was rooted in pan-Islamism. Faiz, Jafri, Majaz, Makhdoom, and Sahir, on the other hand, spoke with feeling about Vietnam, Palestine, Paul Robeson, Martin Luther King, and other champions of freedom and justice.

***

In a very compelling poem titled 'Mauzoo-e Sukhan' (Poetry's Theme), Faiz brings the break between the Progressives and the traditionalists into sharp relief. The poem can be seen as having three separate moments. In the first, Faiz writes about the beloved in the manner of the poets of the past:

Aaj phir husn-e dilaara ki vahi dhaj hogi
Vahi khwaabeeda si aankheñ, vahi kaajal ki lakeer
Rang-e rukhsaar pe halka sa voh ghaaze ka ghubaar
Sandali haath pe dhundli si hina ki tahreer
Apne afkaar ki, ash'aar ki duniya hai yahi
Jaan-e mazmooñ hai yahi, shaahid-e maa'na hai yahi

Today, the beloved's beauty will again be on splendid display
Those half-closed eyes, adorned with kohl
That hint of blush on the colour of the cheeks
The fading lines of henna on the perfumed hands
This is the world of our writing, our thoughts
Here lies the soul of our compositions, this is our true beloved

And then, the progressive poet turns to look at that which has hitherto escaped attention:

In damakte hue shahroñ ki faraavaañ makhlooq
Kyooñ faqat marne ki hasrat meiñ jiya karti hai
Ye haseeñ khet phata padta hai joban jin ka
Kis liye in meiñ faqat bhook uga karti hai

These teeming masses living in the glittering cities
Why do their lives desire nothing but death?
These beautiful fields bursting with abundance
Why do they grow nothing but hunger?

However, Faiz recognizing that he is speaking to an inert body of poets, captured and subjugated by their past and inured to the changing conditions of the times, subjects them to a marvellous bit of sarcasm:

Ye bhi haiñ, aise kaee aur bhi mazmooñ honge
Lekin us shokh ke aahista se khulte hue hont
Hai, us jism ke kambakht dil-aavez khutoot
Aap hi kahiye kahiñ aise bhi afsooñ honge?

Yes, there are these issues, surely others too
But ah, those softly parting lips of that ravishing beauty
Oh, those alluring lines of that body
You tell me; can such magic be found elsewhere?

Apna mauzoo-e sukhan in ke siva aur nahiñ
Tab'e shaayar ka vatan is ke siva aur nahiñ

The subject of our poetry can be nothing but this
A poet's temperament can find place nowhere but here

***

But the progressive poets had their own *mauzoo-e sukhan,* themes that they made their own and by extension those of their readers.

In a reflective piece called 'Jang Aur Aman' (War and Peace) published in *Naya Adab* in 1946, Sahir Ludhianvi contended that the real contribution of the poetry of the progressive writers needed to be judged by a different set of parameters than those used for the norm. He wrote: 'There was a dark windstorm of death which was about to cover the whole globe and hide forever under its thick layers those shining stars that could fill the downtrodden people and classes and impoverished sections of humankind with the hope of light.' According to Sahir, not acting in those circumstances would have amounted to a betrayal of humanity itself. In the conflict between freedom and darkness, love and racial hatred, right and wrong, poets had to contribute to the efforts to 'pull people out of the whirlpool of depression and defeatism and make them aware of their power. And that is why we wrote the way we did.' Sahir, saying more or less the same thing in one of his poems writes:

Mere sarkash taraanoñ ki haqeeqat hai to itni hai
Ke jab maiñ dekhta hooñ bhook se maare kisaanoñ ko
Ghareeboñ, muflisoñ ko, bekasoñ ko besahaaroñ ko
To dil taab-e nishaat-e bazm-e ishrat la nahiñ sakta
Maiñ chaahooñ to bhi khwaabavar taraane ga nahiñ sakta

If there is a reason for my angry songs, it is this
That when I see the hungry farmers
The poor, the oppressed, the destitute, the helpless
My heart cannot participate in assemblies of pleasure
Even if I wish, I cannot write dreamy songs of love

***

So why did this progressive aesthetic thrive in this era? We suggest that the movement worked because it spoke to its time, its place and its politics. Progressive poets created their best work during moments of crisis. The anti-imperialist struggle, the freedom movement, the trauma of Partition, the Telangana uprising, and the failure of the new nation to deliver on its promise of a better life for all its citizens allowed these writers to speak in a voice that resonated with the aspirations of the people.

It is useful to remember that while the progressive poets wrote about workers' and peasants' struggles, their primary audience was the middle class which was unable, and perhaps reluctant, to participate directly in the working-class movements but was willing to champion their cause from the sidelines. The workers would bring about the revolution and the rest would then partake of the just and egalitarian society that would ensue.

But with the passage of time and the creation of the bourgeois independent state, that moment passed. The hope of a mass transformation towards a just society, one that could be fashioned by struggle and solidarity dimmed considerably. Struggles became localized, their intentions less grandiose. The middle class sought its emancipation, not through challenging the system, but by learning to play its game. The ambivalence of the middle class was no longer worth addressing, the presumption of its role in societal transformation abandoned.

As the progressive context dissipated, the progressive aesthetic too lost its broad appeal. But the power of the poets and their contribution to the history of Urdu literature was such that their voice, while no longer dominant, still resonates across time. Poetry appeals to us because it says what we want to say, but more compellingly, because it gives voice to what we did not know we felt till we actually heard it[16]. In Ghalib's words:

Dekhna taqreer ki lazzat ke jo usne kaha
Maiñ ne ye jaana ke goya ye bhi mere dil meiñ hai

Behold the beauty of expression, for when it was uttered
I realized that this sentiment already resided in my heart

***

Cultural spaces are fragile and are constantly negotiated and reconstructed by the politics of the time. They are vital terrains of engagement that must constantly and consciously be brought into the service of ideologies. The progressive poets offered us a vision for which those among us who believe in social justice and in struggle must be grateful. And now, more than ever, we need our Faiz, our Majaz and our Sahir. Ghalib once wrote:

Hooñ garmi-e nishaat-e tassavvur se naghma-sanj
Maiñ andaleeb-e gulshan-e na-aafreeda hooñ

I sing with the warmth of the joy my imagination brings
I am the nightingale of that garden which has not yet been created

That *gulshan-e na-afreeda* may be created soon. Or not. But in the meantime, here is Faiz, reminding us of the value of struggle:

Hai dasht ab bhi dasht, magar khoon-e pa se Faiz
Seraab chand khaar-e mugheelaañ hue to haiñ

The desolate desert we walked through still remains desolate, Faiz
But at least the thirst of some of its thorns has been quenched by the blood of our feet

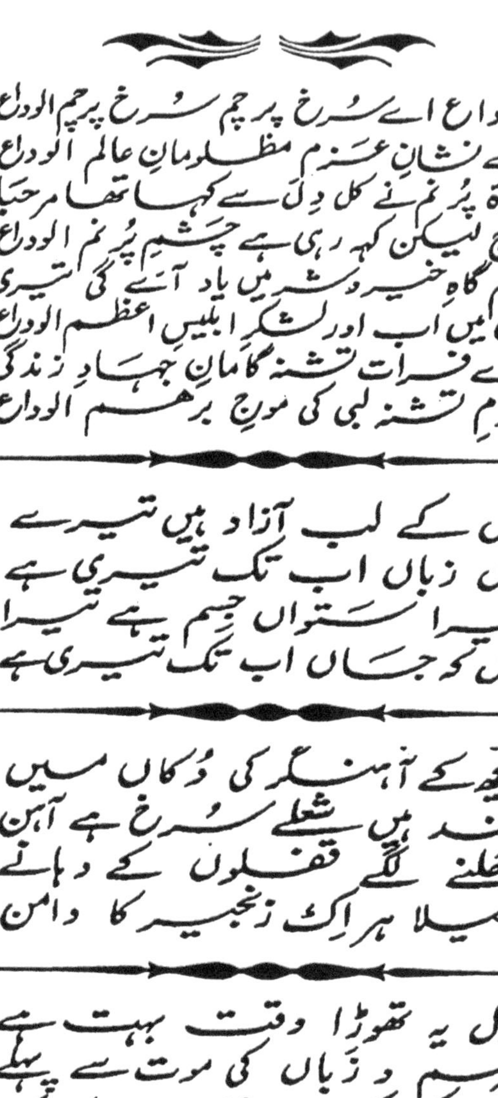

الوداع اے سُرخ پرچم سُرخ پرچم الوداع
اے نشانِ عزمِ مظلومانِ عالم الوداع
دیدۂ پُرنم نے کل دِل سے کہا تھا مرحبا
آج لیکن کہہ رہی ہے چشمِ پُرنم الوداع
رزم گاہِ خیر و شر میں یاد آئے گی تیری
ہاں ہمیں اب اور لشکرِ ابلیسِ اعظم الوداع
اے فراتِ تشنہ گامانِ جہادِ زندگی
قلزمِ تشنہ لبی کی موجِ برہم الوداع

بول کے لب آزاد ہیں تیرے
بول زباں اب تک تیری ہے
تیرا ستواں جسم ہے تیرا
بول کہ جاں اب تک تیری ہے

دیکھ کے آہنگر کی دُکاں میں
تند ہیں شعلے سُرخ ہے آہن
کھُلنے لگے قفلوں کے دہانے
پھیلا ہر اِک زنجیر کا دامن

بول یہ تھوڑا وقت بہت ہے
جسم و زباں کی موت سے پہلے
بول کہ سچ زِندہ ہے اب تک
بول جو کچھ کہنا ہے کہہ لے

کہاں تک یہ بالجبر مر مر کے جینا
بدلنے لگا ہے عمل کا قرینا
لہو میں ہے کھولن جبیں پر پسینا
دھڑکتی ہے نبضیں سلگتا ہے سینہ
گرج اسے بغاوت کہ تیار ہوں میں

ان کالی صدیوں کے سر سے جب رات کا آنچل ڈھلکے گا
جب دکھ کے بادل پگھلیں گے، جب سکھ کا ساگر چھلکے گا
جب عنبر جھوم کے ناچے گا، جب دھرتی نغمے گائے گی
وہ صبح کبھی تو آئے گی

چشمِ نم جانِ شوریدہ کافی نہیں
تہمتِ عشقِ پوشیدہ کافی نہیں
آج بازار میں پابجولاں چلو

ہے دشت اب بھی دشت، مگر خونِ پا سے فیض
سیراب چند خارِ مغیلاں ہوئے تو ہیں

3

SAARE JAHAAÑ SE ACHCHA

Progressive Poets and the Problematic of Nationalism

On 2 March 2002, during the communal pogrom in Gujarat, one act of destruction did not receive much attention, perhaps because it was dwarfed by the scale of violence unleashed in the state. Among the several mosques and *dargahs* that were destroyed was the tomb of one of Urdu's earliest poets, Wali Deccani-Gujrati.

Wali, who lived and worked in the seventeenth century, once spoke about the place he was buried in the following words:

> *Vahaañ saakin ite haiñ ahl-e mazhab, ke ginti meiñ na aaveñ unke mashrab*
> *Agarche sab haiñ voh abnaa-e Aadam, vale beenash meiñ rangaarang-e aalam*
> *Bhari hai seerat-o soorat suñ Surat, har ek soorat hai vhaañ anmol moorat*
> *Sabha Indar ki hai har ek qadam meiñ, chupa Indar, sabha kun le adam meiñ*
> *Kishan ki gopiyaañ ki naiñ hai yeh nasl, rhaeeñ sab gopiaañ voh naql, yeh asl*

> So many people of so many religions live there, their sects cannot possibly be counted

> Even though they are all children of Adam, in their appearance, they are a multi-coloured spectrum
> Surat (the city) is filled with numerous ways and *surats* (forms), each one of these, a priceless image
> At every step, stands the court of Indra, and Indra himself envies these courts
> This generation is not of Krishna's *gopis*
> For those *gopis* were imperfect imitations – this, the real!

Around the same time that Wali's tomb was being torn down, a mob was burning a home that housed the ex-Congress member of Parliament, Ehsan Jafri, and several members of his family. Though we did not know much about Ehsan Jafri, the reports about him after his death seemed to indicate he was a decent man, who had refused to move to a 'safer' Muslim neighbourhood because he thought that would be a betrayal of his secular ideals and whose wife insisted on moving back into the same home to give lie to the contention that the ability of Muslims and Hindus to coexist had been incinerated in the conflagration of Gujarat. We also found out that Ehsan Jafri was a poet who wrote in the vein of the progressive writers. His book *Qandeel* (Lantern) was filled with poems on religious harmony, pacifism and nationalism. Two homes burnt on the same day, two homes of two Urdu poets separated by three centuries. The span of time between their respective deaths contains the story of a language, its engagement with colonialism, fascism, nationalism and secularism.

In this chapter, we intend to examine the deployment of Urdu poetry as a tool of Indian nationalism, particularly by the poets of the Progressive Writers' Association (PWA) and attempt to reflect the story of nationalism in the mirror of Urdu poetry. Specifically, we highlight four moments that mark the modes of engagement of the Progressives with the problematic of nationalism: the anti-colonial struggle against the British, the attitude of the Progressives towards the Second World War, the trauma of the Partition, and the reconfiguration of their politics vis-á-vis the Indian state.

The Anti-Colonial Struggle as Workers' Movement

Saare jahaañ se achcha Hindostaañ hamaara
Hum bulbuleñ haiñ uski, voh gulsitaañ hamaara

This simple 'East or West, India is Best' song, still frequently heard in India, was written by Mohammad Iqbal around 1905 and echoed the sentiments of a generation of Urdu poets. The period of 1850s onwards, sometimes referred to as the *Nishaat-e Saania* (Renaissance) in Urdu literature exhibited a new sensibility that was spurred by an attitude of resentment and rebellion against the yoke of colonialism. Around the turn of the century, the call by Altaf Husain Hali and Mohammad Husain Azad to poets asking for mushairas to be organized on the basis of themes such as the love of the nation also provided an impetus to *qaumi shaa'iri,* or the poetry of nationalism.

Urdu poetry for long had had a tradition of an engagement with the human condition but the period of 1920s onwards saw a new mood, one that Jan Nisar Akhtar calls *avaami bedaari ki lehar* (the awakening of the masses). An anthology of Urdu patriotic poetry called *Hindustan Hamara* (Our India), edited by Akhtar, covering the period 1857-1970 runs into two volumes with its thousand or so pages containing over seven hundred poems.

There were plenty of standard patriotic pieces, but a large number of poems of this period indicated the beginning of a new form of social and political awakening. The interesting thing about this consciousness was that the poems of this time such as 'The Farmer' by Josh, 'The Rise of the New Sun' by Hamidullah, 'The Cry of the New Times' by Sarosh Kashmiri, 'The Challenge of Life' by Firaq Gorakhpuri, 'The Labourer's Flute' by Jameel Manzari, 'Revolution' by Israr-ul-Haq Majaz, 'The Farmer's Song' by Masood Akhtar Jamaal and dozens of others – actively sought to reframe the anti-colonial struggle along the binaries of the exploiters and the exploited, the zamindars and the landless farmers and the *sarmaayadaars* and the *mazdoors* (the capitalists and the labourers). The October Revolution that helped form the Soviet Union was held up as a model and was seen as a source of inspiration. Majaz in his poem 'Inquilab' (Revolution) composed in 1933 writes:

Kohsaaroñ ki taraf se surkh aandhi aayegi
Jabaja aabaadiyoñ meiñ aag si lag jaayegi ...
Aur is rang-e shafaq meiñ ba-hazaraañ aab-o taab
Jagmagaaega vatan ki hurriyat ka aaftaab

A red storm is approaching from over the mountains
Sparking a fire in the settlements ...
And on this horizon, amidst a thousand tumults
Shall shine the sun of our land's freedom

This influence is visible even in Iqbal's poetry of this period, which included some unabashed odes to Lenin. An interesting trilogy in *Baal-e Gibreel* (Gabriel's Wing, 1935) starts with a poem in which a startled Lenin finds himself face to face with God he never believed existed. Undaunted, he lets loose a Marxist critique of the poor job that God was doing, starting with the question:

Maiñ kaise samajhta ke tu hai ya ke nahiñ hai?

How do you expect me to have believed in your existence?

As the poem proceeds, Lenin asks: 'Whose God are you; of the same ones who live under the sky? For as far as I could tell, the gods of the East are the foreigners of the West, while the West prays only to the shining dollar. The appropriators of wealth, power and knowledge exploit the poor while preaching equality; profit for one is death for millions.' Lenin concludes with the following observation:

Tu qaadir-o aadil hai magar tere jahaañ meiñ
Haiñ talq bahut banda-e mazdoor ke auqaat

You may be powerful and just, but in your world
Bitter are the lives of the slaves of labour

The watching angels mull this over and, convinced by Lenin's analysis, offer their own response in the second poem titled 'Farishtoñ Ka Geet' (The Song of the Angels):

Aql hai bezamaam abhi, ishq hai bemaqaam abhi
Naqshgar-e azal tera, naqsh hai natamaam abhi

The Intellect is still unreined, Love still unmoored
Architect of Eternity, your design is still incomplete!

Suitably chastised, God in turn offers his 'Farmaan-e Khuda Farishtoñ Se' (God's Command to the Angels):

Utho meri duniya ke ghareeboñ ko jagaado
Kaakh-e umara ke dar-o deewaar hilaado
Jis khet se dahkhaañ ko mayassar nahiñ rozi
Us khet ke har gosha-e gandum ko jalaado

Rise, awaken the poor of my land
Rattle the palaces of the rich men's band
A field whose crop the farmer can't eat?
Burn, burn every grain of that wheat

In some ways, this mood provided the ground in which the PWA took root in the mid-thirties and flourished in the following decades, spurring the large-scale production of radical cultural leftist fiction and poetry in India. Urdu poetry responded with great enthusiasm, so much so that the PWA defined the social agenda for a whole generation of writers. Since most of the leadership and much of the rank-and-file of the PWA was composed of leftist poets and writers, the goal of the anti-colonial struggle was seen as not merely independence, but the formation of a socialist society. The dawn that was awaited was going to be a red one. In Makhdoom's words:

Lo surkh savera aata hai, aazaadi ka, aazaadi ka
Gulnaar taraana gaata hai, aazaadi ka, aazaadi ka
Dekho parcham lahraata hai, aazaadi ka, aazaadi ka

Behold, the red dawn of independence arrives
Singing the red anthem of liberty
And look, the banner of freedom waves in the wind

For the Progressives, the freedom struggle was inextricably intertwined with their socialist aspirations. The end of one form of oppression, they believed, would come hand in hand with the end of all forms of oppression.

The Second World War and the Progressive Flip-Flop

The advent of the Second World War provided more fodder for the Progressives' pens. When the British asked the people of India to join it in what the Progressives had dubbed the 'imperialist war', Josh Malihabadi responded with a bitingly sarcastic poem titled 'East India Company Ke Farzandoñ Se' (To the Sons of the East India Company)[17]:

Kis zabaañ se kah rahe ho aaj, ai saudaagaro
'Dahr meiñ insaaniyat ke naam ko ooncha karo
Jisko sab kahte haiñ Hitler, *bhediya hai, bhediya*
Bhediye ko maar do goli pa'e amn-o baqaa
Baagh-e insaani pe chalne hi ko hai baad-e khizaañ
Aadamiyyat le rahi hai hichkiyoñ par hichkiyaañ
Haath Hitler *ka hai rakhsh-e khudsari ki baag par*
Tegh ka paani chidak do Germany *ki aag par.'*

Sakht hairaañ hooñ, ke mahfil meiñ tumhaari aur ye zikr
Nau-e insaani ke mustaqbil ki ab karte ho fikr?
Jab yahaañ aaye the tum saudaagari ke vaaste
Nau-e insaani ke mustaqbil se kya vaaqif na the?
Hindiyoñ ke jism meiñ kya rooh-e aazaadi na thi?
Sach bataao, kya voh insaanoñ ki aabaadi na thi?

Apne zulm-e be-nihaayat ka fasaana yaad hai?
Company *ka bhi voh daur-e mujrimaana yaad hai?*
Loot-te phirte the tum jab kaarvaañ dar kaarvaañ?
Sar barahna phir rahi thi daulat-e Hindostaañ
Dastkaaroñ ke angoothe kaat-te phirte the tum
Sard laashoñ se garhon ko paat-te phirte the tum
San'at-e Hindostaañ par maut thi chaayi hui
Maut bhi kaisi? Tumhaare haath ki laayi hui

Allah Allah! Kis qadar insaaf ke taalib ho aaj
Meer Jafar ki qasam, kya dushman-e haq tha Siraaj?
Voh Avadh ki begamoñ ka bhi sataana yaad hai?
Yaad hai Jhaansi ki Raani ka zamaana yaad hai?
Hijrat-e Sultan-e Dilli ka samaañ bhi yaad hai?
Sher-dil Tipu ki khooni daastaañ bhi yaad hai?
Teesre faaqe meiñ ek girte hue ko thaamne
Kin ke sar laaye the tum Shaah-e Zafar ke saamne?

Voh Bhagat Singh jis ke gham meiñ ab bhi dil naashaad hai
Us ki gardan meiñ jo daala tha voh phanda yaad hai?
Zahn meiñ hoga ye taaza Hindiyoñ ka daagh bhi
Yaad to hoga tumheñ Jaliaanwaala Baagh bhi

With what tongue dare you counsel us, O traders!

You say: 'Restore the dignity of humanity in the world
He who they call Hitler is but a wolf
Let us shoot him down, in the name of peace and stability
The winds of bleak autumn are about to ruin the garden
Humanity is gasping in its death throes
Hitler's hand has grasped the mane of the horse of hubris
Let us douse Germany's fire with the water of the sword'

I am amazed by the words that emerge from your assembly!
You talk about the future of humanity now?
When you came here to ply your sorry trade
Were you not acquainted with humanity's future then?
Didn't the bodies of Indians have the soul of freedom?
Speak truthfully, wasn't it a community of humans?

Do you even remember the tales of your unparalleled cruelty?
Of the Company's criminal days in power?
When you went about looting every caravan
While the wealth of India wandered bare-headed
You, who used to cut off the thumbs of weavers,
And fill holes in the earth with cold corpses?
The industry of India was under the shadow of death
And what a wretched death! At your hands!

Allah! Allah! How you demand justice today!
Swear by Meer Jafar[18]; was Siraj such an enemy of truth?
Do you recall how you harassed the noblewomen of Oudh?
Remember the age of the Queen of Jhansi[19]? Remember?
Do you remember the flight of the King of Delhi[20]?
Remember the bloody legend of Tipu[21] the Lion-hearted?
And to support him as he was collapsing on his third hungry day
Whose heads did you bring in front of King Zafar[22]?

That Bhagat Singh whose memory still fills the heart with sorrow
Surely you remember the noose you put round his neck?
The scars that Indians felt must be fresh in your memory
Those that were inflicted at Jalianwala Bagh. You remember, don't you?

Needless to say, this poem was banned immediately after it was published, and Josh's journal *Kaalim* (The Pen-Wielder) was forced to close down. The Urdu press became a platform for the anti-war position of the Progressives, who decried the British position that this was a war for justice. The 'imperialist war' was roundly condemned and there were demands to transform the war into a revolution. Communists across the nation, including Sajjad Zaheer, were arrested and imprisoned. Poets wrote of the war as one that was being waged for wealth and as a sign that capitalism was tottering on its throne. Their sympathies were with the soldiers who were being condemned to die in the service of an imperial order.

This sentiment underwent a profound change with Hitler's launch of Operation Barbarossa – the German invasion of Russia – in June 1941. The jailed leadership of the PWA, most likely under a directive from Moscow, issued a statement from the Deoli detention camp near Ajmer – the 'Deoli thesis' – asking for unflinching support to the anti-fascist cause. Eventually, the poets responded. Makhdoom, who had written a poignant anti-war piece called 'Sipaahi' (Soldier), now produced his 'Jang-e Aazaadi' (The War for Freedom), a poem that reflected the new configuration of allies:

Ye jang hai jang-e aazaadi
Saara sansaar hamaara hai
Poorab, pachchim, uttar, dakshin
Hum Afrangi, hum Amriki
Hum Cheeni jaanbaazan-e vatan
Hum surkh sipaahi zulm shikan
Aahan paikar, faulaad badan
Ye jang hai jang-e aazaadi
Aazaadi ke parcham ke tale

This is a war for freedom
The whole world is ours
The East and the West, the North and the South
We Europeans, we Americans

We Chinese soldiers ready to sacrifice ourselves for our homeland
We, the red soldiers, the destroyers of tyranny
Iron-bodied, steely figured
This is the war for freedom
Under the banner of freedom

The Awaited Dawn of Freedom

Freedom did eventually dawn, but the redness of its colour came not from its revolutionary/socialist fervour but from the bloody Partition, and Urdu poetry reflected the mood of the times in a somber, mournful tone. Faiz Ahmad Faiz's famous lament 'Subh-e Aazaadi' (Freedom's Morning) exemplifies this mood:

Ye daagh daagh ujaala, ye shab gazeeda sahar
Voh intezaar tha jiska ye voh sahar to nahiñ
...
Suna hai ho bhi chuka hai firaaq-e zulmat-o noor
Suna hai ho bhi chuka hai visaal-e manzil-o gaam
Badal chuka hai bahut ahl-e dard ka dastoor
Najaat-e vasl halaal-o azaab-e hijr haraam

Jigar ki aag, nazar ki umang, dil ki jalan
Kisi pe chaara-e hijraañ ka kuch asar hi nahiñ
Kahaañ se aayi nigaar-e saba, kidhar ko gayi?
Abhi charaagh-e sar-e rah ko kuch khabar hi nahiñ

This tarnished light, this ashen dawn
This is not that morning which we were awaiting
...

Now they tell us that Darkness has finally been expunged from the Light
That our Path has already merged with its Destination
That the fortunes of abject lovers have turned such that
The pleasure of union is now Permitted, the hell of separation Forbidden

But the fire in the soul, the yearning in the gaze, the wound of the heart
Are unaffected by the balm of those who seek to heal parting's sorrow

Where did the morning breeze come from, which way did it depart?
No one seems to know, not even the lamp that lights up the path

Offering a similar disillusioned take, but deploying a harsher tone, Sahir's poem 'Mufaahimat' (Compromise) announced:

Ye jashn jashn-e masarrat nahiñ, tamaasha hai
Naye libaas meiñ nikla hai rahzani ka juloos
Hazaar shamm-e aquwwat bujha ke chamke haiñ
Ye teeragi ke ubhaare hue naye faanoos

This is not a celebration of joy, but a vulgar spectacle
The same procession of robbers has emerged wearing new clothes
After extinguishing a thousand lamps of relationships
A new lampshade has been trotted out by the darkness

In a poem that was probably written a few years later, Ahmad Faraz echoes the sentiments that were dominant among the Progressives in Pakistan:

Ab kis ka jashn manaate ho
Us desh ka jo taqseem hua
Us desh ka geet sunaate ho
Jo toot ke hi tasleem hua

In mazloomoñ ka jin ke lahu se
Tum ne firoza raateñ ki
Ya un mazloomoñ ka jin se
Khanjar ki zubaañ meiñ baateñ ki

Now what do you celebrate?
That country that was torn into two
Whose song do you sing?
Of that nation that came into being only upon being broken?

You celebrate the ones with whose blood
You painted your nights a ruby shade?
Or those oppressed with whom you spoke
In the murderous tongue of the blade?

Josh's quiet despair was evident in his couplet:

Apna gala kharosh-e tarannum se phat gaya
Talvaar se bacha, to rag-e gul se kat gaya

The strain of song tore our throats
We escaped the sword, but were beheaded by the rose's vein

The division of the nation along religious lines, particularly the formation of Pakistan as a state founded on the basis of Muslim nationalism, was repugnant to the Progressives. Independence had produced a condition that was far removed from their cherished dream of a socialist, united India. The use of religion as a means to unite, and consequently divide people, was widely condemned by them on both sides of the border. They wrote extensively about the conditions of independence, contending that it was the result of a deal made between the British government and an alliance of the rich and powerful in India and Pakistan. In an editorial published in *Savera,* Sahir Ludhianvi and Nazir Chaudhri asserted that 'the edifices of nationalism ... raised on the false view of religion' would soon 'crumble to dust'.[23]

The newly formed states were seen as oppressive, an assessment that was borne out soon afterwards by the attitude of the governments of both India and Pakistan towards the Left. Abdul Majeed Bhatti's song depicts the irony of self-rule under which women and girls were being abducted and raped:

Beti gaaoñ bhar ki beti
Beti sab ki laaj
Nagar nagar meiñ kaudi-kaudi bik gayi beti aaj
Aaya apna raaj!

The girls who were the entire village's daughters
The girls who were everyone's honour

Are now being sold for a pittance
Self-rule has arrived!

In a comment about this poem, Zaheer Kashmiri contended that it was obvious that 'the riots and the so-called independence are two inevitable aspects of the imperialist policy'[24].

Faiz's 'Subh-e Aazaadi' ended with the following lines asserting that the arrival of Independence was not the end of the struggle:

Abhi giraani-e shab meiñ kami nahiñ aayi
Najaat-e deeda-o dil ki gha<u>d</u>i nahiñ aayi
Chale chalo ke voh manzil abhi nahiñ aayi

The burden of the night still weighs us down
The eye and the heart are still not free
Move on, for our destination hasn't yet been reached

The Disillusionment with the Nation-State

The *manzil* (destination) for many of the Progressives was a socialist revolution. Freedom from the British was seen by many of them as the replacement of one form of imperialism by another. For them, the battle continued. The poets saw their work as a means to build a certain kind of political consciousness among their millions of listeners. The Congress leadership, once valourized, bore the brunt of the attack.

The Telangana peasant movement had been held aloft as the beacon of the revolutionary age to come. The rural poor of this region had generated an uprising that was unique in its caste/class participation and its vision of a new order. This revolutionary movement that had started in 1939 was still strong in 1947 when Makhdoom wrote 'Telangaana':

Dayaar-e Hind ka voh raahbar Telangaana
Bana raha hai nayi ek sahar Telangaana

Bula raha hai ba simt-e digar Telangaana
Voh inquilaab ka paighaambar Telangaana

The leader of a new India, Telangana
The creator of a new dawn, Telangana
Beckoning us towards a new place
The prophet of the revolution, Telangana

Since the ode to Telangana demanded a salute towards the source of its inspiration, the 'Arz-e Cheen' (the land of China), the poem ended with the following lines:

Salaam surkh shaheedoñ ki sar-zameen salaam
Salaam azm-e buland, aahani yaqeen salaam
Mujaahidoñ ki chamakti hui jabeen salaam
Dayar-e Hind ki mahboob arz-e Cheen salaam

Salutations to the land of the red martyrs
To the lofty purpose, its iron-clad certainty
To the shining foreheads of the revolutionaries
To the land of China, India's beloved

But the Telangana Movement was brutally crushed by the newly formed state. Jawaharlal Nehru, once the darling of the Progressives, received his share of the flak and was subjected to vitriolic criticism such as '*Commonwealth ka daas ye Nehru, aur tabaahi laane na paaye*' ('Let us ensure that Nehru, the slave-agent of the Commonwealth does not wreak any more havoc'). The disillusionment with the bourgeois nation-state was expressed in acerbic terms by Sahir in his poem titled 'Chhabbees Janvary' (26th January[25]):

Aao ke aaj ghaur kareñ is savaal par
Dekhe the hum ne jo, voh haseeñ khwaab kya hue?
Bekas barehnagi ko kafan tak nahiñ naseeb
Voh vaada-haa-e atlas-o kamkhwaab kya hue?
Jamhooriyat-navaaz, bashar-dost, amn-khwaah
Khud ko jo khud diye the, voh alqaab kya hue?

> Come, and let us ponder on the question
> Those beautiful dreams of ours, what became of them?
> The helpless and naked cannot even afford a shroud
> What happened to those promises of silk and satin?
> Democrat, humanist, pacifist
> What happened to all those self-conferred titles?

While the critique of the national leadership continued, the PWA lost much steam during this period. The internal struggles of the Communist Party of India, especially between the moderate faction headed by P. C. Joshi and the radicals led by B. T. Ranadive played themselves out in the literary arena as well. The Ranadive doctrine was more or less adopted by the PWA with Abdul Aleem issuing what amounted to a policy statement: 'The so-called nationalist government proclaim themselves as enemies of imperialism but make compromises with it. All their policies are in the interests of capitalists while they pretend to represent the people. This contradiction is demonstrated in every department of culture and civilization, especially literature.'

The world according to the new manifesto (1949) was split between two camps – the democratic and the imperialist. Similarly, India was divided into feudal reactionaries in collusion with foreign and domestic capitalists, and the forces of progressivism. The concept of Socialist Realism, as defined by the Statute of the Union of Soviet Writers, was invoked, demanding a truthful, historically concrete depiction of reality that served the purposes of ideological transformation and the education of the workers in the spirit of socialism. The PWA denounced individualism and those who engaged in art for arts sake (*adab ba ra-e adab adeeb*), taking many of their own to task for failing to live up to these standards. Internal fights and purges followed and while the PWA eventually did weather these storms, it emerged from them as a significantly weaker force. Its period of uncontested hegemony had come to an end.

Notwithstanding the fact that the moment of Independence and the following period had not resulted in the fulfilment of their socialist dream, the Progressives continued to write with great intensity about issues of social justice. But their aspirations were now different, their enthusiasm and hope for an egalitarian society now tempered. This period was marked by the decline of the movement and progressive Urdu poetry spoke chiefly through the remaining voices of those who had carried its banner so proudly in the past. Some of the more interesting poetry was produced through the attempts of the Progressives to seek newer configurations by turning their attention to struggles taking place in different parts of the world. Poems were composed on Palestine, Vietnam, the Congo, Patrice Lumumba, the Rosenbergs, Paul Robeson and Martin Luther King. In some ways, international solidarity with anti-imperialist struggles took the place of nationalist aspirations in the Progressives' repertoire.

***

The trajectory that we have laid out can be read in more ways than one. For example, one can see this account as a failure of the progressive Urdu poets to come to terms with the shifting terrain of nationalism. Or, one could understand it as the failure of nationalism and modernity to live up to their promises of liberty and equality for all. In either case, the Progressives can be seen as critics of nationalism in the revolutionary tradition of anti-colonial black intellectuals like Frantz Fanon and C.L.R. James, positing universal goals like emancipation and giving prominence to what Fanon called social consciousness over national consciousness.

For the Progressives, the world was a secular space; it was the world of Time, the world of History and above all, a world fashioned by human beings. It had no room for revelation, redemption or a transcendental origin. And if it had a telos, it was the socialist revolution. The pursuit of this ideal led them to adopt a variety of strategies based on class solidarity in an attempt to create a socially just form of nationalism.

Ironically, the urge to reject religious and sectarian identities was so overwhelming that the condition of minority existence in a polarizing society was never really addressed. One might argue that progressive Urdu poetry's abdication of the space of religion made it easier for retrograde and communal forces to appropriate it (though it would be unfair to blame the Progressives for this). A more sympathetic reading might be that perhaps the burden of the minority and the urge to prove their fidelity to an India that was growing suspicious of its Muslim citizens weighed heavily on them. One example of this can be found in their attitude towards the Sino-Indian conflict of 1962 and the Indo-Pak war of 1965. Despite the fact that many of the Progressives had maintained a strong anti-war stance in much of their work (with the 'peoples' war' period being a glaring exception), they penned some rather militant verses during this time, exemplified by the following lines from Kaifi's song for the movie *Haqeeqat* (1964):

Khench do apne khooñ se zameeñ par lakeer
Is taraf aane paaye na Raavan koi
Tod do haath gar haath uthne lageñ
Chhoone paaye na Sita ka daaman koi
Raam ho tum, tumhiñ Lakhsman saathiyo
Ab tumhaare havaale watan saathiyo

Draw a line on the sand with your blood
May no Ravan be able to cross it

Break those hands that rise against us
May no one be able to touch Sita's garment again
You are Ram, and you are Lakshman too, O compatriots
We now leave this land in your care

Most Indian writers took a hard stand against Pakistan during the 1965 war (an attitude that was reflected on the other side of the border). The notable exceptions were the old-timer Progressives such as Ali Sardar Jafri, who insisted on writing poetry urging the people of both countries to examine their attitudes and to turn the border from one that separated nations into one that symbolized kissing lips:

Voh din aaye ke aansoo ho ke nafrat dil se bah jaaye
Voh din aaye ye sarhad bosa-e lab ban ke rah jaaye
...
Ye sarhad doobte taaroñ, ubharte aaftaaboñ ki
Ye sarhad khooñ meiñ lithde pyaar ke zakhmi gulaaboñ ki
Maiñ is sarhad pe kabse muntazar hooñ subh-e farda ka

May that day arrive when hatred ebbs from the heart in the form of tears
May that day arrive when this border becomes the kissing lips of the beloved
...
This is the border of setting stars, of rising suns
This the border of love's roses soaked in blood
I, for long, have been waiting at this border for a new morning

Sahir characteristically wrote a strong poem, urging the two nations to turn their attention to other, more important wars:

Jang sarmaaye ke tasallut se
Amn jamhoor ki khushi ke liye
Jang jangoñ ke falsafe ke khilaaf
Amn pur-amn zindagi ke liye

Wage war against the grip of capitalism
Seek peace for the happiness of the common people

Wage war against the philosophy of war
Seek peace for the sake of a harmonious life

Perhaps the most famous of Sardar Jafri's verses are these from a poem 'Kaun Dushman Hai?' (Who is the Enemy?) that was composed during the 1965 war and addressed to his Pakistani counterparts:

Tum aao gulshan-e Lahore se chaman bar-dosh
Hum aayeñ subh-e Banaaras ki raushni le kar
Himaalaya ke havaaoñ ki taazagi le kar
Phir us ke baad ye poochhenge, kaun dushman hai?

You come bearing the gardens of Lahore on your shoulders
We will bring the brightness of Benaras' morning
The freshness of the Himalayan breeze
And then, we can ask one another: who is the enemy?

***

The Partition had divided the nation in more ways than one. The political partition of the region was followed in a gradual fashion by its cultural partition. The tensions between state and literary ideologies, between their durability and mutation were inscribed on the body of Urdu itself.

The year 1947 was not the only partition that the region witnessed. In 1971, following a long and brutal repression of the aspirations of the Bengali population of East Pakistan, the state of Bangladesh came into being. In a poignant poem Faiz, returning from a trip to the new nation, wrote about the hatred and suspicion that now filled the hearts of his once-compatriots:

Hum ke ṯhahre ajnabi itni madaaraatoñ ke baad
Phir banenge aashna kitni mulaqaatoñ ke baad
Kab nazar meiñ aayegi be-daagh sabze ki bahaar
Khoon ke dhabbe dhulenge kitni barsaatoñ ke baad
Dil to chaaha par shikast-e dil ne mohlat hi na di
Kuch gile-shikve bhi kar lete munaajaatoñ ke baad

The bahut be-dard lamheñ khatm-e dard-e ishq ke
Thi bahut be-mahr sub'heñ mehrbaañ raatoñ ke baad
Un se jo kahne gaye the Faiz, jaañ sadqa kiye
Ankahi hi rah gayee voh baat sab baatoñ ke baad

We remain strangers, despite our histories of hospitality
How many more meetings will we need, before we become friends again?
When again will we see the bloom of an unspoiled spring?
How many rainfalls will it take to wash away the bloodstains?
The heart did desire fiercely, but its wounds gave no respite
If only we could share grievances too, after the pleasantries were done
Devastating were the moments when the pain of love came to an end
Very cruel were the mornings after the gentleness of those nights
Faiz, that one thing which I went there to say with all my heart
That very thing was left unsaid, after so much had been spoken

***

The engagement of the progressive poets with the issue of nationalism was complex and contingent. At different points in history, the Progressives were determined nationalists struggling against an imperial order, allies in common cause with other nationalist struggles, patriots averse to letting the promise of the nation-state be subverted by a self-serving leadership and internationalists who recognized no border in their expressions of solidarity with those who were battling injustice. The unifying theme of the Progressives' engagement with nationalism was their insistence that it be reclaimed from the grasp of the elites by the common people, that it be defined by the masses rather than the leaders and that it be held accountable to the consciousness of a universality that was underscored by justice and egalitarianism.

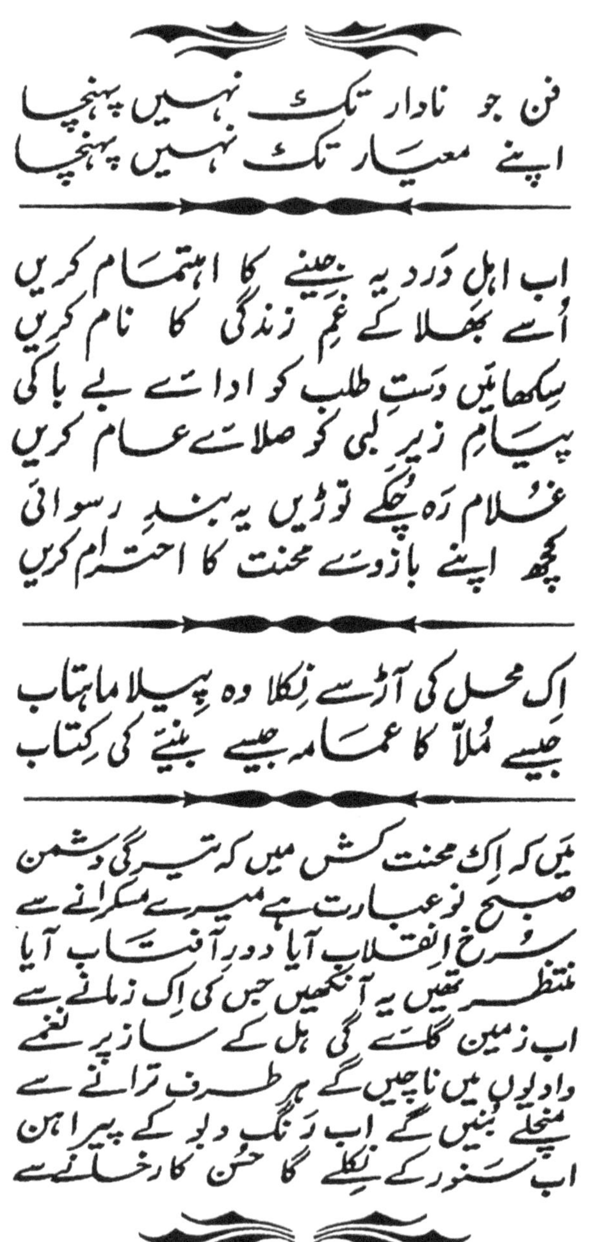

فن جو نادار تک نہیں پہنچا
اپنے معیار تک نہیں پہنچا

اب اہلِ درد یہ جینے کا اہتمام کریں
اُسے بھلا کے غمِ زندگی کا نام کریں
سکھائیں دستِ طلب کو ادائے بے باکی
پیامِ زیرِ لبی کو صلائے عام کریں
غلام رہ چکے توڑیں یہ بندِ رسوائی
کچھ اپنے بازوئے محنت کا احترام کریں

اِک محل کی آڑ سے نِکلا وہ پِیلا ماہتاب
جیسے مُلّا کا عمامہ جیسے بنیے کی کِتاب

میں کہ اِک محنت کش میں کہ تیرگی دشمن
صبحِ نو عبارت ہے میرے مسکرانے سے
سُرخ اِنقلاب آیا دورِ آفتاب آیا
منتظر تھیں یہ آنکھیں جس کی اِک زمانے سے
اب زمین گائے گی ہل کے ساز پر نغمے
وادیوں میں ناچیں گے ہر طرف ترانے سے
منچلے بُنیں گے اب رنگ و بو کے پیراہن
اب سنور کے نِکلے گا حُسن کارخانے سے

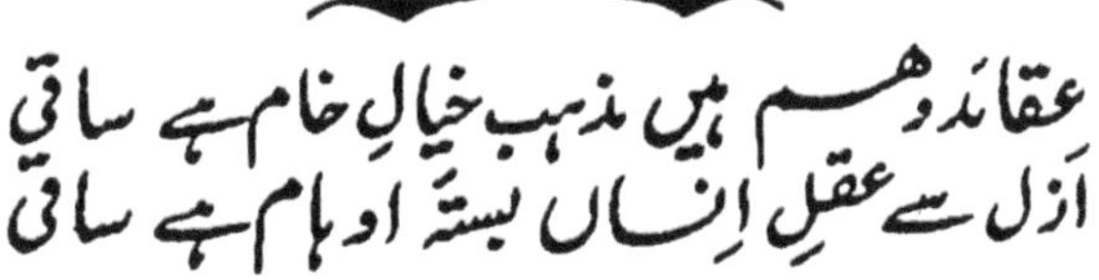

عقائد وہم ہیں مذہب خیالِ خام ہے ساقی
ازل سے عقلِ انساں بستۂ اوہام ہے ساقی

یہ دنیا دو رنگی ہے
ایک طرف سے ریشم اوڑھے ایک طرف سے ننگی ہے
ایک طرف اندھی دولت کی پاگل عیش پرستی
ایک طرف جسموں کی قیمت روٹی سے بھی سستی
ایک طرف ہے سونا گاچی ایک طرف چورنگی ہے
یہ دنیا دو رنگی ہے

کھائیں بھی مزدور کا مزدور پہ غُرّائیں بھی
دِن کو محنت بھی کرائیں رات کو رُلوائیں بھی
بھوک سے مزدور کے بچّے بھی بِلکیں مائیں بھی
تف ہے سرمایہ پرستوں پر کہیں مِٹ جائیں بھی
اِنتقام اے اِنتقام اے اِنتقام

ہم دیکھیں گے
لازِم ہے کہ ہم بھی دیکھیں گے، ہم دیکھیں گے
وہ دِن کے جس کا وعدہ ہے
جو لوحِ ازل پہ لِکھا ہے
ہم دیکھیں گے

4

FROM HOME TO THE WORLD

The Internationalist Ethos

In March 1955, Faiz Ahmad Faiz, still imprisoned in Rawalpindi's Montgomery Jail where he had been interred since 1951 for 'seditious activities', wrote 'Aa Jaao Africa' (Come, Africa), based on a phrase he had heard as a rallying cry among African anti-colonial rebels:

... Aa jaao maiñ ne dhool se maatha utha liya
Aa jaao maiñ ne chheel di aankhoñ se gham ki chhaal
Aa jaao maiñ ne dard se baazoo chhuda liya
Aa jaao maiñ ne noch diya bekasi ka jaal
'Aa jaao Africa'

Dharti dhadak rahi hai mere saath Africa
Dariya thirak raha hai to ban de raha hai taal
Maiñ Africa hooñ dhaal liya maiñ ne tera roop
Maiñ tu hooñ, meri chaal hai teri, babar ki chaal
'Aa jaao Africa'
Aao babar ki chaal
'Aa jaao Africa'

Come, Africa
Come, for I have raised my forehead from the dust

Scraped away the grief from my eyes
Broken away from the grip of pain
Torn away the web of helplessness
Come, Africa!

The earth's heart beats with mine, Africa
The river dances while the moon keeps time
I am Africa, for I have taken on your form
I am you, and my gait is your lion-walk
Come, Africa
Come with a lion-walk
Come, Africa!

If Faiz's poem is a vibrant example of the internationalist ethos of progressive Urdu poetry, it is no exception either. The internationalist commitment of the Progressive Movement was apparent since its very beginning. The anti-fascist struggles of European literary figures had enthused the Progressives, and one of the first official actions taken by the newly formed PWA, in 1935, was to send Sajjad Zaheer and Mulk Raj Anand as their representatives to London to participate in the conference of 'International Writers for the Defense of Culture'[26].

This culture of internationalism was not exactly new to Urdu literature; Mohammad Iqbal had been expanding the horizons of Urdu literature's engagement with the world for a while. The PWA poets, however, took this to new levels. The association had come into being at a time when the freedom movement was at its height, and the initial writings of its members were focused on the struggle against British occupation. Overtures to internationalism took on two forms: an interrogation and critique of colonialism and its related issues (the Second World War, for instance) and an expression of admiration for the Soviet revolution accompanied by a hope that India's freedom would result in a similar socialist society.

The disillusionment with the consequences of Independence – chiefly, the partition of the nation-state and its resultant bloodbath – and the disenchantment with the newly formed bourgeois state, which acted decisively and ruthlessly against the militant peasant movement of Telangana, took a toll on the erstwhile optimism of the progressive poets. In the years that were to follow, they increasingly turned their attention to the anti-colonial and anti-imperialist struggles of their time. The shift of focus towards the international arena was also spurred substantially by Ali Sardar Jafri's essay in *Naya Adab* titled 'Taraqqi Pasand Sha'iri ke Baaz Masaa'el' (Some Issues Facing Progressive Poetry) in which he urged Urdu poets to give expression to and highlight people's movements in other parts of the world. Several poets responded enthusiastically to this call and composed verses about China, Japan, Burma, Malay, Indonesia, Korea, Turkey, Iran, and Tunisia, among others.

The emergence of the Non-Aligned Movement at Bandung, Indonesia in 1955 (coincidentally, the year of the writing of 'Aa Jaao Africa'), concretized the idea of Third World solidarity, and provided another basis for its poetic expression in progressive poetry. The cultural exchange fostered by the Non-Aligned and Afro-Asian movements led to the translation of many of Faiz's poems in Swahili, Chinese and Vietnamese, while the works of progressive poets from around the world[27] were translated into Urdu.

As Carlo Coppola[28] points out, the progressive poets 'studied and borrowed from English literature, but unlike their fellow writers of earlier generations the Progressives also looked to the literature of France and Germany and especially Russia for additional inspiration. No longer were writers confined to the particular problems and concerns of India; they were thrust into the mainstream of international literary and intellectual life. Literary movements and ideas in London, Paris and Moscow had immediate repercussions in Delhi, Lucknow and Lahore.'

This period of Third World solidarity saw the Progressives composing poems on issues such as the struggles of Iranian students in 1959, the McCarthy era of repression of dissent in the United States, the European student uprisings in the 1960s, the Algerian freedom movement, the Palestinian struggle and the anti-apartheid movement in South Africa.

Internationalist sentiment within progressive poetry did not begin, of course, in this period. As socialists, the Progressives were always internationalists and the original focus of their internationalism was, obviously, the communist revolution and the international working-class movement – even Iqbal wrote paeans to it and to its heroes. Decades later (1970 to be precise), Sahir would write the following hagiographic lines on the occasion of the worldwide centennial celebrations of Lenin's birth:

Insaañ ke muqaddar ko aazaad kiya tu ne
Mazhab ke fareboñ se, shaahi ke azaaboñ se

Through you, humanity was released from its fate
And was freed from the deceptions of religion, the depredations of monarchy

When Julius and Ethel Rosenberg were executed in 1953 by the US government on the charge of being Soviet spies, Faiz wrote a lyrical tribute titled 'Hum jo tareek raahoñ meiñ maare gaye' (We who were executed on dark highways):

Tere hontoñ ke phooloñ ki chaahat meiñ hum
Daar ki khushk tahni pe vaare gaye
Tere haathoñ ki shamm'oñ ki hasrat meiñ hum
Neem-tareek raahoñ meiñ maare gaye ...

Jab ghuli teri raahoñ meiñ shaam-e sitam
Hum chale aaye laaye jahaañ tak qadam
Lab pe harf-e ghazal, dil meiñ qandeel-e gham
Apna gham tha gavaahi tere husn ki
Dekh khaayam rahe is gavaahi pe hum
Hum jo tareek raahoñ meiñ maare gaye

In the desire for the flowers that were your lips
We were sacrificed on the dry branch of the scaffold
In the yearning for the light of your hands
We were killed in the darkening streets ...

As the evening of tyranny dissolved in your memory
We walked on as far as our feet could carry us
A song on our lips, a lamp of sadness in our heart
Our grief bore witnesss to our love for your beauty
Look, we remained true to that love
We, who were executed in the dark lanes

The anti-imperialist position of the PWA also found its voice during the Vietnam war. Kaifi Azmi's 'Ibn-e Maryam' (Mary's Son) implored Jesus to come back for the sake of those who were being killed by members of his flock:

Jaao, voh Vietnaam ke jangal
Us ke masloob shahr, veeraañ gaaoñ
Jin ko Injeel padhne vaaloñ ne
Raund daala hai, phoonk daala hai
Jaane kab se pukaarte haiñ tumhe

Go to those jungles of Vietnam
Its crucified cities and desolate villages
That have been crushed and burnt by Bible-readers
They have been calling out to you for a while

***

The last major organizational act by the PWA was to hold an Afro-Asian Writers' conference in 1970, in which poets from Guinea, South Africa, Sudan, North and South Vietnam, Laos, and various parts of the subcontinent participated. This conference was a culmination of over two decades of solidarity between the progressive poets and their African counterparts. By this time, Africa had established a strong presence in the consciousness of the Urdu Progressives. Writing in the late 1960s, Ali Sardar Jafri had sought to articulate a bond with the 'Negro', claiming a special relationship between Indians and Africans:

Habshi mera bhai
Jangal jangal phool chune
Bhai ke paaooñ laal gulaab

This African, my brother
Picks flowers in forest after forest
My brother, whose feet are red
Red as roses

In this poem, Jafri's identification with the Africans and their struggles is obvious. What is lost in the English translation is the affection that accompanies this solidarity. Those who are familiar with the idiom will know that the couplet, *Jangal jangal phool chune, Bhai ke paaooñ laal gulaab,* is from a folk song expressing deep fraternal fondness.

And a brother's suffering compelled the poet to fashion poetry embodying a shared sense of grief and loss. When Patrice Lumumba, the first Prime Minister of the Republic of Congo and a staunch anti-imperialist, was deposed from office and subsequently murdered, Urdu poets celebrated his achievements and mourned his death. Makhdoom captured the feelings of the Progressives in his poem 'Chup Na Raho' (Be Not Silent):

Aur oonchi hui sehra meiñ umeedoñ ki saleeb
Aur ik qatra-e khooñ chashm-e sahar se tapka
Roz ho jashn-e shaheedaan-e wafa, chup na raho
Baar baar aati hai maqtal se sada, chup na raho, chup na raho

On a high scaffold, hope was hanged again in the desert
And another drop of blood fell from the eye of the morn
Let the celebration of martyrs continue, be not silent
The execution grounds cry out: be not silent, do not be silent

One of the more powerful poems written on this occasion was Sahir's 'Khoon Phir Khoon Hai' (Blood, However, is Blood). The poem begins with an epigraph, a fragment of a quote by Nehru (identified by Sahir as simply, Jawahar): A murdered Lumumba is several times more powerful than a living Lumumba ...

Zulm phir zulm hai, badhta hai to mit jaata hai
Khoon phir khoon hai, tapkega to jam jaayega

Khaak-e sehra pe jame ya kaf-e qaatil pe jame
Farq-e insaaf pe ya paa-e salaasil pe jame
Tegh-e bedaad pe ya laasha-e bismil pe jame
Khoon phir khoon hai, tapkega to jam jaayega

Laakh baithe koi chhup chhup ke kameengaahoñ meiñ
Khoon khud deta hai jallaadoñ ke maskan ka suraagh

Saazisheñ laakh udaati raheeñ zulmat ke naqaab
Le ke har boond nikalti hai hatheli pe charaagh

Zulm ki qismat-e naakaara-o rusva se kaho
Jabr ki hikmat-e purkaar ke eema se kaho
Mahmil-e majlis-e aqvaam ki Laila se kaho
Khoon deewaana hai, daaman pe lapak sakta hai
Shola-e tund hai, khirman pe lapak sakta hai

Tum ne jis khoon ko maqtal meiñ chupaana chaaha
Aaj voh koocha-o baazaar meiñ aa nikla hai
Kahiñ shola, kahiñ naara, kahiñ patthar ban kar
Khoon chalta hai to rukta nahiñ sangeenoñ se
Sar uthaata hai to jhukta nahiñ aaeenoñ se

Zulm ke baat hi kya, zulm ki auqaat hi kya
Zulm bas zulm hai aaghaaz se anjaam talak
Khoon phir khoon hai, sau shakl badal sakta hai
Aisi shakleñ ke mitaao to mitaaye na bane
Aise sholay ke bujhaao to bujhaaye na bane
Aise naare ke dabaao to dabaaye na bane

Tyranny is but tyranny; when it grows, it is vanquished
Blood however is blood; if it spills, it will congeal

It will congeal on the desert sands, on the murderer's hand
On the brow of justice, and on chained feet
On the unjust sword, on the sacrificial body
Blood is blood; if it spills, it takes root

Let them hide all they want, skulk in their lairs
The tracks of spilled blood will point out the executioners' abode
Let conspiracies shroud the truth with darkness
Each drop of blood will march out, holding aloft a lamp

Say this to tyranny's worthless and dishonoured Destiny
Say this to Coercion's manipulative intent
Say this to the Laila, the darling of the assembly[29]
Blood is wild, it will splatter and stain your garment
It is a rapid flame that will scorch your harvests

That blood which you wished to bury in the killing fields
Has risen today in the streets and the courts
Somewhere as a flame, somewhere as a slogan, somewhere else as a flung stone
When blood flows, bayonets cannot contain it
When it raises its defiant head, laws will not restrain it

Tyranny has no caste, no community, no status nor dignity
Tyranny is simply tyranny, from its beginning to its end
Blood however is blood; it becomes a hundred things:
Shapes that cannot be obliterated
Flames that can never be extinguished
Chants that will not be suppressed

***

The Civil Rights Movement of the US was similarly a source of great inspiration to the Progressives who saw their own memories of colonial exclusion reflected in the plight of the African-Americans. Gandhi's influence on Martin Luther King and its impact on the black liberation movement had already helped establish a bond between people of the two countries. Langston Hughes, the Harlem-based African-American poet, had written:

Mighty Britain tremble!
Let your empire's standard sway
Lest it break entirely –
Mr Ghandi fasts today

All of Asia's watching
And I am watching too
For I am also jim crowed
As India is jim crowed by you

This powerful expression of solidarity, based on a common racial identity, is echoed by Ali Sardar Jafri's poem on Paul Robeson:

Krishn ka geet hai, Gokhul ki haseeñ shaam hai tu
Aa kaleje se lagaaleñ ke siyaah-faam hai tu

You are Krishna's song, you are Gokul's beautiful evening
Come let us embrace, for you too, like me, are dark-skinned

Jafri's use of a racialized (non-white) identity to make a connection with the colonized communities in other parts of the world, and to implicitly place the opposition to oppression along the fault lines of race is particularly interesting when seen in the context of the fact that the Progressives had rarely deployed racial tropes during the freedom movement. This new sensibility – which coincided with the understanding of the racist underpinnings of colonialism articulated by the likes of Fanon (in *Black Skin, White Masks),* Aimee Cesaire and Amilcar Cabral – emerged from an understanding of and an identification with the anti-colonial struggles in Africa and the Civil Rights Movement in the US.

It was no surprise then that Martin Luther King became a celebrated hero for the Progressives and that his assassination, in 1968, prompted Makhdoom to write this poem, celebrating King's life, mourning his death and placing his politics within the broader context of other international struggles such as Palestine and Vietnam:

Ye qatl qatl kisi ek aadmi ka nahiñ
Ye qatl haq ka, masaavaat ka, sharaafat ka
Ye qatl ilm ka hikmat ka aadmiyat ka
Ye qatl hilm-o muravvat ka khaaksaari ka
Ye qatl ek ka do ka nahiñ, hazaar ka hai
Khuda ka qatl hai, qudrat ke shaahkaar ka qatl
Hai sham sham-e ghareebaañ, hai subha subh-e Hunain
Ye qatl qatl-e maseeha, ye qatl qatl-e Husain

Voh haath aaj bhi maujood-o kaar farma haiñ

Voh haath jis ne pilaaya kisi ko zahr ka jaam
Voh haath jis ne chaḏhaaya kisi ko sooli par
Voh haath vaadi-e Sina meiñ, Vieṯnaam meiñ hai
Har ek gardan-e meena, har ek jaam meiñ haiñ

'Kamina shart-e wafa tark-e sar buvad Haafiz
Baro guzaar-e tu eeñ-kaar gar nami aayad'[30]
This is not just the murder of one man
This is the murder of truth, of equality, of nobility
This is the murder of knowledge, of wisdom, of humanity
This is the murder of clemency, of chivalry, of humility
This is the murder of the alleviators of oppression
This is not just the murder of one or two, but of a thousand
This is the murder of God, of God's masterpiece
This night is the night of the wretched[31], this morning the morning of Hunain[32]
This is the murder of the messiah, this the murder of Husain

Even today, those hands remain and wreak havoc
Those hands that raised the poisoned chalice to someone's lips
Those hands that pushed someone to the gallows
Those same hands are still at work in the valley of Sinai, in Vietnam
Around the neck of every flask, around every goblet

'Fidelity demands, at the least, the willingness to sacrifice oneself, Hafiz
If you are not capable of this, then leave!'

The mention of the valley of Sinai in Makhdoom's poem was no isolated incident. Over a period of time, the Palestinian struggle for a nation-state had become an issue close to the hearts of the Progressives. Following the defeat of the Arab forces in the June 1967 war, Faiz wrote 'Sar-e Vaadi-e Seena' (Atop the Sinai Valley), which was, among other things, a scathing indictment of the hypocrisy of elitist pan-Islamists that urged his readers to cast off the chains of theocratic exploitation:

Phir barq farozaañ hai sar-e vaadi-e Seena
Ai deeda-e beena
Phir dil ko musaffa karo is lauh pe, shaayad
Maabain-e man-o tu naya paimaañ koi utre
Ab rasm-e sitam hikmat-e khaasaan-e zameeñ hai
Taa'eed-e sitam maslehat-e mufti-e deeñ hai
Ab sadiyoñ ke iqraar-e itaa'at ko badalne
Laazim hai ke inkaar ka farmaañ koi utre

Yet again, lightning shimmers atop the Sinai valley
O seeing eye
Ask the hearts to line up again
That between you and I, a new promise may descend
For now, the elite of the earth have decreed Tyranny to be normal
And the *mufti* has pronounced oppression worth obeying
To break this centuries-old cycle of acquiescence
A new proclamation must descend, the proclamation of dissent

Faiz, exiled to Lebanon under the dictatorship of General Zia-ul-Haq, wrote several poems dealing with the Middle Eastern conflict: a piece on the city of Beirut ('Ishq Apne Mujrimoñ Ko Pabajaulaañ Le Chala'/Love Leads its Prisoners Away in Chains), an anthem for Palestinian freedom fighters ('Ek Taraana Filastini Mujaahidoñ Ke Naam'), a dirge for those Palestinian martyrs who died in foreign lands ('Filastini Shohada Jo Pardes Meiñ Kaam Aaye'), and perhaps the most famous, a lullaby to a Palestinian orphan ('Mat Ro Bachche'/Weep Not, Child), and even dedicated his book 'Mere Dil, Mere Musaafir' (My Heart, My Wanderer) to the Palestinian leader Yasser Arafat.

In response to his call, a legion of Pakistani poets wrote with great feeling and empathy about Palestine[33], comparing the fate of the Palestinians to their own oppression under the dictatorship of Zia-ul-Haq. The most vocal of these was, of course, Habib Jalib, who taunted Zia-ul-Haq in a ghazal that quickly became a popular anthem:

Jahaañ khatre meiñ hai Islaam, us maidaan meiñ jaao
Hamaari jaan ke dar pe ho kyooñ, Lebnaan meiñ jaao
Ijaazat maangte haiñ hum bhi jab Beirut jaane ki
To ahl-e hukm ye kahte haiñ tum zindaan meiñ jaao

Go to the battleground where Islam actually is in danger
Why are you after our lives? Go to Lebanon
And when we ask for permission to go to Beirut
Our rulers instead tell us to head for the dungeons

Jalib was, of course, exposing the hypocrisy of the Zia regime whose battle cry (both before it usurped power and afterwards when justifying the need to 'Islamize' Pakistani state and society) was 'Islam in danger', but which refused to even pay lip service to the actual struggles of the people of Lebanon and Palestine.

***

Ultimately, the internationalist vision and solidarity of the Progressives came directly out of their politics and the general sensibility of the time. The realities of colonialism, and later neocolonialism/neo-imperialism, both required and provided a global frame of reference and a basis for shared political engagement with other colonized and/or oppressed peoples. Internationalism in this period, however, was not of a piece; the internationalism of the Progressives, for example, was a far cry from the pan-Islamism of Iqbal and his followers. It was instead informed by an understanding of the shared material conditions of oppression and struggle and was inspired by the international working-class movements and the struggles of colonized peoples across the world. There were other Urdu poets who wrote paeans to the Algerian freedom fighters and the Palestinian cause, but from within a pan-Islamic sensibility. Not so the Progressives, for whom internationalism meant a common struggle against imperialism and for a new world order.

کوہساروں کی طرف سے سُرخ آندھی آئے گی
جابجا آبادیوں میں آگ سی لگ جائے گی
اور اس رنگِ شفق میں باہزاراں آب و تاب
جگمگائے گا وطن کی حریت کا آفتاب

اُٹھو میری دنیا کے غریبوں کو جگا دو
کاخِ اُمرا کے در و دیوار ہلا دو
جس کھیت سے دہقاں کو میسّر نہیں روزی
اُس کھیت کے ہر گوشۂ گندم کو جلا دو

وہ بھگت سنگھ جس کے غم میں اب بھی دِل ناشاد ہے
اُس کی گردن میں جو ڈالا تھا وہ پھندا یاد ہے
ذہن میں ہوگا تازہ یہ ہندیوں کا داغ بھی
یاد تو ہوگا تمہیں جلیان والا باغ بھی

اپنا گلا خروشِ ترنّم سے پھٹ گیا
تلوار سے بچا تو رگِ گُل سے کٹ گیا

ابھی گرانیِ شب میں کمی نہیں آئی
نجاتِ دیدہ و دِل کی گھڑی نہیں آئی
چلے چلو کہ وہ منزل ابھی نہیں آئی

سلام سُرخ شہیدوں کی سرزمین سلام
سلام عزمِ بُلند، آہنی یقین سلام
مجاہدوں کی چمکتی ہوئی جبین سلام
دیارِ ہند کی محبوب ارضِ چین سلام

آؤ کہ آج غور کریں اِس سوال پر
دیکھے تھے ہم نے جو، وہ حسیں خواب کیا ہوئے؟
بےکس برہنگی کو کفن تک نہیں نصیب
وہ وعدہ ہائے اطلس و کمخواب کیا ہوئے؟
جمہوریت نواز، بشر دوست امن خواں
خود کو جو خود دیئے تھے، وہ القاب کیا ہوئے؟

5

DREAM AND NIGHTMARE

The Flirtation with Modernity

> The full power of the idea of modernity lay in a desire to wipe out whatever came earlier, so as to achieve a radically new departure, a point that could be a true present ...
>
> – Marshall Berman[34]

In 1958, when the Sputnik blasted into space, it received one of its most lyrical tributes from an unlikely source, Sahir Ludhianvi. In a poem titled 'Mere Ah'd Ke Haseeno' (Beauties of my Generation), Sahir presented the event as a success of humanity over nature. Taking aim at those who thought that their futures were determined by fate (the stars), Sahir saw in the Sputnik's rise yet another sign that humans had conquered those very heavenly bodies that purportedly held their fortunes hostage:

Voh buland-baam taare, voh falak-maqaam taare
Jo nishaan de ke apna, rahe be-nashaañ hamesha
Voh haseeñ, voh noor-zaade, voh khala ke shaahzaade
Jo hamaari qismatoñ par rahe hukm'raañ hamesha ...

Mere a'hd ke haseeno, voh nazar-navaaz taare
Mera ishq-e husn parvar tumheñ nazr de raha hai
Voh junooñ jo aab-o aatish ko aseer kar chuka tha

Voh khala ki vus'atoñ se bhi khiraaj le raha hai

Mere saath rahne vaalo, mere baad aane vaalo
Mere daur ka ye tohfa, tumheñ saazgaar aaye
Kabhi tum khala se guzro kisi seem-tan ki khaatir
Kabhi tum ko dil meiñ rakh kar koi gul-'izaar aaye

Those exalted stars, those heaven dwellers
Who revealed themselves, but remained beyond our reach
Those beautiful children of light, those princes of space
Who established their vain kingdom over our fates ...

O beautiful people of the new age, these very stars
Are hereby bequeathed to you by my generation
The passion that has already enslaved water and fire[35]
Now commands obeisance even from the depths of space

You who live with me, and you who will follow me in time
May this gift from my generation bring you joy
May you fly in space looking for a silver-bodied beauty
And may some rosy-cheeked one come looking for you

There is a passionate optimism in Sahir's poem, which works at several levels. It exhibits an unselfconscious internationalism in the way in which it appropriates a foreign achievement[36] as a matter of course. It curiously uses an unabashedly romantic tone and imagery to describe a technological event (the reference to *seem-tan*, silver-bodied beauties, reflects a futuristic aesthetic infused with romance). There is undisguised awe in the face of this wonder that has rendered familiar the same stars which, for all of human history, had been synonymous with unreachability and remoteness. The poem demonstrates an abiding faith in technology, expressing a belief that nature will ultimately bow down to the power of human endeavour. But above all, it is about the march of humanity over the seemingly insurmountable barriers in its path, and consequently of the ability of human beings to triumph over the erstwhile symbols of fatalism.

Sahir's *nazm* is a powerful example of the fascination of the PWA poets with the phenomenon of modernity, especially its technological and scientific aspects. Modernity, whether understood as a particular phase of world history or a particular episteme, is a slippery and multilayered concept, but it has some characteristic features that the Progressives were drawn towards and inspired by. Central to the concept of modernity is a deep and abiding faith in 'progress' in terms of a telos or end point towards which humanity marches inexorably. This telos does not represent a utopian ideal, but a goal that is well within the grasp of human endeavour (for the Progressives, the telos was a classless society). And it is the human being which is understood to be the driving force of this progress, and the agent of History. This understanding is accompanied by a belief in the power of science and technology to conquer nature and bend it to human will, and a conviction that logic and reason can triumph over moribund traditions, superstitions and religion.

But the Progressives were not the first – even within the Urdu literary tradition – to be so enamoured by and infused with the spirit of modernity. It is customary, for example, to regard Ghalib's letters, which were published and widely read, as the first instance of modernity in Urdu prose; even though some of his poems did engage with contemporary social conditions, they did so in an oblique fashion. The writings of Mohammad Husain Azad (1830-1910) and Altaf Husain Hali (1837-1914)[37] along with the works of Sayyid Ahmed Khan (1817-1898) and Shibli Nomani (1857-1914) pushed the agenda of social reform and modernity in Urdu literature, significantly transforming its preoccupations and aesthetics in the process.

The first authentically and quintessentially modern poet within the Urdu literary tradition was Mohammad Iqbal whose work explicitly engaged with nationalism, capitalism, socialism, imperialism and a host of other political and social issues of his time. Iqbal's revolutionary concept of *khudi* (selfhood), or a subject-centred rationality, dealt with in his 1915 collection titled *Asraar-e Khudi* (Intimations of Selfhood), celebrated free will and consequently the ability of human beings to determine their fate as the most important aspect of human nature. In one of his most famous couplets, Iqbal says:

Khudi ko kar buland itna, ke har taqdeer se pahle
Khuda bande se khud poochhe, bata, teri raza kya hai

Exalt your Self thus, that before every twist of fate
God himself asks you, 'My creation, let me know your desire'

But for the expression of unapologetically in-your-face, unconditional, take-no-prisoners paeans to modernity, we had to wait for the Marxist writers, especially those whose agenda was formalized under the institutional leadership of the PWA. The concept of modernity held a very seductive appeal to the Urdu writers of the PWA lineage. Committed as they were to radical social change, they were drawn to an ideology that was unabashedly iconoclastic and delighted in undermining sacred cows. Ironically, they sometimes fell into a different trap, that of making a sacred cow out of modernity itself.

That the promise of modernity was one of the most abiding influences on the PWA is obvious even on the most cursory of examinations[38] and is evident from the assertions made in its first manifesto. The PWA believed that older socio-political institutions stood in the way of progress and advocated a transformation of society that was predicated upon the transcendence of religion, culture and traditions. It constantly underscored the contention that literature ought to reflect material reality; literature that was produced for its own sake was frowned upon. It focused obsessively on 'rationality', often deriding extant literature for not being rational enough for the times. It took aim at the priestly class, exhibiting a disdain for religion that went far beyond the sly iconoclasm of earlier Urdu poetry.

Sahir's poem on the flight of the Sputnik was hardly an isolated instance of the celebration of modernity by the Urdu poets. Progressive poets deployed modern themes, developed new tropes in their writings as markers of their era and posited modernity itself as the solution to the problems that beset Indian society. The modernist dream of these poets appeared to acquire its own agency over time, becoming a vitally important part of their project. They frequently venerated artefacts of the industrial revolution such as mills, trains, electricity and rockets. Majaz's 'Raat Aur Rel' (The Night and the Train) is nothing less than an elegy to one of the most classic tropes of modernity – the train – and offers an interesting inventory of its admirable attributes. Like Sahir's poem, the mood here is romantic:

Phir chali hai rel, istayshan se lehraati hui
Neem-shab ki khaam'shi meiñ zer-e lab gaati hui
Daalti behis chataanoñ par hiqaarat ki nazar
Koh par hansti, falak ko aankh dikhlaati hui
Daaman-e taariki-e shab ki udaati dhajjiyaañ
Qasr-e zulmat par musalsal teer barsaati hui
Zad meiñ koi cheez aa jaaye to us ko pees kar
Irteqaa-e zindagi ke raaz batlaati hui

Al-ghharaz, badhti chali jaati hai, be-khhauf-o khhatar
Shaayar-e aatish-nafas ka khhoon khaulaati hui

Once again, the train jauntily leaves the station
Breaking the silence of the night with its whispered song
Casting scornful glances on the placid cliffs
Laughing at mountains, making eyes at the sky
Tearing the black fabric of the night to shreds
Shooting constant arrows of sparks at the palace of darkness
Crushing anything that comes in its way
Revealing the secrets of the evolution of life
Ultimately it flies, fearlessly,
Roiling the blood of the poet's fiery soul

It is easy to see why the train functions as the sign of modernity in Majaz's poem. The path of a train is straight, its destination unambiguous, its contours sharp-edged and its relationship with nature contemptuous. It emits fire and piercing whistles, leaps through mountains and ultimately fascinates the modernist poet in much the same way that doe-eyed and languid beauties captivated Ghalib and Zafar; he is as irresistibly drawn to it as the moth (*parvaana*) is to the taper (*sham'a*). It is interesting to note that while the theme of this poem is extremely unconventional, its language and form continue to be inspired by an earlier tradition, and deploy a set of metaphors and images quite recognizable by anyone who is familiar with ghazals and classical poetry.

***

A commitment to modernity also simultaneously reflected and necessitated a strident disavowal of certain cultural traditions, especially religious ones. Given the history of communalism in the subcontinent, the PWA poets were critical of the role of organized religion in creating inter-religious strife and the obstacles it placed in the path of peace and progress. In their eyes, religious orthodoxy and theological obscurantism were the 'Other' of Progress, and stood in the way of its liberatory promise. Given that many of them were Muslim, it was Islamic religious practices and traditions which tended to be the focus of their ire.

It is worth noting that this unrelenting critique of religion which was characteristic of the PWA was markedly different from its earlier expressions in Urdu poetry. Urdu poets like Ghalib and Mir had developed a style of sly attacks on religion, but their modus operandi had stayed within the bounds of the tradition of *gustaakhaana shaa'iri* (literally: irreverent poetry). For Ghalib and Mir, the object of the poet's ridicule was often the self-important yet ultimately bumbling religious figure: the *shaikh* (the holy man), the *waa'iz* (the preacher/adviser), the *safeer-e haram* (ambassador of the mosque) or the *naaseh* (the counsellor). For example, Ghalib says:

Kahaañ maikhaane ka darvaaza, Ghalib, aur kahaañ waa'iz
Par itna jaante haiñ, kal voh jaata tha ke hum nikle

Whither the tavern door, and whither the holy man, Ghalib?
But all I know is this; he was entering as I left

The implicit criticism here is not directed so much at the prescriptions of the *waa'iz* as at his hypocrisy and the fact that he does not practise the temperance he preaches. Note that religion itself is not under attack; only its self-righteous invocation by the unworthy is lampooned. Sometimes, in a different vein, the poet positioned a lover as a *kaafir*, the beautiful infidel who had the power to lead the poet-protagonist away from the *siraat-al mustaqeem*, the righteous path. This deviation from the straight and narrow was projected in light-hearted terms, as in this couplet by Mir in which a spartan religious existence comes up short against a gloriously misguided but tempting epicurean lifestyle:

Dekhi hai jab se us but-e-kaafir ki shakl, Mir
Jaata nahiñ hai jee tanik Islaam ki taraf

Ever since I saw that infidel statue, O Mir
My heart is not even mildly inclined toward Islam[39]

The Progressives, on the other hand, went beyond this playful mischievousness and upped the ante in their attacks on religion, supplementing the critique of the holy men with a direct condemnation of faith itself. For example, Sahir cuts to the chase:

Aqaaid vahm hai, mazhab khayaal-e khaam hai saaqi
Azal se zahn-e insaañ basta-e auhaam hai saaqi

O Saqi, faith is but superstition, religion an inferior idea
Since the dawn of time, this blindness has imprisoned our imagination

Here we have a broadside against the very notion of Faith, which is seen as no more than fraudulent obscurantism. The Progressives expressed a defiant atheism that sought to create a new world through the repudiation of faith (Sahir says elsewhere: *Ilhaad kar raha hai murattab jahaan-e nau;* Atheism is building a new world). Likewise, Majaz writes brusquely to an imaginary lover, who is inviting the poet to become a believer as a preamble to their relationship. His verse is not only dismissive of religious fervour, but of the very fruits that such an endeavour promises:

Dair-o kaabe ka maiñ nahiñ qaayal
Dair-o kaabe ko aashiyaañ na bana
Mujh meiñ tu rooh-e sarmadi mat phoonk
Raunaq-e bazm-e aarifaañ na bana

I believe neither in the temple nor the Kaaba,
Do not make them your home
Breathe not an eternal soul into me
I am not going to grace the company of the faithful

This audacious refusal to be co-opted into any spirituality or religion was a novel and interesting turn in Urdu poetry. Once religion was put in the dock with such ferocity, the Progressives felt free to subject its practitioners and ambassadors to acerbic calumny. Their mocking of religious evangelists also became increasingly intransigent and uncivil. Josh Malihabadi collared the *mufti* thus:

Teri baatoñ se padi jaati hai kaanoñ meiñ kharaash
Kufr-o eemaañ, kufr-o eemaañ, ta kuja? Khaamosh-baash!

Your drivel now gives me an earache
Infidelity and faith, infidelity and faith, how long? Shut up!

Expectedly, such epithets ran afoul of the religious establishment and the PWA poets were ostracized by Islamic groups who discouraged the reading of these works by their wards. Despite this, the Progressives continued to be hugely popular among the youth of the times. In the tumultuous period that characterized the anti-colonial struggles and the emergence of the nation-state, the progressive poets offered a cavalier disregard for religious prescription that must have been a heady contrast to the conservatism of their times.

***

Given their unabashed commitment to socialism, it is hardly surprising that the poems of the PWA paid considerable attention to the social conditions of the time, particularly to the contributions of the common labourers towards the movement of humanity on the path of progress. In his famous poem 'Makaan' (House), for instance, Kaifi Azmi wrote evocatively about construction workers and their role in facilitating the transformation of human beings from tree-dwelling animals to civilized citizens residing in towns and cities:

Ye zameeñ tab bhi nigal lene pe aamaada thi
Paaoñ jab toot-ti shaakhoñ se utaare hum ne,
Un makaanoñ ko khabar hai, na makeenoñ ko khabar
Un dinoñ ki jo gufaaoñ meiñ guzaare hum ne
Haath dhalte gaye saanchoñ meiñ to thakte kaise
Naqsh ke baad naye naqsh nikhaare hum ne
Ki ye deewaar buland, aur buland, aur buland
Baam-o dar aur zaraa aur sanwaare hum ne
Aandhiyaañ töd liya karti thi shammoñ ki laveñ
Jad diye is liye bijli ke sitaare hum ne

The earth had forever threatened to swallow us
Since we descended from the breaking branches of trees,
Neither these houses, nor their residents care to remember
Of all those days we spent in caves
Once our hand learnt the craft however, how could they tire?
Design after design took shape through our work
And then we built the walls higher, higher and yet higher,
Lovingly brought an even greater beauty to the ceilings and doors
Storms used to extinguish the flames of our lamps
So we fixed stars made of electricity in our skies

However, as the poem proceeds, Kaifi produces a moment of dissonance in which we are introduced to the possibility that modernity and progress are not all 'good'. The labourers, having constructed the edifice, are evicted from its premises and forced to sleep on the dirt outside, watching the walls of the palace of their creation with smouldering eyes. The poet comes face to face with the problem of modernity, understanding that while modernity can facilitate the conquest of nature resulting in the creation of wealth, it has no say in its equitable distribution. Kaifi responds by exhorting the labourers to revolt, promising to participate in the uprising. This is the poet's moment of recognition that a modernity in the service of capital cannot ensure the fulfilment of its liberatory potential:

Ban gaya qasr, to pahre pe ko'ee baith gaya
So rahe khaak pe hum shorish-e taameer liye
Apni nas nas meiñ liye mehnat-e paiham ki thakan
Band aankhoñ meiñ usi qasr ki tasveer liye
Din pighalta hai usi tarha saroñ par ab bhi
Raat aankhoñ meiñ khatakti hai siyaah teer liye
Aaj ki raat bahut garm hava chalti hai
Aaj ki raat na footpaath pe neend aayegi
Sab utho, maiñ bhi uthooñ, tum bhi utho, tum bhi utho
Koi khidki isi deewaar meiñ khul jaayegi

Once the palace was built, they hired a guard
While we slept in the dirt, with our screaming craft,
Our pulses pounding with exhaustion
Bearing the picture of that very palace in our tightly shut eyes
The day still melts on our heads
The night pierces our eyes with black arrows
A hot air blows tonight
It will be impossible to sleep on the pavement
Arise everyone! Me. You. And you too
That a window may open in these very walls

The poem is remarkable because while celebrating modernity, it also acknowledges its shortcomings from the point of view of the socialist: modernity by itself is incapable of ensuring a just and egalitarian society and thus fails the very subjects who were promised freedom in return for their labour. The failure of modernity hurts because it eventually crushes the flamboyant optimism it had generated in the dispossessed; the betrayal of its promise is poignant and heartbreaking. But at the same time, this realization is liberating for it points the way towards the path that leads to the promised future.

Ultimately, however, the betrayal which was the unkindest cut of all was the one they suffered at the hands of another quintessentially 'modern' artefact: the nation-state. The failure of nationalism itself, especially its inability to construct a national community which had overcome the barbarism of communalism and communal violence, was a harsh blow to the Progressives. In his characteristically direct poem, 'Mera Maazi Mere Kaandhe Pe' (My Past on My Shoulders), Kaifi, wondering at the persistence of sectarian violence in the subcontinent despite years of 'progress', concludes:

Ab tamaddun ki ho ye jeet ke haar
Mera maazi hai abhi tak mere kaandhe pe savaar

Padta rahta hai mere maazi ka saaya mujh par
Daur-e khoonkhaari se guzra hooñ, chhupaaooñ kyooñkar
Daant sab khoon meiñ doobe hue aate haiñ nazar

Mal liya maathe pe tahzeeb ka ghaala lekin
Barbariyat ka hai jo daagh, voh chhoota hi nahiñ
Gaaoñ aabaad kiye, shahr basaaye hum ne
Rishta jangal se jo apna hai, voh toota hi nahiñ

Now whether Civilization wins or suffers defeat
My past is still seated on my shoulders

> The shadow of my past continues to fall on me
> I have been blood-thirsty, how can I deny it?
> My teeth are still blood stained
>
> I have smeared civility on my face
> Which is still pockmarked by the scars of barbarity
> I have populated villages, moved to cities
> But never severed my relationship with the jungle

Modernity, even after the successful culmination of the anti-colonial struggle, was ultimately unable to vanquish the demons of the past which live on as a kind of bestiality within human beings.

The Progressives' initial optimism became tempered with time and with disillusionment over the nationalism project. Their poems were forced to negotiate the terrain of a modern landscape that was littered with the debris of destruction and violence. Their attempts to theorize this condition took forms that were often highly contrived and defensive. For instance, in a later poem 'Saanp' (Snake), Kaifi uses the snake as a symbol of the fundamentalism that technological progress had purportedly eliminated:

> *Ye saanp aaj jo phan uthaaye*
> *Mere raaste meiñ khada hai*
> *Pada tha qadam chaand par mera jis din*
> *Usi din use maar dala tha maiñ ne*
>
> This snake that blocks my way,
> Poised to strike
> I had killed it the day
> I set foot on the moon

Kaifi asserts that humankind had decisively exorcised the beast of sectarianism the day it had set foot on the moon. Modernity, signified by the landing on the moon, had triumphed over the atavistic aspects of human nature. However, the poem goes on to describe how the snake did not die, but was merely wounded; it took refuge in a temple, a mosque and a church, where it was well looked after and made stronger by various religious fundamentalisms. So far it appears that Kaifi is working within a more conventional mode, identifying religious obscurantism as the problem for the failure of modernity. However, at its end, the poem takes a different turn:

Hui jab se science zar ki ghulaam
Jo tha ilm ka aitbaar uth gaya
Aur is saanp ko zindagi mil gayi

Ever since science has become the slave of capital
Knowledge has been proven untrustworthy
And this snake has found life

In this moment, Kaifi identifies the true villain of the piece: capital and its enslavement of science. One can see at work in the poem a sense of despair about the emancipatory possibilities of 'progress' as long as 'science and reason' are held hostage by an exploitative system.

***

Ultimately, the Progressives' unconditional optimism with regard to the liberatory potential of modernity was undermined by circumstances which left them disillusioned and sometimes confused. Modernity cruelly announced its failure to its ardent believers in several ways. The tainted moment of freedom and decolonization, the rampant and ugly sectarian conflict in urban South Asia, and above all, the inability of the independent state to ensure a decent and dignified life for its citizens weighed heavily on the progressive poets. And when this failure looked deep into their eyes, the PWA poets wrote their best poems, poems of anguish and rage, producing several heartbreakers that may only be described as modernity's laments, its dirges.

One poem that, while written in the early days of the movement, captures this ambivalence vis-à-vis modernity's promise is Majaz's 'Aawaara' (Vagabond). The poem was written to highlight the deep sense of alienation that the Progressives felt with feudal Indian society and tells its story from the point of view of an intensely alienated protagonist who walks the streets at night, giving voice to his feeling of despair. His estrangement is derived from an understanding of his own poverty, a feeling that is exacerbated as he walks past merry streets where the elite have constructed artificial islands of prosperity surrounded by walls behind which one can pretend that all is well with the world. It also comes from his knowledge that all this wealth and gaiety could have been his too, had he been willing to make some compromises. He is, however, held back by his 'worthless' commitments to honesty and fealty. His unease with the scene around him is reflected in several images, sometimes of religious exploitation (a *mullah's* turban), sometimes of penury (a moneylender's ledger). The beauty of stars itself becomes the source of great anguish, which turns into a sense of fury at the end of the poem. However, in the new century, we can read it not as the impatient anger of the revolutionary, but the inchoate, ineffable and the tragic rage of the human being who is caught in a dilemma against a world that is neither comprehendable nor changeable. It is the rage of the utterly helpless and mirrors the condition of the PWA poets struggling to make sense of the nightmare that their modernist dream had turned into.

Shahr ki raat aur maiñ naashaad-o naakaara phirooñ
Jagmagaati jaagti sadkoñ pe aawaara phirooñ
Ghair ki basti hai, kab tak dar-ba-dar maaraa phirooñ
Ai gham-e dil kya karooñ, ai vahshat-e dil, kya karooñ

Jhilmilaate qamqamoñ ki raah meiñ zanjeer si
Raat ke aanchal meiñ din ki mohini tasveer si
Mere seene par magar dahki hui shamsheer si
Ai gham-e dil kya karooñ, ai vahshat-e dil, kya karooñ

Ye roopaheli chhaaoñ, ye aakaash par taaroñ ka jaal
Jaise Sufi ka tasavvur, jaise aashiq ka khayaal
Aah lekin kaun jaane, kaun samjhe ji ka haal
Ai gham-e dil kya karooñ, ai vahshat-e dil, kya karooñ

Phir voh toota ek sitaara, phir voh chhooti phuljhadi
Jaane kiski göd meiñ aayi ye moti ki ladi
Hook si seene meiñ uthi, chot si dil par padi
Ai gham-e dil kya karooñ, ai vahshat-e dil, kya karooñ

Raat hans hans kar ye kahti hai ke maikhaane meiñ chal
Phir kisi Shahnaaz-e la'ala-rukh ke kaashaane meiñ chal
Ye nahiñ mumkin to phir ai dost, veeraane meiñ chal
Ai gham-e dil kya karooñ, ai vahshat-e dil, kya karooñ

Har taraf bikhri hui rangeeniyaañ ra'anaaiyaañ
Har qadam par ishrateñ leti hui angdaaiyaañ
Badh rahi hai göd phailaaye hue rusvaaiyaañ
Ai gham-e dil kya karooñ, ai vahshat-e dil, kya karooñ

Raaste meiñ ruk ke dam le looñ meri aadat nahiñ
Laut kar vaapas chala jaooñ, meri fitrat nahiñ
Aur koi ham-nava mil jaaye ye qismat nahiñ
Ai gham-e dil kya karooñ, ai vahshat-e dil, kya karooñ

Muntazir hai ek toofan-e bala mere liye
Ab bhi jaane kitne darvaaze haiñ va mere liye
Par museebat hai mera ahd-e wafa mere liye
Ai gham-e dil kya karooñ, ai vahshat-e dil, kya karooñ

Jee meiñ aata hai ke ab ahd-e wafa bhi tod dooñ
Un ko pa sakta hooñ maiñ, ye aasra bhi tod dooñ
Haañ, munaasib hai ye zanjeer-e wafa bhi tod dooñ
Ai gham-e dil kya karooñ, ai vahshat-e dil, kya karooñ

Ek mahal ki aad se nikla voh peela maahtaab
Jaise mullah ka amaama, jaise baniye ki kitaab
Jaise muflis ki javaani, jaise beva ka shabaab
Ai gham-e dil kya karooñ, ai vahshat-e dil, kya karooñ

Dil meiñ ek shola bhadak utha hai, aakhir kya karooñ
Mera paimaana chhalak utha hai, aakhir kya karooñ
Zakhm seene ka mehak utha hai, aakhir kya karooñ
Ai gham-e dil kya karooñ, ai vahshat-e dil, kya karooñ

Jee meiñ aata hai, ye murda chaand taare noch looñ
Is kinaare noch looñ, aur us kinaare noch looñ
Ek do ki qadr kya, saare ke saare noch looñ
Ai gham-e dil kya karooñ, ai vahshat-e dil, kya karooñ

Muflisi, aur ye manaazir haiñ nazar ke saamne
Sainkdoñ Sultan-o jaabir haiñ nazar ke saamne
Sainkdoñ Changez-o Naadir haiñ nazar ke saamne
Ai gham-e dil kya karooñ, ai vahshat-e dil, kya karooñ

Le ke ek Changez ke haathoñ se khanjar tod dooñ
Taj par us ke damakta hai jo patthar tod dooñ
Koi tode ya na tode, maiñ hi badh kar tod dooñ
Ai gham-e dil kya karooñ, ai vahshat-e dil, kya karooñ

Badh ke is Indarsabha ka saaz-o saamaañ phoonk dooñ
Is ka gulshan phoonk dooñ, us ka shabistaañ phoonk dooñ
Takht-e Sultaañ kya, maiñ saara qasr-e Sultaañ phoonk dooñ
Ai gham-e dil kya karooñ, ai vahshat-e dil, kya karooñ

Night has fallen in the city, and I, unhappy and defeated
Roam, a vagabond on dazzling, awake streets
It is not my neighbourhood, how long can I loiter thus?
Anguished heart, desperate heart, what should I do?

In the glittering sky, the streetlights seem linked like a chain

The bosom of the night holds the image of a beautiful day
But the lights fall on my heart like the flash of a scimitar
Anguished heart, desperate heart, what should I do?

These beautiful shadows, this net of stars on the sky
Like a Sufi's contemplation, a poet's thought
But ah, who is to know, to understand a heart's plight?
Anguished heart, desperate heart, what should I do?

There falls a shooting star, like a sparkler
A string of pearls fell in somebody's lap, perhaps?
Desolation rises in my chest, hitting the heart like a blow
Anguished heart, desperate heart, what should I do?

The night laughs gaily, and invites me to a tavern
Or come then, to the boudoir of a rose-cheeked beauty
'If not, then join me O friend, among the ruins'
Anguished heart, desperate heart, what should I do?

Bright colours and lovely images lie scattered
At every step, joys beckon languorously
But look here, sorrows and defeats also proffer their laps
Anguished heart, desperate heart, what should I do?

To stop and rest on the way is not my habit
To admit defeat and return is not my nature
But to find a companion, alas, is not my fate
Anguished heart, desperate heart, what should I do?

A storm of misfortune lies, ready to waylay me
And though several open doors still beckon me
An old promise of fealty holds me back, like a curse
Anguished heart, desperate heart, what should I do?

Sometimes I wonder, should I break those foolish vows?
Should I even surrender the hope that love will be rewarded?
It is possible, is it not, that I could break this chain made of air?
Anguished heart, desperate heart, what should I do?

From behind a palace, emerged the yellow moon

Like a mullah's turban, like a moneylender's ledger
Like a poor man's youth, a widow's beauty
Anguished heart, desperate heart, what should I do?

My heart burns like a flame, what should I do?
The cup of my patience brims over, what should I do?
The wound in my chest is fragrant, what should I do?
Anguished heart, desperate heart, what should I do?

I want to pluck this dead moon, these dead stars from the sky
Pluck them from this end of the horizon and from that corner
Not just one or two, I want to pluck them all out
Anguished heart, desperate heart, what should I do?

My poverty, and these beautiful sights to behold
Hundreds of wealthy kings pollute my gaze
Hundreds of Chengizes, hundreds of Nadirs to behold[40]
Anguished heart, desperate heart, what should I do?

Ah that I could break every sword in the hands of every Chengiz
Pull out the jewel from his crown and break it too
Why wait for anyone else, let me break it myself
Anguished heart, desperate heart, what should I do?

I want to walk into the Indrasabha[41] and burn it to the ground
Burn down this garden, and burn down that bedchamber
Not just the king's crown, I want to burn the entire palace!
Anguished heart, desperate heart, what should I do?

جنگ سرمایہ کے تسلّط سے
امن جمہور کی خوشی کے لیے
جنگ جنگوں کے فلسفے کے خلاف
امن پُر امن زندگی کے لیے

تم آؤ گلشنِ لاہور سے چمن بر دوش
ہم آئیں صبحِ بنارس کی روشنی لے کر
ہمالیہ کی ہواؤں کی تازگی لے کر
پھر اس کے بعد یہ پوچھیں گے کون دشمن ہے!

یہ قتل قتل کسی ایک آدمی کا نہیں
یہ قتل حق کا مساوات کا شرافت کا
یہ قتل علم کا حکمت کا آدمیت کا
یہ قتل حلم و مُروّت کا خاکساری کا
یہ قتل ایک کا دو کا نہیں، ہزار کا ہے
خدا کا قتل ہے قدرت کے شاہکار کا قتل
یہ شام شامِ غریباں ہے صبحِ صبحِ حُنین
یہ قتل قتلِ مسیحا یہ قتل قتلِ حُسین

وہ ہاتھ آج بھی موجود و کارفرما ہیں
وہ ہاتھ جن نے پلائے کسی کو زہر کا جام
وہ ہاتھ جن نے چڑھایا کسی کو سولی پر
وہ ہاتھ وادیٔ سینا میں دیٹ نام میں ہیں
ہر ایک گردن مینا ہر ایک جام میں ہیں

"کمینہ شرطِ وفا ترکِ سر بود حافظ
برو گزار تو ایں کار بر نمی آید"

تیرے ہونٹوں کے پھولوں کی چاہت میں ہم
دار کی خشک ٹہنی پہ وارے گئے
تیرے ہاتھوں کی شمعوں کی حسرت میں ہم
نیم تاریک راہوں میں مارے گئے
جب گھلی تیری راہوں میں شامِ ستم
ہم چلے آئے لائے جہاں تک قدم
لب پہ حرفِ غزل دِل میں قندیلِ غم
اپنا غم تھا گواہی تیرے حسن کی
دیکھ قائم رہے اِس گواہی پہ ہم
ہم جو تاریک راہوں میں مارے گئے

6

PROGRESSIVE POETRY AND FILM LYRICS

Eeshwar Allah tere jahaañ meiñ, nafrat kyooñ hai jang hai kyooñ
Tera dil to itna badha hai, insaañ ka dil tang hai kyooñ
...
Is duniya ke daaman par, insaañ ke lahu ka rang hai kyooñ
...
Dil ke darwaazoñ par taale, taaloñ par ye zang hai kyooñ

O Eeshwar, O Allah, why this hatred, this war in your world?[42]
Your heart knows no bounds, why are the hearts of humans
so small and petty?
...
Why is the garment of the world stained with human blood?
...
Why are the doors of hearts locked, why are these locks rusted?

So goes the hauntingly beautiful song from the 1998 film *Earth*. Written by Javed Akhtar and set to music by A.R. Rahman (and incidentally, put to good use by Gauhar Raza as the recurring theme of *Evil Stalks the Land*, a documentary on the 2002 Gujarat violence), the song is obviously a homage to another one that was written earlier by Sahir Ludhianvi:

Khuda-e bartar, teri zameeñ par, zameeñ ki khaatir ye jang kyooñ hai
Har ek fath-o zafar ke daaman pe khoon-e insaañ ka rang kyooñ hai
...
Jinheñ talab hai jahaañ bhar ki unheeñ ka dil itna tang kyooñ hai
...
Saroñ meiñ kibr-o ghuroor kyooñ hai, diloñ ke sheeshe pe zang kyooñ hai

O great God, why do people of your earth wage war over land?
Why is the garment of every conqueror stained with human blood?
...
Why are the hearts of those who desire the whole world so small and petty?
...
Why are their heads swollen with pride and arrogance, why are the mirrors of their hearts rusted?

Do these two songs represent bookends of a line that ran from Sahir through Kaifi Azmi and Majrooh Sultanpuri to Javed Akhtar? Is there a generational continuity of progressive sentiment that Urdu poets deployed in the arena of popular culture through their Hindi film lyrics? After all one can, without much effort, recall a number of progressive film songs written by the Urdu poets of the PWA. In order to answer these questions, we bought books of lyrics, cross-checked with online databases and asked friends to tell us about the progressive songs that came to their mind. Surprisingly, the search yielded a far smaller output than we had first imagined. Nevertheless, there is a story to be told here, a narrative to unfold, a lesson or two to be learnt.

***

The deployment of songs to propel a narrative has a long and varied tradition in India. Many of the country's popular art forms have used this technique for a long time: the Kutiyattam and Kathakali in Kerala, the Jatra in Bengal, the Nautanki and Ramlila traditions in North India, the Marathi Tamasha, the Terukuttu from Tamil Nadu, the Burrakatha in Andhra Pradesh, the Yakshgana from Karnataka, the Bhavai from Gujarat, the Ojapali from Assam, the Lila from Orissa and, of course, the various enactments of the Ramayana and the Mahabharata.[43]

The early Parsi theatre, the precursor to Indian cinema, also had its share of songs. As Javed Akhtar says in an interview[44], in a play about Marcus and Helena set in Rome, for instance, Helena pining for her love would burst out into a song *Piya morey aaj nahiñ aaye* (My beloved hasn't come today). The original plays of the likes of Agha Hashr Kashmiri were subsequently adapted into Hindi cinema. Here is a typical dialogue from *Aseer-e Hirs* (Prisoner of Greed). The conver-sation is between Changez Khan and his love, Naushaba[45]:

N: *Pyaar se ek savaal hai* (I have a question for my love).

C: *Farmaaiye voh kya khayaal hai?* (Pray, what are you thinking?)

N: *Kumhaar jo mitti ka khilona banaata hai, voh kis kaam aata hai?* (The clay toy a potter makes, what good is it?)

C: *Us se dil bahlaaya jaata hai. Agar voh kisi ke haath se choot jaaye, ya thokar se toot jaaye, to kumhaar ko sakht malaal hoga* (It is to amuse one's heart. But if it slips through one's fingers, or is broken by a careless foot, the potter will be very sad).

N: *Kyonñ aisa khayaal hoga?* (Why would he feel so?)

C: *Kyoñke us shakhs ne kumhaar ki mehnat barbaad kar di* (Because the person has destroyed the potter's effort).

N: *Waah waah, subhaanallah. Khoob baat irshaad kar di* (Lord be praised. That was beautifully said).

Given this history, it is no surprise then that Indian cinema took so easily to including songs as a form of theatrical narrative.

The history of Hindi film lyrics actually predates the talkies. The standard practice during the silent era was to provide musical accompaniment to the film from the orchestra pit. Each movie theatre had its own band of musicians that played along with the film itself. The first instance of playback singing seems to have occurred in 1921 for the movie *Bhakt Vidur*. Vidur's wife, spinning a charkha, mouthed the words of a song that was lip-synched for the audience by a live singer in the theatre (the audience sang along, often demanding encores). By the time the first talkie, *Alam Ara*, was released in 1931, songs had taken centre stage in Indian cinema (according to one account, *Alam Ara* had fifty five!).

***

The use of Hindi film lyrics as a means of articulating a progressive sentiment was, not surprisingly, intertwined with the freedom struggle. While some film screenings in the North used the interval between the changing of the reels to lead the audience into singing nationalist songs, the deployment of lyrics to propagate resistance was first popularized in the South. Daring film-makers in Tamil Nadu and Andhra Pradesh defied the British censors by using the poems of the banned revolutionary poet Subramanya Bharati in films, sometimes without credit (for example, in *Navayuvan*/Modern Youth, 1937; *Menaka*, 1935; *Adrishṯam*/Fate, 1939; and *Naam Iruvar*/We Two, 1947). Hindi cinema, initially cautious, soon followed suit. The 1936 film *Janmabhoomi* (Land of Birth) was one of the first to have an explicitly nationalist song (written by J.S. Cashyap): 'Jai jai janani janmabhoomi' (Hail to the land of our birth).

One lyricist who consistently wrote patriotic songs for films was Ramchandra Narainji Dwivedi, better known as

Pradeep, whose most famous song is probably this one from the film *Jagriti* (Awakening, 1954):

Aao bachcho tumheñ dikhayeñ jhaanki Hindustaan ki
Is mitti se tilak karo, ye dharti hai balidaan ki
Vande Mataram, Vande Mataram
Come children, let me offer you a peek into Hindustan
Adorn your foreheads with its soil, for this is the land of martyrs
Vande Mataram, Vande Mataram

Writing first for Bombay Talkies, Pradeep soon joined the newly created Filmistan, whose first film *Chal Chal Re Naujawan*/Walk on, Youth, 1944 (scripted by the PWA writer Saadat Hasan Manto) included a song extolling the unity of Hindus and Muslims:

Manzil sabhi ki ek hai, raaheñ alag alag
Voh ek hai, par apni nigaaheñ alag alag
Mandir meiñ hai bhagwaan, voh Masjid meiñ khuda hai
Kisne kaha Hindu se Musalmaan juda hai
Bolo Har Har Mahaadev, Bolo Allah-o Akbar

Though our paths are different, our destination is the same
There is but one God, just different ways of looking at Him
In the temple He is called Bhagwaan, in the mosque, Khuda
Who says that Hindus and Muslims aren't but one
Say Har Har Mahadev, say Allah-o Akbar

In the 1940 film, *Aaj Ka Hindustani* (Today's Indian), directed by Jayant Desai and featuring Miss Rose, Prithviraj, Ishwarlal, Sitara and comedian Charlie[46], Prithviraj, playing a nationalist, is picturized walking through his village singing:

Charkha chalaao behno
Kaato ye kachhe dhaage
Dhaage ye kah rahe haiñ

Bhaarat ke bhaag jaage
Charkhe ke geet gaao
Duniya ko ye sunaao
Charkha chalaane waala
Gandhi hai aage aage

Spin the charkha O sisters
And as you cut these threads
Listen as they say that
India's destiny has awakened
Tell this to the world
That the charkha spinner Gandhi
Leads us all

Some of the songs that were written during the Quit India Movement consciously pushed the censor-imposed bounds of acceptability. The opening song in *Kismat* (Fate, 1943), written by Pradeep and composed by Anil Biswas, had the following chorus:

Aaj Himaalay ki choṯi se, phir hum ne lalkaara hai
Door hato, door haṯo ai duniya vaalo Hindustaan hamaara hai

From the peak of the Himalayas, we defiantly announce
Get out O foreigners, for India is ours

Gautam Kaul, in his book *Cinema and the Indian Freedom Struggle* documents an anecdote about how the censors were hoodwinked into thinking that the reference to 'foreigners' in the song was about the Japanese army and not the British. *Kismat* was first released in Kanpur at the Imperial Talkies. The British authorities received information that this song was being played repeatedly on public demand. Officer Dharmendra Gaur (the brother of Vrajendra Gaur, author, lyricist and screenplay writer of many films) was sent to investigate. A detention order under Section 26 of the Defense of India Rules was readied to arrest Pradeep. Dharmendra Gaur reportedly saw the film four times and filed a report saying that another line in the same song, *Tum na kisi ke aage jhukna, German ho ya Jaapaani* (Do not bow before anyone, be they German or Japanese), demonstrated that the song was not anti-British. *Kismat* ended up running for 186 weeks at Roxy Cinema in Calcutta. Other lyricists such as Pandit Narendra Sharma (*Hamari Baat*/Our Story, 1943), Qamar Jalalabadi (*Chand*/Moon, 1944), D.N. Madhok (*Pehle Aap*/You First, 1944), Zia Sarhadi (*Badi Maa*, 1945), and Gopal Singh Nepali (*Amar Asha*/Eternal Hope, 1947) took heart from this and penned freedom songs with increasing frequency.

Gramophone records served the purpose of popularizing film music beyond the cinema halls. Since the recordings were not of a great quality, the lyrics were printed on cheap booklets and distributed with the records. The British administration banned several of these songs, but the booklets circulated freely carrying the word around.

Independence unshackled film-makers from the limitations placed by the censors on patriotic songs and lyricists celebrated. Songs such as the one from *Ahimsa*/Non-violence (1947; *Azaad hum haiñ aaj se, jailoñ ke taale toḏ do;* We are free from today, let us break the locks of our jails) and *Majboor*/Helpless (1948; *Chala gaya gora angrez, ab kaahe ka ḏar*; The white British have departed, what do we have to fear now?) became more and more common.

***

In the meantime, the PWA was gathering momentum. This radical movement breathed a new life into cultural production and rapidly gained popularity. Not surprisingly, the medium of cinema was seen by the PWA as a space for intervention. The mood of the nation allowed members of the association to make inroads into the film industry and leftist writers were soon penning scripts and stories for large film studios, exposing the large movie-going audience to socially conscious ideas.

Another institution that had a considerable impact on the evolution of Indian cinema was the Indian People's Theatre Association (IPTA), the cultural wing of the Communist Party of India (CPI). Launched in 1943 'to defend culture against fascism and imperialism', IPTA worked towards the development of an avant-garde culture in India, largely in theatre – its primary field of engagement – but also in the arena of cinema.

A large number of the country's cultural intelligentsia – actors, directors, screenplay writers, journalists, lyricists, musicians and technicians – came together to produce work that was in line with their politics of social justice. Writer-director Khwaja Ahmad Abbas, cinematographer-director Bimal Roy, director Chetan Anand, music composer Salil Choudhary, poet-lyricists Sahir Ludhianvi and Majrooh Sultanpuri and actors Balraj Sahni and Utpal Dutt were all linked to IPTA.

K.A. Abbas, a cofounder of the IPTA, made *Dharti Ke Lal* (Children of the Earth, 1946) from a story by Krishen Chander, a film that examined the Bengal famine in a documentary-like fashion. Mohan Bhavnani's *Mazdoor*/Labourer (1934), inspired by IPTA's play *The Factory* based on a story by Premchand, was one of the first of its kind and offered a realistic portrayal of the plight of industrial workers. Chandulal Shah's *Acchut*, a film focusing on the theme of untouchability, Mehboob Khan's *Manmohan* (1936) which critiqued the patriarchal order, *Jagirdar*/Feudal Landlord (1937) which questioned the issue of land ownership, and *Hum Tum Aur Woh*/I, You, and the Other (1938), a film about a woman who seeks sexual and emotional comfort through an extramarital relationship – all challenged existing social norms in a probing fashion.

While writers and directors belonging to the Progressive Writers' Movement made a number of films that exhibited a political consciousness and a desire to precipitate social change, it took a while for the Urdu poetry of the movement to enter the arena of film lyrics. Although Sahir Ludhianvi made his debut in 1941 (in *Naujawan*/Youth) and Majrooh Sultanpuri in 1946 (with *Shahjahan*), their early lyrical output belonged to the traditional genre of love poetry.

For reasons that are too complex to go into in detail, the leading Hindi poets of the time had shied away from writing film lyrics. The leadership of the Hindi poets was at that time dominated by an orthodoxy which insisted that its members refuse to degrade their art by writing for popular cinema or theatre in the common or *bazaari* language of Hindustani. As Yogendra Malik points out 'literary traditions in Hindi tended to be dominated by Hindi revivalism, nationalism and romanticism'.[47] The leading Hindi writers and poets of the time frowned upon socialism as 'an alien philosophy unsuitable for the Indian context as well as upon popular culture as a medium for their work'[48].

The Urdu poets, on the other hand, were more than eager to explore this new medium of expression. Kaifi Azmi, Majrooh Sultanpuri and perhaps most significantly Sahir Ludhianvi started writing for cinema and dominated the landscape of its lyrical production for the next few decades. Other progressive poets such as Shailendra, Ali Sardar Jafri,

Jan Nisar Akhtar, Neeraj and Gulzar joined the fray in due course.

***

The decade of the 1950s proved to be the time when progressive lyrics came of age. This was the period dominated by the auteurs of Hindi cinema, the movie-makers with a vision. K.A. Abbas, Bimal Roy, Raj Kapoor, Kamal Amrohi and, of course, Guru Dutt sought to use cinema as a pedagogical tool and a space for constructing social critique. Their expression found a cause in the failure of the free nation to fulfil its promise of an egalitarian society with justice for all citizens. As the euphoria of Independence dissipated, and as people understood that the end of British occupation did not mean the end of their misery, disenchantment with the Nehru government grew.

Some like the IPTA poet Prem Dhawan, who had written 'Jhoom jhoom ke gaao aaj' celebrating the exit of the British, continued to urge the youth of the Nehruvian era to engage in the process of nation building:

Chhoro kal ki baateñ, kal ki baat puraani
Naye daur meiñ likhenge hum mil kar nayi kahaani
Hum Hindustaani, hum Hindustaani

Forget yesterday, yesterday is gone
We shall write a new story for the new times
We Indians, we Indians

But for a host of others, Nehru became the symbol of the betrayal of the promise of Independence. As Rajadhyaksha and Willemen point out, this was a period reflecting 'the emotional and social complexities affecting the artist when the reformism associated with Nehruvian nationalism disintegrated under the pressure of industrialization and urbanization creating the space for Indian modernism but also generating social dislocation[49].'

Sahir strode on to this stage like a giant, writing songs for movies like *Naya Daur*/The New Age (1957) and *Phir Subha Hogi*/Morning Will Come (1958) in a manner that was in keeping with his reputation as a revolutionary poet.

Saathi haath badhaana, saathi haath badhaana
Ek akela thak jaayega mil kar bojh uthaana
Saathi haath badhaana

Comrades, lend your hand!
One alone will tire soon, let us bear this burden together,
Comrades lend your hand!

Maati se hum laal nikaaleñ, moti laaeñ jal se
Jo kuch is duniya meiñ bana hai, bana hamaare bal se
Kab tak mehnat ke pairoñ meiñ daulat ki zanjeereñ
Haath badhaakar chheen lo apne sapnoñ ki tasveereñ
Saathi haath badhaana

We are the ones who extract rubies from the earth, pearls from the sea,
All that is of value in this world has been created by us
How long will labour be chained by those who own wealth?
Reach out and snatch that which you have always dreamed of
Comrades, lend your hand!

Pyaasa (1957), of course, is the movie that is best remembered as Sahir's vehicle. A Guru Dutt film about a struggling poet coming to terms with post-independence India, the story gets its radical edge mainly from its songs. The poet-protagonist of the story, after an agonized search for meaning, offers this disdainful take on the current times:

Ye mahloñ ye takhtoñ ye taajoñ ki duniya

Ye insaañ ke dushman samaajoñ ki duniya
Ye daulat ke bhooke rivaajoñ ki duniya
Ye duniya agar mil bhi jaye to kya hai?

This world of palaces, thrones and crowns
This world of societies that hate humanity
This world that hungers for nothing but wealth
Even if one obtains this world, so what?

And as the poet, played by Guru Dutt himself, wanders through the red-light district and observes the desperation that forces women to sell their bodies, he sings a song that is a minor reworking of a poem that Sahir had written earlier (called *Chakle*, or Brothels) which went: *Sanaakhaane tasdeeq-e mashriq kahaañ haiñ?* (Where are those who praise the purity of the East?). The story goes that Nehru had given a speech in which he had remarked 'I am proud of India.' Guru Dutt asked Sahir to work this line into the refrain of the song. The result was:

Ye kooche, ye neelaam-ghar dilkashi ke
Ye lut-te hue kaarvaañ zindagi ke
Kahaañ haiñ, kahaañ haiñ, muhaafiz khudi ke?
Jinheñ naaz hai Hind par voh kahaañ haiñ?

These streets, these auction houses of pleasure
These looted caravans of life
Where are they, the guardians of self-hood?
Those who are proud of India, where are they?

This taunt was followed by a harsh indictment of the national leadership:

Zara mulk ke rahbaroñ ko bulaao
Ye kooche, ye galiyaañ, ye manzar dikhaao
Jinheñ naaz hai Hind par unko laao
Jinheñ naaz hai Hind par voh kahaañ haiñ?

Go, fetch the leaders of the nation
Show them these streets, these lanes, these sights
Summon them, those who are proud of India
Those who are proud of India, where are they?

***

This mode of film-making soon ran into problems. The censor board, now under the control of the Indian government, kicked into gear, reflecting the government's hypersensitivity towards any reference to people's struggles, particularly in the cause of socialism. Director Ramesh Saigal was asked to delete a line from his movie *Kafila*/Caravan which went: The caravan of the people of Asia is on the move. Sahir's line *Paise ka raj miṯa dena* (End the rule of the wealthy) was axed from another film. Pradeep's song from the film *Amar Rahe Ye Pyaar*/May This Love Be Forever (1961) was deleted in its entirety, presumably because of the lines:

Hai! Siyaasat kitni gandi
Buri hai kitni firqa bandi
Aaj ye sab ke sab nar-naari
Ho gaye raste ke ye bhikaari

Alas! How dirty are the politics of the time
How despicable this sectarianism
Today, all these men and women
Have been turned into beggars

The lyrics of *Phir Subha Hogi* were considered so radical that two songs from the film were banned in India. One was:

Aasmaañ pe hai k̲h̲uda aur zameeñ pe hum
Aaj kal voh is taraf dekhta hai kam
Kis ko bheje voh yahaañ k̲h̲aak chaan-ne
Is tamaam bheeḏ ka haal jaan-ne
Aadmi haiñ anginat, devata haiñ kam

God is in the heavens while we are here on earth
These days, He does not pay us much attention
Who can He send here to sift through these sands,
To figure out the condition of these teeming masses?
For there are too many people, not enough deities

And the other was a parody of the famous Iqbal poem, *Saare jahaan se achcha Hindostaañ hamaara* (Our India is better than the rest of the world):

Cheen-o Arab hamaara, Hindostaañ hamaara
Rahne ko ghar nahiñ hai, saara jahaañ hamaara

China and Arabia are ours, so is India
Yet we have no home to live in; the whole world is ours

Jitni bhi buildingeñ thiñ, sethoñ ne baanṯ li haiñ
Fooṯpaath Bambayi ke, haiñ aashiyaañ hamaara

The wealthy have distributed all the buildings among themselves
While we are left to take refuge on the footpaths of Bombay

***

After Independence, the Indian government maintained monopolistic control over its radio broadcasting. When B.V. Keskar succeeded as the Minister for Information & Broadcasting in 1952, he decided to ban the broadcast of film music on All India Radio, considering it simultaneously too vulgar, too Westernized and too steeped in Urdu, choosing instead to promote light classical music. Most listeners simply tuned over to Radio Ceylon or Pakistani stations, both of which were broadcasting Hindi film songs. In 1957, film music was back on All India Radio on a new channel called Vividh Bharti. It is probably fair to say that most Hindustani-speaking Indian households had their radios perennially tuned to this station.

Since the only medium through which the public got to hear film music was the radio, station programming determined the songs that the public listened to. Popular demand, expressed through write-ins to programmes like *Man Chaahe Geet* (Favourite Songs), began to play a significant role in the kind of music that was heard on the airwaves and, therefore, in the kind of music that was produced.

***

Eventually, the social sensibility of the 1950s and early 1960s lost its appeal, shrinking the space available for progressive cinema and consequently progressive lyrics. There were two major reasons behind this.

The first was the break-up of the studio system in the 1960s, a phenomenon that changed the rules of the film-making game rather significantly. Serious, socially conscious cinema gave way surely but steadily to popular entertainment and the space provided by the studios to the maverick film-makers, writers and poets withered away. The growing urban population, which formed the largest chunk of the viewing public, gravitated towards escapist films seeking perhaps to forget their frustrations. Opulent sets, well-choreographed songs and a formulaic script were the order of the new day. As the critic Aruna Vasudev puts it, the films that were produced were mostly 'absurd romances packed with songs and dances, made like fairytales with a moral'.[50]

The second, as Peter Manuel elaborates in his book *Cassette Culture*[51], was the advent of the portable cassette-players, the early ones arriving in the country in the late 1970s in the hands of the guest workers returning from the Gulf. The fetishization of the cassette-player (everyone wanted to have one) symbolized the changing aspirations of the middle class and its freshly discovered consumer power (which was beginning to be unleashed by the newly instituted policies of economic liberalization). With foreign collaboration now a possibility, new tie-ups like Bush-Akai, Orson-Sony, BPL-Sanyo and Onida-JVC started manufacturing cheap cassettes. Sales of recorded music consequently went up from $1.2 million in 1980 to $12 million in 1986 and over $21 million in 1990.

Bourgeois democracy, thus unleashed, paved the way for what can be called the age of Bappi Lahiri. Foot- tapping, easily consumable and subsequently disposable tunes became the order of the day, and banal lyrics were welcomed:

D se hota hai Dance
I se hota hai Item
S se hota hai Singer
C se hota hai Chorus
O se Orchestra!
I am a Disco Dancer!!

D for Dance,
I for Item,
S for Singer,
C for Chorus,
O for Orchestra!
I am a Disco Dancer!!

The allegedly anti-establishment films of the 'angry young man' days did not provide much scope for progressive writing either. We say 'allegedly' because there was nothing really anti-establishment about this cinema; all it did was to promote the image of an alienated, disillusioned youth who sought vigilante justice by taking the law in his own hands. It must be recalled that *Sholay*/Flames (1975, possibly the biggest blockbuster produced in India and a film whose influence can still be seen on Indian cinema) is essentially a story about two mercenaries fighting subaltern dacoits on behalf of the feudal zamindar of the village. Songs in these films were used merely to interrupt the narrative and to provide some light moments. Rhyme became the handmaiden of the tune, and relatively meaningless lyrics fitted comfortably in this setup:

Koi haseena jab rooṯh jaati hai to aur bhi haseen ho jaati hai
Station se gaadi jab chooṯ jaati hai to ek-do-teen ho jaati hai

When a beauty gets upset, she becomes even more beautiful
When a train leaves the station, it departs from sight

Even the likes of Sahir were reduced to writing love songs of, shall we say, dubious merit (such as the one in *Trishul* that went *Gapuchi gapuchi gam gam, kishiki kishiki kam kam*); his light and frothy songs in *Deewaar* (*Kah dooñ tumheñ ya chup rahooñ dil meiñ mere aaj kya hai?* Shall I tell you what is in my heart, or shall I remain silent?) were in popular demand while the only semi-progressive song he wrote for the film (*Deewaroñ ka jangal jis ka aabaadi hai naam*; This forest of walls that we call a city) was deleted from the movie.

Ironically, the one space which could have provided refuge to the progressive poets, the so-called parallel cinema movement, did not open its doors to their lyrics. In this genre, songs were seen as an unnecessary impediment to the narrative. In their attempt to produce a cinema of calculated, purposeful naturalism that anxiously sought to distance itself from the *bazaari* Hindustani of commercial films, the alternate film-makers adopted a self-consciously Sanskritized Hindi, as is evident even from the titles of the films by Shyam Benegal,

Govind Nihalini and others: *Ankur*/Seedling, *Nishant*/Night's End, *Manthan*/Churning, *Bhumika*/Actor, *Aakrosh*/Anguish, *Ardhasatya*/Half-truth.

***

A further wrinkle was added to the development of film lyrics with the emergence of A.R. Rahman whose genius captured the nation's imagination with a fresh brand of music that was a breathtaking amalgamation of classical Hindustani and Carnatic ragas, syncopated jazz rhythms, meticulous orchestration inspired by his Western classical training and complex changes of tone and tune. His musical scores for south Indian films were such huge hits that these movies were dubbed in Hindi and re-released for a wider audience. The unfamiliar actors and the crude dubbing were more than offset by the wild popularity of the music. Lyricists were brought in to write fresh words for the songs and operated under the constraint of trying to write songs that would provide an acceptable level of lip synchronization[52]. The subordination of the lyrics to the tune became so overwhelming that we were treated to gems like *Strawberry aankhen* (Strawberry eyes) and *Telephone dhun meiñ hansne vaali* (The one who laughs like a telephone ringing).

This about-turn was quite dramatic since, at least until the 1980s, most lyricists were poets in their own right and first wrote out the words to the song based on the requirements of the script and then handed them over to the composers who set them to a tune. In an interview, a disgruntled Kaifi Azmi complained bitterly about the new trend of lyricists being asked to fit words around already composed musical scores '*Ye to vahi baat hui*', he said, '*ke kisi ne kaha ke ye khabar khudi hai; is size ki laash le aao!*' ('It is like being told that a grave has already been dug and now an appropriately sized corpse has to be found to fit in it').

The most successful lyricist of today, Javed Akhtar, says that the emphasis is now on the tune and it is up to the song writer to find the right words, and just as importantly, the appropriate sound that works for the melody. The following comment by Akhtar is interesting in and of itself, but also points to the diminishing importance of the words vis-à-vis the sound:

> The meaning of the words is important but so is their phonetic effect. Ultimately the song is being written to be sung. So it should sound extremely good ... What I'm going to say might sound very strange, but every sound has a certain visual effect. If you take 'j': now 'ja' has a sparkle that is very white. While the sound of 'cha' also has a sparkle, it's somehow yellow or golden. 'Ta' sounds like throwing a ball on a solid floor. But if you throw the ball on wet ground, then you get the sound 'tha'. If you hit the ball against a hollow wooden wall, you'll hear a 'dha'. Sounds create different images in your mind. Like 'dha' is a sticky sound, 'gha' is a dense sound, 'ga' is clean[53].

Despite the constraints under which he writes, Javed Akhtar does produce the occasional lyric that reminds one of the time that once was, when Hindi film songs pressed the cause of social justice, a time that seems to have long gone:

Footpaathoñ ke hum rahne vaale
Raatoñ ne paala hum voh ujaale
Aakaash sar pe, pairoñ tale, hai door tak ye zameeñ
Aur to apna koi nahiñ, aur to apna koi nahiñ

Bachpan meiñ khele gham se, nirdhan gharoñ ke bete
Phooloñ ki sej nahiñ, kaanton pe hum haiñ lete

Dukh meiñ rahe, sau g̲h̲am sahe, dil ye kahe
Roṯi jahaañ, hai swarg apna vahiñ
Aur to apna koi nahiñ, aur to apna koi nahiñ

We are the pavement dwellers
We the light that has been sheltered by the nights
Our companions are the sky ahead, the ground beneath our feet
And none else

Our childhood spent playing with sorrow
Our beds made not of flowers but thorns
We live with unhappiness, suffer sadness, and say with our heart
That our heaven is where we can find bread

***

Peter Manuel, describing the Frankfurt School's analysis of popular culture, writes that 'modern capitalism operated through the acquiescence of a depoliticized, alienated and generally stupefied public. The mass media (and in Adorno's thought, popular music), played essential roles in legitimizing the status quo by stultifying critical consciousness, commodifying and disarming oppositional art, and promoting consumerism and the myth of a classless society'[54]. In this context, the media function as 'manipulative instruments' that seek to promote the voices of those who are comfortable with the status quo while delegitimizing the voices of those who challenge and subvert the relationships of power and domination in inequitable social systems. It is no surprise then that the content that is produced in Hindi cinema, including its lyrics, tends towards escapist fantasies and commodity fetishism played out in chimerical dreamscapes.

But at the same time, it is important to remind ourselves that popular culture is a site of contestations, negotiations, mediations and rearticulations, a space where hegemonic and oppositional values symbolically and explicitly engage one another. This chapter then, is partly the mourning of that which has passed, but it is simultaneously both an attempt to remind ourselves that the current struggles for social justice have a history and a celebration of those who helped produce it.

***

In the movie *Kabhi Kabhie* (Sometimes, 1976), Sahir wrote a song that anticipates the end of his period as a poet:

Maiñ pal do pal ka shaayar hooñ
Pal do pal meri kahaani hai
Pal do pal meri hasti hai
Pal do pal meri javaani hai

I am a poet of a brief moment or two
My story is a passing one
My life is ephemeral
My youth, transient

Kal aur aayenge naghmoñ ki khilti kaliyaañ chun-ne vaale
Mujh se behtar kahne vaale, tum se behtar sun-ne vaale
Kal koi mujh ko yaad kare, kyooñ koi mujh ko yaad kare
Masroof zamaana mere liye, kyooñ waqt apna barbaad kare?
Maiñ pal do pal ka shaayar hooñ

Tomorrow, there will be others harvesting the blooming buds of fresh songs
Others who will write better than I could, others who will listen better than you can
Who will remember me tomorrow, why should anyone?
Why would this busy world waste its time on me in the future?
I am a poet of but the moment

But Sahir did more than just write in and for the moment. He not only left behind an oeuvre that still plays on our radios and stereos, but also inspired a whole lot of others like Shailendra, Hasan Kamal, Javed Akhtar, and occasionally, even the not-quite-progressive Anand Bakshi to follow in his footsteps. Listening to a tape of songs from the 1971 movie *Dushman*/Enemy (lyrics: Anand Bakshi), we did a double-take when a song (*Dilli ka Qutub Minaar dekho, Bambayi shahar ki bahaar dekho*; Look at Delhi's Qutub Minar, look at Bombay's spring) suddenly sprung the lines:

Logoñ ko paise se pyaar dekho
Zaalim ye sarmaayaadaar dekho

Look at how people love wealth
Look at the oppressive capitalist

The word *sarmaayaadaar* sticks out because it is a legacy of the progressive poets, their contribution to our popular vocabulary. Its explicit use reminds us of the time when lyrics and poetry were defined by the PWA, and when film songs could, almost unselfconsciously, offer a critique of social conditions.

Perhaps because he recognized his influence, or perhaps merely in hope, Sahir, in a rare moment of self-assertion, added a coda to his *Kabhi Kabhie* song that in our opinion is an apt comment on the generation of PWA poets:

Maiñ har ek pal ka shaayar hooñ
Har ek pal meri kahaani hai
Har ek pal meri hasti hai
Har ek pal meri javaani hai

I am a poet for all times
My story is forever
My life, unending,
My youth, eternal!

کرشن کا گیت ہے گوکل کی حسیں شام ہے تو
آ کلیجے سے لگا لیں کہ سیاہ فام ہے تو

ظلم پھر ظلم ہے بڑھتا ہے تو مٹ جاتا ہے
خون پھر خون ہے ٹپکے گا تو جم جائے گا

خاکِ صحرا پہ جمے یا کفِ قاتل پہ جمے
فرقِ انصاف پہ یا پائے سلاسل پہ جمے
تیغ بیداد پہ یا لاشۂ بسمل پہ جمے
خون پھر خون ہے ٹپکے گا تو جم جائے گا

ظلم کی بات ہی ظلم کی اوقات ہی کیا
ظلم بس ظلم ہے آغاز سے انجام تلک
خون پھر خون ہے سو شکل بدل سکتا ہے
ایسی شکلیں کہ مٹاؤ تو مٹائے نہ بنے
ایسے شعلے کہ بجھاؤ تو بجھائے نہ بنے
ایسے نعرے کہ دباؤ تو دبائے نہ بنے

مَیں قتل تو ہو گیا تمہاری گلی میں لیکن
میرے لہو سے تمہاری دیوار گل رہی ہے

مگر تجھی خوابوں کے لشکر میں کس کو اتنی خبر
ہر ایک قصّہ کا اِک اختتام ہوتا ہے
ہزار لکھ لے کوئی فتح ذرّہ ذرّہ پر
مگر شکست کا بھی اِک مقام ہوتا ہے

جیون جیون ہم نے جگ میں کھیل یہی ہوتے دیکھا
دھیرے دھیرے جیتی دُنیا دھیرے دھیرے ہارے لوگ
نیکی اِک دِن کام آئے گی ہم کو کیا سمجھاتے ہو
ہم نے بے بس مرتے دیکھے کیسے پیارے پیارے لوگ

وصل کا سکوں کیا ہے ہجر کا جُنوں کیا ہے
حسن کا فسوں کیا ہے عشق کے دروں کیا ہے
تم مریضِ دانائی مصلحت کے شیدائی
راہِ گمرہاں کیا ہے تم نہ جان پاؤ گے

7

VOH YAAR HAI JO KHUSHBOO KI TARAAH, JIS KI ZUBAAÑ URDU KI TARAAH

Dil na-umeed to nahiñ, naakaam hi to hai
Lambi hai gham ki shaam, magar shaam hi to hai

Defeated it may be, but the heart does not despair
Sorrow's evening is long, but it too will pass

Thus begins a song from the 1994 Hindi movie *1942 – A Love Story*. The lyrics of the song are credited to Javed Akhtar, but the verse above comes from a poem by Faiz Ahmad Faiz. The contribution of Faiz to this song is unstated, unobtrusive, seamless, and is emblematic of the symbiotic relationship between Urdu poetry and Hindi film songs. This chapter contends that Hindi film music not only offered a new space to Urdu poetry, ensured its performative presence in the cultural landscape and nurtured its heritage but also transformed it in the process, keeping it in tune with the cultural milieu in India.

In order to appreciate the association between Urdu

poetry and Hindi film songs, one must place the relationship in the context of the diminishing institutional patronage of Urdu by the post-independence Indian state as a result of the identification of Urdu as the language of Muslims and therefore the language of outsiders. The attempts to conflate language, script and religion, especially with respect to the Hindi-Urdu divide, have a long history dating back to at least the 1860s[55]. Various colonial decrees, including Anthony MacDonnell's '1900 resolution' only added fuel to the fire[56]. The bitter disputes over the language policy of the colonialist administration, the antagonisms between the proponents of a 'pure' Sanskritized Hindi and a 'pure' Persianized Urdu, the espousal of a common language (Hindustani) by a number of people including Mahatma Gandhi and the political fallouts of these debates are well detailed in a number of books[57] and the interested reader can find a wealth of information in them. Despite the attempts to compartmentalize the spoken tongue into two different languages, it was obvious that the lingua franca of what is now called the 'Hindi-speaking' population of the country was Hindustani, the linguistic heir of Khari Boli and the fount of both Hindi and Urdu. As a matter of fact, even the 1931 census of the subcontinent did not list Hindi and Urdu as separate languages; the divide between the two *zabaans/bhashas* emerged only in subsequent census tabulations. By 1961, Hindustani had been eliminated from the census as a language[58], forcing respondents to choose between Hindi and Urdu and thereby burning a significant bridge that linked Urdu to the spoken traditions in the subcontinent. The fallout of the Partition and the decision by the Pakistani elite to adopt Urdu as the national language had a significant impact on the language in India. Now identified as the tongue of the enemy, Urdu came to be seen as a 'foreign' language and began to be viewed with suspicion by the state and certain proponents of religious nationalism. State patronage, particularly in Uttar Pradesh and Bihar, dwindled considerably resulting in the erosion of the formal, institutional spaces in which the language thrived, pushing it into the penumbra of national relevance. Phrases like 'dying language' are often used to describe the condition of Urdu in India and indicators like 'the number of Urdu-medium schools' present a litany of bad news with respect to the present conditions and future of the language.

While the impact of the poor treatment meted out to Urdu has been substantial, one cannot merely use inert and sterile touchstones to gauge the viability of a language. A casual glance around the Indian cultural landscape reveals that Urdu is still very much alive in the performed linguistic traditions of India. Further, it is a language that is often accorded a mystifyingly high status and viewed as a sign of refinement in middle-class and upper-crust Indian society and Urdu ghazals are frequently quoted by Hindi speakers to punctuate mellow moments. Most ironically, the deep-rooted presence of Urdu in India can be gauged from the fact that the speeches of even the most rabid of anti-Muslim religious nationalists are replete with Urdu phrases, metaphors and poetry[59].

What social avenues then allowed Urdu's performance and enactment in India to survive in an atmosphere where the traditional institutions were under retreat? Our simple thesis here is that the medium of Hindi film songs has proven to be one of the most valuable repositories for the safe-keeping and nurturing of Urdu poetry and idiom. It is obvious that cinema plays a dominant role in Indian cultural life and that songs form a cornerstone of this art form. What is less apparent is the preponderance of Urdu[60] words, phrases and metaphors in Hindi film songs. A random perusal of four songs, for instance, turns up words like *ilteja* (request, in the song *O mere Sona* from the film *Teesri Manzil*, 1966), *jaaneman* (my life, in *Jaaneman jaaneman* from *Chhoṯi Si Baat*, 1975), *mahsoos* (aware, in *Tu hi tu* from *Dil Se*, 1998), and *saaqi* (wine-bearer, in *Kaise rahooñ chup* from *Inteqam*, 1969). Those who are familiar with Hindi film music will agree that far from being isolated examples, these are fairly common words found extensively in Hindi film lyrics. These words that have Persian (Farsi) roots, along with many others, routinely find a place in the Hindustani vocabulary spoken in India, simply because of their repeated usage in the Hindi film songs.[61]

Hindi film music provides refuge to Urdu poetry in many different ways. Here, we look at some of these: the utilization of Urdu poems, both classical and contemporary, in Hindi cinema; the incorporation of Urdu poetic idiom in songs; the influence of Urdu poetry on songs and the reciprocal impact of films on Urdu poetics; and the deployment of famous Urdu poetical phrases and couplets in lyrics.

Classical and Contemporary Urdu Poems as Film Songs

Urdu poetry written by classical poets has frequently been used as lyrics in Hindi films, a sample of which is shown in Table 1 below[62]. From the fifteenth century Deccani intonations of Quli Qutub Shah to Ghalib's metaphysical imagery to the tortured alienation of Bahadur Shah Zafar, classical Urdu poems have found their way through these songs into the lexicon of the Indian public.

Table 1

Examples of Works of Classical Poets Used as Hindi Film Songs		
Poet	Song	Film
Amir Khusrau	*Kaaheko biyaahe bides*	Umrao Jaan (1981)
Bahadur Shah Zafar	*Lagta nahiñ hai jee mera*	Laal Qila (1957)
Mir Taqi Mir	*Dikhaayi diye yooñ, ke bekhud kiya*	Bazaar (1982)
Mirza Ghalib	*Dil-e naadaañ, tujhe hua kya hai*	Mirza Ghalib
Mohammad Iqbal	*Kabhi ai haqeeqat-e muntazar*	Dulhan Ek Raat Ki (1967)
Quli Qutub Shah	*Piya baj pyaala piya jaaye na*	Nishant (1975)
Wajid Ali Shah	*Baabul mora, naihar chhooto hi jaaye*	Street Singer (1938)

Apart from the works of poets from the distant past, Hindi films have also used contemporary Urdu poems as lyrics for songs. Since an inventory of such works would be a bit too large to deal with in any detail[63], we focus our attention on the PWA song-writers in Hindi cinema[64] whose impact on the lyrics of Hindi films was formidable. Consider the 1982 film *Bazaar*, where Farooq Sheikh serenades Supriya Pathak with the song *Phir chhidi raat, baat phooloñ ki* (The tale of flowers was retold tonight). The 1993 film *Muhafiz* (Protector), where Deven, the Hindi teacher played by Om Puri, rushes to the house of the old poet Noor (Shashi Kapoor) to meet him, only to find he is too late; Noor's funeral procession is passing by to the tune of *Aaj baazaar meiñ paa-bajaulaañ chalo* (Today, come in fetters to the marketplace). Or take a walk down memory lane to the 1965 film *Haqeeqat* (Reality), when the forlorn soldier played by Sanjay Khan remembers the parting with his lover thus: *Maiñ ye soch kar us ke dar se utha tha* (I left her door hoping…). All these wondrous moments appear so seamlessly integrated in the narratives of the movies that one would think that the words had been written specifically for the scene, while, in fact, these songs were earlier poetical compositions by Makhdoom, Faiz and Kaifi, respectively. Film-makers had access to this reserve of poetry that they could draw upon depending on their needs. The poems also benefitted enormously from this; rather than remaining confined to a select audience, they suddenly became available to the masses and were brought to the attention of a wide public.

Progressive Urdu poets took advantage of this exposure to introduce a new brand of poetry to their audience, pioneering a new aesthetic of realism and thereby producing a corpus of profound yet accessible verse. Hindi films also served to provide a source of income to these poets; apart from the highly successful lyricists like Sahir Ludhianvi and Majrooh Sultanpuri, other PWA poets like Faiz Ahmad Faiz, Firaq Gorakhpuri, Israr-ul-Haq Majaz, Kaifi Azmi, Jan Nisar Akhtar, Makhdoom Mohiuddin and Hasrat Mohani had their published work occasionally deployed in Hindi film songs (see Table 2 for a partial list).

Table 2

Examples of Works of Progressive Poets Used as Hindi Film songs		
Poet	Song	Film
Faiz Ahmad Faiz	*Mujh se pahli si mohabbat*	Qaidi (1957)
Israr-ul-Haq	*Ai g̲h̲am-e dil kya karooñ*	Thokar (1939)
Majaz Kaifi Azmi	*Ho ke majboor mujhe us ne bhulaaya*[65]	Haqeeqat (1964)
Majrooh Sultanpuri	*Hum the, mataa-e koocha-o bazaar*	Dastak (1970)
Makhdoom Mohiuddin	*Ek chameli ke mand̲ve tale*	Cha Cha Cha (1953)
Sahir Ludhianvi	*Chalo ek baar phir se ajnabi*	Gumraah (1963)

Such songs not only infused an Urdu sensibility into the Hindi film song but also contributed to the development of a distinct lyrical style. Be it Faiz's anguished entreaty to a beloved to forego love for a commitment to social change, Majaz's paean to the wandering urban 'outsider', Kaifi's wistful recount of a breaking relationship, Majrooh's description of the commodification of love in the marketplace of desire, Makhdoom's fiery invocation of the emergence of love in the hearts of the passionate, or Sahir's resigned acceptance of lost love, progressive poets used their existing body of work to enrich Hindi film songs immeasurably.

These poems, classical and contemporary, found their way into movies in a variety of ways. Historical films, of course, had a ready reason for using the poems from the period that the movie was set in. The 1954 film *Mirza Ghalib* could not but use Ghalib's ghazals (choosing to focus on his simpler ones such as *Dil-e-naadaañ tujhe hua kya hai*; What has become of you, my innocent heart?). The 1957 release *Lal Qila* (Red Fort) on the life of Bahadur Shah Zafar incorporated Zafar's poetry like *Na kisi ke aankh ka noor hooñ* (Nor am I the light of any eye).[66] Sometimes the character in the story was a singer giving a public performance; Supriya Pathak, for instance, in *Bazaar* (1982) is shown singing Mir's ghazal *Dikhaayi diye yooñ ke bekhud kiya* (You made me lose myself).

In the case of contemporary poems, film-makers either selected a poem from the repertoire of the lyricist or asked the poets to 'tweak' a particular poem to make it more amenable to the situation or to make some of the words more accessible to the public at large. Writing for a broad audience meant that poets had to impose certain restrictions on themselves, particularly in the choice of the song's vocabulary. For instance, when Guru Dutt chose to adopt Sahir's despairing commentary on Bombay's brothels *Sanakhaan-e taqdees-e mashriq kahaañ haiñ* (Where are they who sing praises of Eastern culture?) for his 1957 movie *Pyaasa* (The Thirsty One), he asked Sahir to alter the opening stanza to make it simpler. Sahir's new *mukhda*, *Jinheñ naaz hai Hind par, voh kahaañ haiñ* (Where are they who are so proud of India?) integrates seamlessly with the rest of the poem and adds new value to the song. Likewise, Kaifi Azmi simplified the lyrics of one of his best-known poems *Aurat* (*Uth meri jaan, mere saath hi chalna hai tujhe,* Arise, my darling, we must walk together) for use in the 1997 movie *Tamanna* (Desire). Sometimes poets would rework their poems in some fashion to convert them into songs, as Javed Akhtar did by expanding his already published *qata* (quatrain) *Kathhai aankhoñ vaali ek ladki* (A girl with brown eyes) for use in *Duplicate* (1998), or as Sahir did by writing a different version of his poem *Maiñ pal do pal ka shaayar hooñ* (I am a poet but for a moment or two) for a song in the film *Kabhi Kabhie* (1976) which went *Maiñ har ek pal ka shaayar hooñ* (I am an eternal poet).

Film Lyrics Written by PWA Poets

Having established themselves as successful lyricists in Hindi cinema, the progressive poets transformed the genre of lyric-writing substantially by introducing a variety of new themes, injecting a modern, urban and realistic sensibility and bringing in a variety of new metaphors into songs which through generations of humming have now become an integral part of Hindustani usage. Thus their own brand of word and word-play was unobtrusively incorporated into the linguistic mosaic of the subcontinent. At the same time, the act of song-writing had a reciprocal impact on their own poetry too, enriching their idiom, expanding their vocabulary and extending their styles.

Lyricists worked under a variety of constraints. They had to write songs that were relevant to the situation, produce words that worked with the tune and write songs that were relatively short. The cinematic situations that were presented to them were rather limited. For reasons that can be partly attributed to accepted social conventions and partly to the prudishness of the censors, Hindi films chose the medium of song to express romantic emotions and sexual desire. Consequently, film songs were predominantly written for situations related to love and erotic passion. The collaborative nature of song-writing meant that songs had to be the result of a joint effort between the director, script-writer, music composer and lyricist. Increasingly, as the tunes assumed greater importance, the lyricist was asked to write words to an already composed piece of music[67]. Finally, the lyricists operated under the demands of brevity; till the advent of the 33-rpm LPs, songs could only be about three minutes long, and even now, rarely go on for more than five minutes.

These constraints, one can argue, produced very distinct changes in the Urdu poem. Demands to write love song after love song must have weighed heavily on the creativity of the poets, especially the Progressives who hankered for the opportunity to write about 'real life' and push a certain social agenda through the powerful medium of song. Possibly in response, the Progressives managed to introduce a variety of other themes into their songs while keeping them within the cinematic and situational requirements. Often, this was accomplished by producing a set of binaries between the purity of love (*ishq, pyaar*) and the corruption of the world, represented by tyranny, wealth, the throne or even God (*zulm, zar/daulat, takht, khudaai*). The struggle between the subaltern lovers and the dominant social order was invoked by the poet as a symbol of other battles between those who were driven by passion and those who valued money and power. Sahir's defiant words resound in a song from the 1963 film *Taj Mahal*:

Takht kya cheez hai, aur laal-o javaahar hai kya?
Pyaar vaale to khudaai bhi luta dete haiñ

What price this throne, what value these jewels?
True lovers will even spurn God's kingdom

One could also claim that the collaborative nature of the song-writing had a positive impact of sorts on the works of many Urdu poets. The constraints imposed by this setup allowed them to engage with innovative rhythms, rhyming structures and tonal restrictions. It would not be unfair to say that one detects the influence of film lyrics in some of Javed Akhtar's non-film poetry and one can only speculate about the impact of the 'lyric habit' on Sahir's multiple rhyme structures. But writing for cinema did allow poets to freely experiment with structures and forms of poetry that were considered 'inferior' in the canon. Classical Urdu poetry, nurtured as it was by the courtly patronage of kings, had developed an aesthetic and cultural sensitivity that catered primarily to emotions that were far removed from the material realities of people's lives[68]. Under this patronage, the ghazal became the dominant form of poetry[69]. The Progressives frequently chafed against the constrictions imposed on their subject matter by the ghazal[70] and attempted to push different poetic forms or to use the ghazal subversively to depict non-traditional ideas. Their desire to experiment with form found a space in their lyrical production while their yearning for mass-outlets was partly fulfilled when their songs began to be hummed on streets all over the country. The *nazm*, traditionally considered a lower form of poetic expression found popularity in the cultural space, partly because of its use in songs (for example, Sahir's *Chalo ek baar phir se ajnabi ban jaayeñ hum dono*/Come that we may start afresh as strangers; in *Gumraah*/Astray, 1963).

The need for brevity in the song-situation imposed another framework on the creativity of the poets, compelling them to use words with care and economy, which suited them just fine, since this was already a part of the grammar of Urdu poets schooled in the austere ghazal tradition. The training of these poets in this tradition is apparent, especially in the way their words come across as multilayered, and on their ability to make the same lines communicate multiple emotional states. For instance, Sahir's song in *Hum Dono* (We Two, 1960) can be read either as an act of ideological compromise or of defiant optimism:

Maiñ zindagi ka saath nibhaata chala gaya
Har fikr ko dhueñ meiñ udaata chala gaya

I learnt to walk apace with life
Blowing all my worries into smoke

One wonderful example of pithy expression is the song from *Boot Polish* (1954), in which Sahir brings an exquisite sense of irony to bear while highlighting the plight of the poor and the homeless. All those who have ever sung Iqbal's *Saare jahaañ se achcha Hindostaañ hamaara* (Our India is Better Than Any Land in the World) with pride are forced to come to terms with a different sentiment when listening to the song which goes:

Jebeñ haiñ apni khaali, kyooñ deta varna gaali
Voh santari hamaara, voh paasbaañ hamaara

Our pockets are empty, why else would he abuse us?
Our glorious sentry, our protector

The sentry in the song is not the lofty Himalayan range of Iqbal that protects India from invasion (*Parbat voh sab se ooncha, humsaaya aasmaañ ka, voh santari hamaara, voh paasbaañ hamaara*; That highest among mountains, that equal of the sky, that is our sentry, our protector). Instead the *santari* here is the beat constable, who drives away the homeless from park benches and railway stations at night. In a few lines, the song not only paints a picture of the life of the poor, but offers a stark critique of the nation-state as well.

The PWA's Shadow on Current Hindi Film Lyrics

Even casual followers of Hindi film music could not have but noted the alarming dip in the standards of film lyrics in the 1980s. Most aficionados think of this period as the nadir of popular music, characterized as it was by waning originality and a growing tendency to borrow tunes from Western hits and populate them with inane lyrics[71]. It is not coincidental that the deterioration of film music followed the death of some of its best lyricists such as Shailendra, Hasrat Jaipuri, Raja Mehdi Ali Khan and Shakeel Badayuni. However, Sahir's untimely death in 1980 not only robbed Hindi cinema of its premier song-writer, but also dealt a major blow of a certain style of progressive lyrical expression. Majrooh, who seemed to have established a watertight separation between his lyrics and his literary work, continued to innovate and kept up with the changing times remarkably; but his songs, while remaining a marvel of inventive vocabulary, rarely spoke of the material conditions of the times. However, other poets such as Nida Fazli, Hasan Kamal and Shahryar used the aesthetic popularized by the PWA when the occasion presented itself and when film-makers offered them that luxury. Shahryar's ghazal in *Gaman* (Disappearance; 1978) gave voice to the sense of urban anomie experienced by the Bombay taxi-driver who wonders:

Seene meiñ jalan, aankhoñ meiñ toofaan sa kyooñ hai
Is shahr meiñ har shaqs pareshaan sa kyooñ hai

Kya koi nayi baat nazar aati hai hum meiñ
Aa'ina hameñ dekh ke hairaan sa kyooñ hai

Why does the heart burn, why is there a storm in the eyes?
Why is everyone in this city so unsettled?

Is there something new about me?
Why is the mirror so surprised at my sight?

Likewise, Hasan Kamal's song in *Mazdoor* (1983) harks back to an older sensibility by deploying imagery made popular by the PWA and expresses a call by workers for their rightful share of the wealth they help create:

Hum mehnat-kash is duniya se jab apna hissa maangenge
Ek baagh nahiñ, ek khet nahiñ, hum saari duniya maangenge[72]

When we labourers demand our share of this world
Not just an orchard, not merely a field, we will demand the entire world

With Majrooh's death in 2000 and the subsequent demise of Kaifi Azmi in 2002, progressive Urdu poetry lost most of its film lyricists. However, the expression of the progressive aesthetic is a responsibility that has been shouldered admirably (if often solitarily) by Javed Akhtar, who acknowledges his debt to the PWA in various places[73]. While Javed Akhtar's lyrics come closest to the traditions established by his PWA predecessors, he manages to infuse them with contemporaenity and his own original sensibility. But one cannot help but notice the shades of Sahir in some of his work such as his song written for *Mashaal* (Torch, 1983):

Ka'ee yaadoñ ke chehre haiñ, ka'ee qisse puraane haiñ
Teri sau daastaaneñ haiñ, tere kitne fasaane haiñ
Magar ek voh kahaani hai, jo ab mujh ko sunaani hai
Zindagi, aa raha hooñ maiñ

Mere haathoñ ki garmi se, pighal jaayegi zanjeereñ
Mere qadmoñ ki aahaṯ se, badal jaayegi taqdeereñ
Umeedoñ ke diye le kar, ye sab tere liye le kar
Zindagi, aa raha hooñ maiñ

Memories have several faces; there are several tales from the past
You have a hundred stories, and as many parables
But there is one little story, which is now mine to tell
Life, I am on my way

The warmth of my hands will melt chains
The sound of my footsteps will change fortunes
Carrying these lamps of hope for you
Life, I am on my way

Akhtar's film songs are at times inflected with a delectable Persian (not many current lyricists would use *posheeda*/hidden and *k͟hwaabeeda*/dreamy in a movie song, as he does in *Wajood*, 1998). But he can just as easily deploy an Awadhi flavour (in the songs of *Lagaan*/Tax, 2001, for instance: *Bijuri ki talvaar nahiñ, boondoñ ke baan chalaao*/Don't wield merely the sword of lightning, shower us with the arrows of raindrops) or invoke the Ramlila tradition (*Swades* /My Country, 2005) and has shown his comfort with traditional genres such as the ghazal (*Saath Saath*/Together, 1982). While these examples are a testimony to Javed Akhtar's versatility, the fact that they are all the product of one poet is also indicative of the common heritage of Hindi, Urdu and Hindustani.

Sampling as Homage

Urdu poetry and film songs from Hindi films are intertwined in other ways as well. There is another fashion in which Urdu poetry and film songs from Hindi films are intertwined. Snippets and phrases from famous Urdu poems find their way into the lexicon of Hindi film songs. For instance, while writing the title song of the 1981 film *Ek Duuje Ke Liye* (For Each Other), Anand Bakshi, a career lyricist, inserts a Ghalib phrase in the line *Ishq par zor nahiñ, Ghalib ne kaha hai isi liye* (As Ghalib says: Love is not bound by compulsion). Momin's couplet *Tum mere paas hoti ho goya, jab koi doosra nahiñ hota* (It is as if you are with me, when there is no one else around) is used inventively by lyricist Rajinder Kishan for the song *Ai meri shah-e khoobaañ* in *Love in Simla* (1960). Ghalib's line *Jee dhoondta hai phir vahi fursat ke raat din* (The heart searches for those days and nights of leisure) forms the *mukhda* (chorus) of a song by Gulzar in *Mausam* (Season, 1975). These seamless incorporations, while clearly a form of homage, are also reflections of the understanding by these lyricists that the film audience will know the source of these phrases, recognize the sampling and appreciate the tribute.

Urdu lives and breathes in the medium of the Hindi film song, while enriching it with its vocabulary and its poetic tradition, negating the efforts of linguistic fundamentalists to wipe it out of India's national consciousness. Fittingly, it is Gulzar, the Ghalib aficionado, who provides us with lines that symbolize the love of Urdu so caringly fostered by Hindi film songs. In *Chhaiyyaañ Chhaiyyaañ*, the super-hit song from *Dil Se* (From the Heart, 1998), Gulzar offers a referential (reverential?) ode to the language itself:

Voh yaar hai jo khushboo ki taraah
Jis ki zubaañ Urdu ki taraah

A friend is like a fragrance
Whose language is (sweet) like Urdu

Indeed.

اور آج جب اِن پیڑوں کے تلے
پھر دو سائے لہراتے ہیں
پھر دو دِل مِلنے آتے ہیں
پھر موت کی آندھی اُٹھتی ہے
پھر جنگ کے بادل چھاتے ہیں
مَیں سوچ رہا ہوں اُن کا بھی
اپنی ہی طرح انجام نہ ہو
اُن کا بھی جُنوں ناکام نہ ہو
اُن کے بھی مُقدّر میں لِکھی
اِک خون میں لِتھڑی شام نہ ہو

قفس ہے بس میں تمہارے تمہارے بس میں نہیں
چمن میں آتشِ گُل کے نِکھار کا موسم
بَلا سے ہم نہ دیکھا تو اور دیکھیں گے
فروغِ گُلشن و صوتِ ہزار کا موسم

دیکھ رفتارِ انقلاب فراق
کِتنی آہستہ اور کِتنی تیز

گزشتہ جنگ میں گھر ہی جلے مگر اِس بار
عجب نہیں کہ یہ تنہائیاں بھی جل جائیں
گزشتہ جنگ میں پیکر جلے مگر اِس بار
عجب نہیں کہ یہ پرچھائیاں بھی جل جائیں

برتری کے ثبوت کی خاطر
خوں بہانا ہی کیا ضروری ہے
گھر کی تاریکیاں مٹانے کو
گھر جلانا ہی کیا ضروری ہے

بیزار ہے کنشت و کلیسا سے یہ جہاں
سوداگرانِ دین کی سوداگری کی خیر
اِلحاد کر رہا ہے مرتّب جہانِ نو
دَیر و حرم کی ہیولۂ غارت گری کی خیر
اِنساں اُلٹ رہا ہے رُخِ زیست سے نقاب
مذہب کے اہتمام فسوں پروری کی خیر

وجہ بے رنگیٔ گلزار کہوں تو کیا ہو
کون ہے کتنا گنہگار کہوں تو کیا ہو
تم نے جو بات سرِ بزم نہ سُننا چاہی
میں وہی بات سرِ دار کہوں تو کیا ہو

8

AN EXEMPLARY PROGRESSIVE

The Aesthetic Experiment of Sahir Ludhianvi

Mujh ko is ka ranj nahiñ hai, log mujhe fankaar na maaneñ
Fikr-o sukhan ke taajir mere sheroñ ko ash'aar na maaneñ

I do not regret that people do not consider me an artist
That the traders of thought and words do not think of my poems as poetry

With this characteristically bold verse, Sahir Ludhianvi announced his aesthetic experiment: his poetry would not cater to the whims of his critics, he would not be bound by tradition or the dominant metaphors of classical poetry, he would not succumb to the desire to be known as an artist. Instead, his work would serve as a voice of the movement, as a manifesto for the working class and as a contribution to the vision of the Left.

Sahir's corpus of work deserves a close look in the context of the history of the Progressive Writers' Association (PWA) simply because more than any other poet (with the possible exception of Ali Sardar Jafri), he responded to the Progressives' call to subordinate art to the service of the goals of the movement. In this sense, Sahir can be seen as a loyal soldier of the PWA and its exemplary poet.

It is not unusual for poets to position themselves as aesthetic rebels or to claim that they do not write for popular acclaim. After all, even Ghalib, despite his periodic moments of self-assertion, had written:

Na sataa'ish ki tamanna na silay ki parvaah
Gar nahiñ haiñ mere ash'aar meiñ maane, na sahi

Neither a craving for appreciation, nor a care for reward
If my verses appear meaningless to you, so be it

But while Ghalib brushes off the contention that he wrote verses that were difficult to comprehend, Sahir takes issue with a different opposition. Speaking to those who label him too didactic and too programmatic to deserve serious attention, he asserts that for him poetry's theme ought not be confined to the exalted sphere of metaphysical conundrums, but should engage with the material realities of the times. Seeking to explain the source of his inspiration, Ghalib had eloquently said:

Aate haiñ ghaib se ye mazaameeñ khayaal meiñ
Ghalib, sareer-e khaama, navaa-e sarosh hai

These ideas come to me from the void
Ghalib, the sound of pen on paper is the flutter of angels' wings

Sahir, in direct contrast, stakes claim to a different fount for his words through the lines he uses as the epigraph on the frontispiece of his book *Talkhiyaañ* (Bitter Words):

Duniya ne tajrubaat-o havaadis ki shakl meiñ
Jo kuch mujhe diya hai, voh lauta raha hooñ maiñ

What the world, in the form of experiences and accidents
Has bestowed upon me; I hereby return

***

Abdul Hai, as Sahir was known before he adopted his famous *ta<u>kh</u>allus*[74], was born into a zamindar family. His parents, however, separated soon after his birth, and he never really enjoyed the material comforts of his class position. Evidently a fractious and combative, if emotionally mercurial, youth he was expelled from college, but by 1943, this twenty-three-year-old had already published a collection of poems, *Talkhiyaañ*, perhaps the best-selling work of Urdu poetry after the *Deevaan-e Ghalib*. While still in his twenties, Sahir began to edit a number of journals including the fortnightly *Savera* (Dawn). After the partition of the subcontinent, he stayed on in Lahore but left for India in 1949 to avoid persecution by the Pakistani state, which was unhappy with the tone of the critique it was subjected to in his periodical[75]. Sahir moved to Bombay, which was to be his home till his death, where he went on to have a spectacularly successful career as a lyricist for Hindi films. His songs spanned an enormous range of style, emotion and content. Angry denouncement (*Ye duniya agar mil bhi jaaye to kya hai*/Even if this world is attained, so what), loving playfulness (*Hum aap ki aankhoñ meiñ is dil ko basaa deñ to*/What if I domiciled this heart in your eyes?), charming buffoonery (*Sar jo tera chakraaye, ya dil <u>d</u>ooba jaaye, aaja pyaare paas hamaare, kaahe ghabraaye?*/If your head spins, or your heart sinks, come on buddy, come to me [have a massage], why worry?), resigned sorrow (*Jaane voh kaise log the jinke pyaar ko pyaar mila?*/I wonder who those were whose love was reciprocated), political critique (*Jinheñ naaz hai Hind par voh kahaañ haiñ?*/Where are they who claim to be proud of India) – all found their way in the songs of a single movie (*Pyaasa*, 1957).

After *Talkhiyaañ,* Sahir's poetry was mostly confined to lyrics though he did bring out another collection of works in 1971 called *Aao Ke Koi Khwaab Buneñ* (Come That We May Weave a Dream). However, he continued to be active in the mushaira circles, and his book of selected film songs *Gaata Jaaye Banjaara* (The Gypsy Sings On) finds pride of place alongside the *deevaans*, *kulliyaats* and *kalaams* of other poets. In effect, Sahir was a public intellectual who sought to shape the poetic sensibilities of the common people. His poems are still hummed in streets, his songs keep an idiom alive and his books continue to be bestsellers till today.

In this chapter, we examine Sahir's contributions to the aesthetic of the Progressive Movement, focusing on the themes that recur frequently in his work: his attempts to give voice to the workers, his ardent espousal of pacifism in an age characterized by war and violence, his critique of the bourgeois nationalist state, his unequivocal condemnation of religion and its attendant ills and his assumed role both as the spokesperson and the interlocutor of the Left.

Giving Voice to the Subaltern

In the mould of the other Progressives, Sahir constantly sought to use his poetry to speak on behalf of the unsung workers whose labour lay unacknowledged, obscured and forgotten by history even while the creations of their endeavours were celebrated. One poem that immediately comes to mind is the dramatic 'Taj Mahal' in which Sahir uses a powerful rhetorical device to turn our attention from our admiration of this edifice towards the blood, sweat and tears of the workers who slaved in order to construct it. The poem is written in the voice of the protagonist who refuses to meet his lover at this grand monument:

Taaj tere liye ek mazhar-e ulfat hi sahi
Tujh ko is vaadi-e rangeeñ se aqeedat hi sahi
Meri mahboob, kahiñ aur mila kar mujh se ...

For you, the Taj may be the expression of Love
And you might be enamoured by its beautiful setting
But my love, meet me elsewhere ...

Meri mahboob, unheñ bhi to mohabbat hogi
*Jin ki sannaa'i ne ba*k͟h*shi hai ise shakl-e jameel*
Un ke pyaaroñ ke maqaabir rahe be naam-o numood
Aaj tak un pe jalaayi na kisi ne qandeel.

My beloved, they too must have loved passionately
They, whose craft has gifted this monument its beautiful visage
Their loved ones lie in unmarked graves
Dark, forgotten, unvisited

By the end of the poem, the image of the Taj Mahal as an object of beauty and reverence is deconstructed by Sahir and exposed for what it really is: the vulgar advertisement of the love of an exploitative king and the shameful exhibitionism of the elite, an obeisance to which would be an insult to the love of ordinary people, including that of the very workers who built it. Sahir famously concludes:

Ye chamanzaar, ye Jamuna ka kinaara, ye mahal
Ye munaqqash dar-o deewaar, ye mehraab, ye taaq
Ek shahenshaah ne daulat ka sahaara lekar
Hum g͟h*areeboñ ki mohabbat ka u*ḏ*aaya hai mazaaq*
Meri mahboob, kahiñ aur mila kar mujh se

These gardens, the banks of the Jamuna, this palace
These wonderfully carved walls, doors, awnings
Are but an emperor's display of wealth
That mocks the love of the poor
My love, meet me elsewhere

War and Peace

While Sahir's poetry is a call for social justice of various kinds, his most poignant and heart-felt work was written in the cause of peace, or more specifically, against the cry of war. Growing up in the aftermath of the First World War, and as a youth seeing the destruction caused by the Second World War, Sahir wrote his best poems when he advocated against conflict. In 1956, following the Suez Canal crisis, when the British forces invaded Port Said threatening to escalate the Arab-Israel conflict into yet another global holocaust, he wrote his magnum opus 'Parchaaiyaañ' (Silhouettes), which is without doubt the finest anti-war poem in the entirety of Urdu literature. This incredibly moving *nazm* is simple in its language, powerful in its imagery and devastating in its ability to bring home the depravity of war. The poem begins by speaking in the forlorn voice of a man who is visiting the scene of his once-furtive trysts with his lover:

Fiza meiñ ghul se gaye haiñ ufaq ke narm khutoot
Zameeñ haseen hai, khwaaboñ ki sarzameeñ ki taraah
Tasavvuraat ki parchaaiyaañ ubharti haiñ
Kabhi gumaan ki soorat, kabhi yaqeeñ ki taraah
Voh ped, jin ke tale hum panaah lete the
Khade haiñ aaj bhi saakat, kisi ameeñ ki taraah

The horizon's features have dissolved in the wind
The world is pretty, like the landscape of dreams
Silhouettes of memories arise
Sometimes like a doubt, and occasionally like certitude
The trees under which we had sought refuge
Still stand, silent, like sentinels

The return brings back memories of the meetings, stolen intimacies and shared dreams of a carefree life, dreams that were soon to be shattered by the arrival of troops from the West in preparation for a great war:

Maghrib ke mohazzib mulkoñ se kuch khaaki vardi-posh aaye
Uthlaate hue maghroor aaye, lehraate hue madhosh aaye
Khaamosh zameeñ ke seene meiñ, khaimoñ ki tanaabeñ gadne lagiñ
Makkhan si mulaayam raahoñ par, bootoñ ki kharaasheñ padne lagiñ
Faujoñ ke bhayaanak band *tale charkhoñ ki sadaayeñ doob gayiñ*
Jeepoñ ki sulagti dhool tale phooloñ ki qabaaeñ doob gayiñ

From the 'cultured' nations of the West, came a few khaki-clad men
Sneering braggarts, lurching in their intoxication
Tent-nails were dug in the breast of the quiet earth
The scratches of boots wounded the paths once soft like butter
The soothing sounds of spinning wheels were lost in the deafening military bands
The fragrance of flowers sank in the smouldering fumes of jeeps

The war ravages the economy of the village, and takes a heavy toll on its social fabric. Young men are conscripted in the army and leave their homes, often never to return. The struggle for survival and its costs are described in the following heart-rending words:

Iflaas-zada dehqaanoñ ke, hal-bail bike, khaliyaan bike
Jeene ki tamanna ke haathoñ, jeene hi ke sab saamaan bike
Kuch bhi na raha jab bikne ko, jismoñ ki tijaarat hone lagi
Khilvat meiñ bhi jo mamnoo' thi voh jalwat meiñ jisaarat hone lagi

Beggared farmers sold ploughs, bullocks and fields
In the mad desire to live, the very implements of livelihood were sold
And when there was nothing left to sell, bodies began to be traded

> That which was prohibited even in private, began to be conducted in public

The war devours the dreams of the story's lovers, who are condemned to wretched lives, unable to quite erase the thoughts of that which could have been, of that which has been sacrificed on the bloody horizon:

> *Sooraj ke lahu meiñ lithḏi hui voh shaam hai ab tak yaad mujhe*
> *Chaahat ke sunahre kẖwaaboñ ka anjaam hai ab tak yaad mujhe*
> *Us shaam mujhe maaloom hua, khetoñ ki taraah is duniya meiñ*
> *Sahmi hui dosheezaaoñ ki muskaan bhi bechi jaati hai*
> *Us shaam mujhe maaloom hua, is kaargah-e zardaari meiñ*
> *Do bholi bhaali roohoñ ki pahchaan bhi bechi jaati hai*
> *Us shaam mujhe maaloom hua, jab baap ki kheti chhin jaaye*
> *Mamta ke sunahre kẖwaaboñ ki anmol nishaani bikti hai*
> *Us shaam mujhe maaloom hua, jab bhaa'i jang meiñ kaam aaye*
> *Sarmaaye ke qahba kẖaanoñ meiñ, behnoñ ki javaani bikti hai*
>
> I still remember that evening reddened by the sun's blood
> I still remember the denouement of the golden dreams of love
> That evening I realized that even the tentative smiles of young women
> Are traded in this world like farms and land
> That evening I realized that in the commerce houses of wealth
> The intimacy of two innocent souls is also traded
> That evening I realized that when a father loses his farm
> The priceless symbol of a mother's love is also traded
> That evening I realized that when a brother dies at war
> In the marketplace of capital, a sister's youth is also traded

The protagonist, assailed by these memories of hope and loss, notices another couple under the same tree that had once provided shade for him and his beloved and his heart fills with trepidation, for he knows that the clouds of war are gathering again. This dread leads towards a resolve not to let the war claim yet another dream:

Hamaara pyaar havaadis ki taab la na saka
Magar inheñ to muraadoñ ki raat mil jaaye
Hameñ to kashmakash-e marg-e be amaañ hi mili
Inheñ to jhoomti gaati hayaat mil jaaye

Our love did not survive the savage power of circumstance
At least they should reach the destination of their desires
We found ourselves in the maelstrom of a pitiless death
At least their life should be filled with dance and song

The poem ends with a passionate call for organized pacifism, an appeal to strengthen the will to resist war, and a warning that paints a grim picture of the cost of remaining silent:

Kaho ke aaj bhi hum sab agar khamosh raheñ
To is damakte hue khaakdaañ ki khair nahiñ
Junooñ ki dhaali hui atomi balaaoñ se
Zameeñ ki khair nahiñ, aasmaañ ki khair nahiñ

Guzishta jang meiñ ghar hi jale, magar is baar
Ajab nahiñ, ke ye tanhaaiyaañ bhi jal jaayeñ
Guzishta jang meiñ paikar jale, magar is baar
Ajab nahiñ ke ye parchaaiyaañ bhi jal jaayeñ

Speak, for if we remain silent today
This burnished treasure of earth has no future
In the lunacy of nuclear proliferation
Not just the earth, even the sky has no future

In the last war, homes were burned, but this time
Even the loneliness may burn away
In the last war, only bodies burnt, but this time
Even the silhouettes may burn away

Sahir went on to write other anti-war poems including ones to protest the Indo-Pak conflict of 1965 and to mark the Tashkent peace accord in 1970. In 'Ai Shareef Insanoñ' (O Civil Humans), he says:

Bartari ke saboot ki khaatir
Khooñ bahaana hi kya zaroori hai?
Ghar ki taareekiyaañ mitaane ko
Ghar jalaana hi kya zaroori hai?

Jang to khud hi ek masla hai
Jang kya mas'aloñ ka hal degi?
Aag aur khoon aaj bakhshegi
Bhook aur ehtiyaaj kal degi

To prove one's superiority
Is it necessary to shed blood?
To eliminate the darkness of the house
Is it necessary to set it ablaze?

War itself is the problem
Not the solution to any
All it will give is fire and blood today
Hunger and beggary tomorrow

The only wars that Sahir saw as necessary were those against poverty, hunger, exploitation and oppression. For spilt blood, whether of friend or foe, was human blood after all; whether war was fought in the East or West, it shattered peace for everyone; whether fields were burnt on one side of the border or the other, human beings writhed with the pain of starvation. And whether bombs fell on houses or borders, and be it the celebration of a victory or the mourning of a defeat, post-war lives were forever scarred by the memories of the dead. Sahir passionately sought a world where war would be endlessly postponed by human will and where the only flames that lit up homes would be those of cheerfully luminescent lamps.

Nationalism in the Dock

Sahir, a staunch nationalist, was, like the rest of the Progressives, disillusioned with the policies of the state following Independence. As time wore on and the new state proved to be as oppressive as the displaced colonialists, Sahir took its leadership to task in his song in *Pyaasa*:

> *Zara mulk ke rahbaroñ ko bulaao*
> *Ye kooche, ye galiyaañ, ye manzar dikhaao*
> *Jinheñ naaz hai Hind par un ko laao*
> *Jinheñ naaz hai Hind par voh kahaañ haiñ*
>
> Pray, call the leaders of this country
> Show them these lanes, these sights
> Call upon those who are so proud of India
> Where are they, who are so proud of India?

There is a bitterness in these verses that contrasts with, say, Faiz's gentle and almost wistful reproach directed at the state which imprisoned him on the trumped-up charge of treason:

> *Nisaar maiñ teri galiyoñ pe ai vatan, ke jahaañ*
> *Chali hai rasm ke koi na sar utha ke chale*
>
> I sacrifice myself to your lanes, my country
> Where it has been decreed that none should walk with head held high

Sahir's voice, however, was uncompromising and even harsh. Although he did write occasionally in a tempered tone, penning patriotic songs like *Ab koi gulshan na ujde, ab vatan aazaad hai* (Let no more gardens be destroyed, the homeland is free now), his critique of the nation-state was usually delivered in a direct and passionate manner. In a poem titled 'Chhabbees Janvary' (26th January), Sahir launches into a critique of the state, accusing it of failing to live up to its promises:

Daulat badhi to mulk meiñ iflaas kyoñ badha?
Khush-haali-e avaam ke asbaab kya hue?
Jo apne saath saath chale, koo-e daar tak,
Voh dost, voh raqeeb, voh ahbaab kya hue?
Har koocha shola-zaar hai, har shahr qatl-gaah,
Ekjahti-e hayaat ke aadaab kya hue?
Sahra-e teeragi meiñ bhatakti hai zindagi
Ubhre the jo ufaq pe voh mahtaab kya hue?

If the wealth of the nation has increased, why this growing poverty?
What ever happened to the path towards ordinary peoples' prosperity?
Those that had once walked with us towards the gallows,
Where are those friends, those companions, those beloveds?
Every street is aflame, every city a killing field,
Where did the etiquette of togetherness disappear?
Life wanders aimlessly through the desert of darkness,
The moons that had once risen on the horizon, where have they gone?

The Atheist in the Middle

Even while Sahir championed the right of Indian Muslims to live in their own country free of persecution and without being viewed with suspicion, he was a strong opponent of Islamic orthodoxy. Often, he reserved his harshest critique for the institution of religion, which he saw as nothing more than a tool of exploitation. He not only challenged the very basis of religion but also despaired of a world where religious leaders were allowed to control the aspirations of the people and conjured up the image of an era where the sensibility of atheism would find a prominent place in society. The following poem almost reads like a declaration of war against Faith, its establishments and its proponents:

Bezaar hai kanisht-o kaleese se ye jahaa.N
Saudagaraan-e deen ki saudaagari ki khair
Ilhaad kar raha hai murattab jahaañ-e nau
Dair-o haram ki hay'ola ghaaratgari ki khair
Insaañ ulat raha hai rukh-e zeest se naqaab
Mazhab ke ehtemaam-e fusooñ parvari ki khair

This world is sick of the temple, mosque, church
You who peddle religion, beware
Atheism is now laying the foundation of a new world
The plundering edifices of faith, beware
Humanity is unveiling the real face of life
Religion's wily artifice, beware

Here, Sahir gives full-throated voice to his disdain of religious institutions, bestowing upon them the most derogatory of adjectives, making them out to be shrill and dishonest, while atheism *(ilhaad)* becomes the saviour of the day. It must, however, be noted that Sahir's criticism appears to be directed towards formal, organized and institutionalized religion rather than its cultural practice, for he often wrote the gentlest and most soothing of *bhajans* and *duaas* for his film songs. His *ilhaad* was not averse to the expression of sentiments such as *Allah tero naam, Eeshwar tero naam.* But when the situation presented itself, he managed to inject his critique of religious divides through a song in the 1959 film *Dhool Ka Phool* (Flower of the Dust). The song is set up by the story in which a villager finds an abandoned baby and decides to bring it up himself. Since there is no way of telling whether the child is a Hindu or a Muslim, the villagers want to know what faith the child will be raised to follow. The man, addressing the child, sings:

Tu Hindu banega na Musalmaan banega
Insaan ki aulaad hai, insaan banega

Achcha hai abhi tak tera kuch naam nahiñ hai
Tujh ko kisi mazhab se koi kaam nahiñ hai
Jis ilm ne insaanoñ ko taqseem kiya hai
Us ilm ka tujh par koi ilzaam nahiñ hai
Tu amn ka aur sulha ka paighaam banega
Insaan ki aulaad hai, insaan banega

You will neither become a Hindu nor a Muslim
You are a child of humans, you will be a human being

It is good that you do not yet have a name
That you are not yet associated with any religion
That you are not accused of possessing the knowledge
Which has divided human beings
You will embody the message of peace and tolerance
You are a child of humans, you will be a human being

A Party Worker, an Interlocutor

Vajh-e berangi-e gulzaar kahooñ to kya ho?
Kaun hai kitna gunehgaar, kahooñ to kya ho?
Tum ne jo baat sar-e bazm na sun-na chaahi
Maiñ vahi baat sar-e daar kahooñ to kya ho?

What if I told you the reason the garden had no colour?
And what if I became the accountant of sins?
The words you did not want to hear in the civil assembly,
What if I spoke those very words on the gallows?

Sahir exemplified the credo of 'speaking truth to power', both of his own accord and at the behest of the movement, both in his poetry and his prose, both through his own writing and through the work he published in the periodicals he edited. While his critique of social conditions was certainly his own, he was also known for loyally toeing the party line, subordinating his poetic will to it when required to do so. Carlo Coppola, in his unpublished dissertation, offers us an anecdote[76] that illustrates this. When Sahir first wrote 'Taj Mahal', the poem included the following lines, referring to the ornate designs of the Taj:

> *Seena-e dahr pe naasoor haiñ, kohna naasoor*
> *Jin meiñ shaamil hai tere aur mere ajdaad ka khooñ*
>
> These decorations are nothing but chronic boils on the body of the earth
> Which have been painted with the blood of our ancestors

The party machinery expressed its unhappiness with the sentiments since it thought that the words debased the product of the labour of ordinary workers. Rather than trying to explain or defend himself, Sahir simply reworked the lines to read thus instead:

> *Daaman-e dahr pe us rang ki gulkaari hai*
> *Jis meiñ shaamil hai tere aur mere ajdaad ka khooñ*
>
> These decorations are embroidered with the colour
> That comes from the blood of our ancestors

Sahir's commitment to the PWA cause and his wholesale adherence to the doctrine of Socialist Realism allowed him to position himself as an interlocutor of his fellow bards. He was especially trenchant in his criticism of poets who had chosen not to write about the Bengal famine, a tragedy that was widely seen as having been caused by capitalist and colonialist policies[77]. In his characteristic direct fashion, he took his own comrades like Faiz, Majaz and Jazbi to task for their silence on the issue, while lauding Ali Sardar Jafri, Jigar Muradabadi and Ahmad Nadeem Qasmi for their attempts to rouse the masses against this outrage. Needless to say, Sahir himself wrote a long poem, 'Bangaal', on the famine and made several references in his other poems to its catastrophic effects on the people of the region.

Clearly, Sahir saw himself as a companion of the revolutionary working class and sought to contribute to its success. And he visualized himself as playing a role as its song-writer, its troubadour and perhaps even its vanguard:

Tum se quvvat le kar ab maiñ tum ko raah dikhaaoonga
Tum parcham lehraana saathi, maiñ barbat par gaaoonga

From you I will take strength, and to you I will be a guide
Raise the banner of revolution, comrades, and I will sing
your anthem

Theorizing the Aesthetic

Zamaana bar-sar-e paikaar hai pur-haul sholoñ se
Tere lab par abhi tak naghma-e Khayyaam hai saaqi!

The world is in mortal combat with deadly flames
And yet you continue to sing the songs of Omar Khayyam,
O saaqi!

Notwithstanding the short shrift he has received, Sahir's work does not allow the serious critic to wave it off, not simply because it is so popular, nor because it offers its own best defence through periodic references to its raison d'etre, but because of the fact that Sahir pushed the boundaries of an explicitly political brand of poetry that served as an aesthetic experiment of the time.

The socialist literary theorist Nikolai Bukharin contended

that 'poetic creation is one of the forms of ideological creation', and that poetry 'is one of the most powerful factors in social development as a whole' since 'the word itself is the product of social development and represents a definite condensing point in which a whole series of social factors find their expression'[78]. Christopher Cauldwell, referring to the power of poetry as a unifying tool for the masses, writes that 'poetry is characteri-stically song, and song is characteristically something which, because of its rhythm, is sung in unison, and is capable of being the expression of a collective emotion'[79], while George Thomson defines the poet as a prophet of the working class, only 'at a higher level of sublimation'[80]. Sahir was Bukharin's poet, Cauldwell's song-writer and Thomson's prophet.

In a self-referential moment, Sahir carefully, yet passionately, opens up the politics behind his poetics in a poem called 'Mere Geet' (My Songs):

Mere sarkash taraane sun ke duniya ye samajhti hai
Ke shaayad mere dil ko ishq ke naghmoñ se nafrat hai
Mujhe hangaama-e jang-o jadal se kaif milta hai
Meri fitrat ko khooñ-rezi ke afsaanoñ se raghbat hai

Magar ai kaash dekheñ voh meri pursoz raatoñ ko
Maiñ jab taaroñ pe nazreñ gaad kar aansoo bahaata hooñ
Tasavvur ban ke bhooli vaardaateñ yaad aati haiñ
To soz-o dard ki shiddat se pahroñ tilmilaata hooñ

Mai shaayar hooñ, mujhe fitrat ke nazzaaroñ se ulfat hai
Mera dil dushman-e naghma saraa'i ho nahiñ sakta
Javaañ hooñ maiñ, javaani naazishoñ ka ek toofaañ hai
Meri baatoñ meiñ rang-e paarsaa'i ho nahiñ sakta

Mere sarkash taraanoñ ki haqeeqat hai, to itni hai,
Ke jab maiñ dekhta hooñ bhook ke maare kisaanoñ ko
Ghareeboñ, mufllisoñ ko, bekasoñ ko, besahaaroñ ko

To dil taab-e nishaat-e bazm-e ishrat la nahiñ sakta
Maiñ chaahooñ bhi to khwaabaavar taraane ga nahiñ sakta

When the world hears my angry songs, it assumes
That perhaps my heart abhors love songs
That I derive pleasure from the turmoil of war and conflict
That by nature, I get pleasure from stories of bloodshed

But alas! That they could witness those anguished nights
When I cast my eyes on the stars and weep
When forgotten encounters flash upon memory's eye
When for hours, I tremble with the intensity of my grief

I am a poet, the love of nature is my instinct
My heart can never be the enemy of song writing!
I am young, and youth is a storm of passion
My words can never be inflected by the colour of temperance!

If there is a reason for my angry songs, it is this
That when I see the tillers of land go hungry
When I see the poor, the oppressed and the helpless
My heart cannot countenance the celebration of high culture
Even if I wish, I cannot give voice to dream-laden songs.

Here and elsewhere, Sahir readily and without the trace of apology admits that his work is programmatic and has a purpose. His poetic attempt to render art into manifesto is a conscious aesthetic choice on his part, not the product of his inability to write songs of love, resulting in a sinewy intensity, a near-unpalatable bitterness, a brusque tone and an impatience with those who did not agree with him. In 'Mujhe Sochne De' (Let Me Think), Sahir, addressing a beloved, writes:

Nau-e insaañ pe ye sarmaaya-o mehnat ka tazaad
Amn-o tahzeeb ke parcham tale qaumoñ ka fasaad
Lahlahaate hue khetoñ pe javaani ka sama
Aur dehqaan ke chhappar meiñ na batti na dhuaañ
Ye bhi kyoñ hai, ye bhi kya hai, mujhe kuch sochne de

Kaun insaañ ka khuda hai, mujhe kuch sochne de
Apni mayoos umangon ka fasaana na suna
Meri nakaam mohabbat ki kahaani mat ched

Writ on humanity is this contradiction of capital and labour
While under the banner of peace and culture, communities riot
The wavy fields bestow a promise of youth
While under the farmer's roof, there is neither lamp nor stove
What is this and why? Let me think!
Who is this God of ours? Let me think!
Do not bring up the story of your defeated youth
Do not bring up the issue of my lost love

The Urdu Freiligrath

Despite the certitude that underscores his writing, Sahir's work is characterized by a certain sense of humility. Never averse to writing as the movement saw fit and always ready to change words and phrases in his poetry that were seen as improper, he appears to have seen himself as someone who was playing his small part in the larger scheme of things. In the tradition of many PWA poets, he never used his poetic signature (*takhallus*) in any of his ghazals, understood the temporality of his intervention and accepted the likelihood of his eventual effacement from public memory, writing the following in *Maiñ Pal Do Pal Ka Shaayar Hooñ* (I am a Poet of a Moment or Two):

Kal koi mujh ko yaad kare?
Kyooñ koi mujh ko yaad kare?
Masroof zamaana mere liye,
Kyooñ waqt apna barbaad kare?

Will anyone remember me tomorrow?
Why should anyone remember me?
Why should this busy world
Waste its time on me?

But ultimately, Sahir was a poet. And despite his assertions to the contrary, possibly yearned for acknowledgement. After all, it comes with the territory. Given Sahir's political leanings, it might be interesting to see what Marx himself had to say on the subject of poets and adulation. In a letter to his friend Joseph Weydemeyer, Marx wrote: 'Write a friendly letter to Freiligrath. Don't be afraid to compliment him, for all poets, even the best of them ... have to be cajoled to make them sing. Our Freiligrath ... is a real revolutionary and an honest man through and through – praise that I would not mete out to many. Nevertheless, a poet – no matter what he may be as a man – requires applause, admiration. I think it lies in the very nature of the species ...'

Since one searches in vain for a verse in Sahir's poetry where he truly thumps his chest *à la* Ghalib (*Kahte haiñ ke Ghalib ka hai andaaz-e bayaañ aur*/It is said that Ghalib's way of speech is unique), let us do it on his behalf and accord him his rightful pride of place in the canon of Urdu poetry.

Sahir was a powerful poet of dissent, a conscience of society, an uncompromising critic of the Right and a strident persuader of the Left. He was a relentless opponent of reactionary cultural and social institutions. His verses were never lacking in virtuosity or depth. His poetry could be as fine-grained as Ghalib's and Mir's ghazals, as lyrical as Faiz's *nazms* and as inflected with philosophy as Hali's or Iqbal's *musaddas*. He was a principled interlocutor who insistently and powerfully critiqued the structures of exploitation and their agents: the ruthless capitalist, the greedy usurer, the decadent priest, the bourgeois nationalist, the besotted lover, the rapacious colonialist and the self-absorbed poet. We were fortunate to have had him in our midst.

وہ یار ہے جو خوشبو کی طرح
ہے جس کی زباں اُردو کی طرح

مجھ کو اِس کا رنج نہیں ہے لوگ مجھے فنکار نہ مانیں
فکر و سخن کے تاجر میرے شعروں کو اشعار نہ مانیں

آتے ہیں غیب سے یہ مضامیں خیال میں
غالبؔ صریرِ خامہ نوائے سروش ہے
دُنیا نے تجرُبات و حوادث کی شکل میں
جو کچھ مجھے دیا ہے وہ لوٹا رہا ہوں مَیں

یہ چمن زار یہ جمنا کا کِنارا یہ محل
یہ منقّش در و دیوار یہ محراب یہ طاق
اِک شہنشاہ نے دولت کا سہارا لے کر
ہم غریبوں کی محبّت کا اُڑایا ہے مذاق
میری محبوب کہیں اور مِلا کر مجھ سے

ہمارا پیار حوادث کی تاب لا نہ سکا
مگر اُنھیں تو مُرادوں کی رات مِل جائے
ہمیں تو کشمکشِ مرگِ بے اماں ہی مِلی
اُنہیں تو جھُومتی گاتی حیات مِل جائے

اگر پلک پہ ہیں موتی تو یہ نہیں کافی
ہنر بھی چاہیے الفاظ میں پرونے کو

اِس ایک ہاتھ میں ہے جیت اُس کی
دوسرے ہاتھ میں تنہائی ہے

جانے کیسا دور ہے جس میں یہ جرأت بھی مشکل ہے
دِن ہو اگر تو لِکھوں اسے دِن رات اگر ہو رات لکھوں

لو دیکھ لو یہ عِشق ہے یہ وصل ہے یہ ہجر
اَب لوٹ چلے آؤ بہت کام پڑا ہے

قاتِل بھی مقتول بھی دونوں نام خدا کا لیتے تھے
کوئی خدا تھا تو وہ کہاں تھا میری کیا اوقات لِکھوں

آج
یہ شہر اک سہمے ہوئے بچے کی طرح
اپنی پرچھائی سے بھی ڈرتا ہے
جنتری دیکھو
مجھے لگتا ہے
آج تیوہار کوئی ہے شاید

9

JAVED AKHTAR'S QUIVER OF POETIC ARROWS

A Legacy Survives

Agar palak pe haiñ moti to ye nahiñ kaafi
Hunar bhi chaahiye alfaaz meiñ pirone ka

It is not enough if pearls of tears abound on eyelashes
One must have the craft to weave them into a necklace of words

In 1995, Urdu poetry received an unexpected gift in the shape of Javed Akhtar's collection of poems titled *Tarkash* (Quiver). It had been a long time since a new book of poetry had generated such enthusiasm. Eager as we all were for a fresh voice, we devoured this well-produced volume (printed incidentally by 'Sahir Publishing House', certainly no coincidence), and marvelled at the poet, whose style, as the author Gopi Chand Narang declared on the dust cover, 'is an original voice, not someone else's echo'. In a flowery foreword to the book, Qurratulain Hyder, the famous Urdu novelist, declared, 'Urdu poetry flows like the Niagara Falls, and its spray produces countless spectra, in which Javed now has added his own little rainbow.'

Each poem in *Tarkash* was a wondrous joy, and an exquisite pain. The book was startlingly familiar in the way it brought back memories of the era of the progressive poets, yet radically different in the new, contemporary sensibility it claimed for itself. The relentless engagement with social conditions was evident in every poem, but the ringing promise of the revolutionary had been replaced by the wistful demeanour of the realist.

In his preface to the book, Akhtar records his remarkable life in unassuming language: an idyllic beginning in Lucknow and Aligarh, a complex adolescence, the early days in the Bombay film industry as a ghost scriptwriter, the decision to turn down a steady job for the uncertain livelihood of a professional writer and the eventual triumph over circumstances. His wry comments about the personal toll exacted by success barely conceals a wealth of pain, masquerading as experience. This experience was to find expression in Akhtar's poetry in extraordinary ways.

To understand Javed Akhtar's *Tarkash*, one needs to contextualize his work in the light of the progressive tradition in Urdu poetry for the last half a century and more. In many ways, Akhtar is an inheritor of this tradition. He is related to many of the iconic poets of the Progressive Writers' Movement (he is Jan Nisar Akhtar's son, Israr-ul-Haq Majaz's nephew, Kaifi Azmi's son-in-law). However, as we shall see, his poetry represents as many departures from this tradition as it does continuities. In this chapter, we highlight five themes in Javed Akhtar's poetry and examine them in terms of their relationship to the work of the Progressives of an earlier generation.

The New Protagonist

Akhtar's poems carry neither the raw anger of Sahir's

Talkhiyaañ (Bitterness) nor the avowedly modern bent of Kaifi Azmi's *Aavaara Sajde* (Vagabond Obeisances). Instead, they appear to be a lot closer to the gentle pain found in Faiz's later works, invoking the mood of the line: *Aaj ek harf ko phir dhoondta phirta hai khayaal* (Today, my thoughts, once again, search in vain for words to express themselves). Javed's protagonist is neither the poor and oppressed labourer nor the fervent revolutionary bent on changing the world, but a modern, alienated subject who lives in a world that has been tainted by compromise and where the grandiose promises of a new dawn have already unravelled. The complex and alien landscape he inhabits produces a tortured ambivalence within him while he attempts to deal with the forces that tug at him from different directions.

Consider for example, the poem titled 'Mother Teresa'. Akhtar begins in a laudatory manner, praising the saintly figure for her work with the destitute, the impoverished and the dispossessed, and offers the following tribute:

Tera lams maseeha hai
Aur tera karam hai ek samandar
Jiska koi paar nahiñ hai
Ai Ma Teresa
Mujh ko teri azmat se inkaar nahiñ hai

Your touch is that of the healer
And your grace is like a boundless ocean
Mother Teresa
I cannot deny your greatness

Having acknowledged her status as a demi-god, he begins to sow the seed of doubt in the narrative he has just formulated. But his questioning is gentle and eschews any form of self-righteousness. His critique, unlike those of the PWA poets, does not come from a position of moral certitude but is articulated in a rather tentative tone. It is the critique of a man who understands his own complicity in the injustice and is consequently uncertain about his right to express his reservations:

Maiñ thahra khudgarz
Bas ek apni hi khaatir jeene vaala
Tujh ko maiñ kis moonh se poochhooñ
Tu ne kabhi ye kyooñ nahiñ poochha
Kis ne in bad-haaloñ ko bad-haal kiya hai?
...
Tu ne kabhi ye kyooñ nahiñ dekha
Vahi nizaam-e zar
Jis ne in bhookoñ se roti chheeni hai
Tere kahne par
Bhookoñ ke aage
Kuch tukde daal raha hai

I stand before you
A selfish being, living merely for my own self
What right do I have to ask you this:
Why did you never wonder?
Who has brought misfortune on these wretches?
...
Why have you never noticed
That the very system of wealth
Which has snatched the bread from these poor
Now, on your demand
Tosses some morsels
Towards the hungry

The poem gradually ups the ante, ultimately holding Mother Teresa accountable for her role in a system which throws a few scraps towards those it destroys and for failing to advocate that the poor demand their right to a life of dignity rather than having to beg for it. The implicit suggestion of the poem is that the Mother is colluding with the forces of tyranny:

Aisa kyooñ hai
Ek jaanib mazloom se tujh ko hamdardi hai
Doosri jaanib
Zaalim se bhi aar nahiñ hai

Why is it
That you have sympathy for the oppressed
And yet you don't spurn the tyrant?

What follows separates Akhtar dramatically from the earlier PWA tradition. Unlike Kaifi's passionate protagonist, Sahir's vanguard or Faiz's resignedly resolute martyr, Akhtar's voice chooses to abdicate the moral battleground of critique:

Lekin sach hai
Aisi baateñ maiñ tum ko kis moonh se poochhooñ
Poochhoonga to
Mujh pe bhi voh zimmedaari aa jaayegi
Jis se maiñ bachta aaya hooñ
Behtar hai khaamosh rahooñ maiñ
Aur agar kuch kahna hai to
Yahi kahooñ maiñ
Ai Ma Teresa
Mujh ko teri azmat se inkaar nahiñ hai

But it is true
I can scarcely ask you such questions
For if I do, I will be saddled with a responsibility
That I have escaped thus far.
Perhaps it is best I remain silent
And if I must say something, let me say just this
Mother Teresa
I can never deny your greatness

The exquisitely troubled irony of the poem treads the fine line between critique and confession. The point comes across, and is arguably rendered more potent by Akhtar's tentativeness, for in it the readers can see themselves reflected along with all of their own contradictions. A similar sentiment runs through several of Akhtar's other poems. For example, in 'Uljhan'(Dilemma), he reflects on a dog-eat-dog world where survival depends on the willingness to disregard others. It is a world without any real choice where one's conscience is forever and always-already compromised. The protagonist of this poem, jostled by a crowd of millions, has to decide between being trampled by others and crushing them in the course of his own march forward:

Chaloon̈
To auron̈ pe zulm d̲haaoon̈
Rukoon̈
To auron̈ ke zulm jheloon̈
Zameer
Tujh ko to naaz hai apni munsifi par
Zara sunoon̈ main̈
Ke aaj kya tera faisla hai

If I walk
I will cause pain to others
If I stop
I will suffer their tyranny
Conscience
You are proud of your own judgement
Let me hear
What your decision is today

This tired frustration is a marker of Akhtar's uniqueness, for the characters in his poem have no dependable moral compass that can guide them in making the right decision. Gone is the certitude expressed by the Progressives and the optimism that accompanied it; the just path, if there ever was one, cannot be found.

One can see this poem's sense of dystopic loss in several other pieces as well. For instance, 'Ek Mohre Ka Safar' (A Pawn's Journey) describes the journey of an ordinary pawn which, aware of the dangers it faces, skilfully dodges powerful enemies and ends up as a larger piece, only to find that now the very power that ensures its safety also produces an alienating distance from all others, friends and foes alike, none of whom can come meaningfully close to it. Victory exacts its price.

Us ke ek haath meiñ hai jeet us ki
Doosre haath meiñ tanhaai hai

In one hand, Victory
And in the other, Loneliness

The New Critic

While the Progressives wrote in the voice of the champions of the downtrodden who sought to change the system, Akhtar's protagonists often learn to play its game of hypocrisy, exploitation and greed. Faced with a cut-throat world in which he finds himself hopelessly implicated, Akhtar does not pitch camp on a moral high ground, choosing instead to deploy sharp cynicism as a tool of his critique:

Aaj ki duniya meiñ jeene ka qareena samjho
Jo mile pyaar se un logoñ ko zeena samjho

Learn the protocols of living in today's world
Treat those who offer you love as stepping stones

There is none of Faiz's optimistic avowal of the poet's commitment to truth and experience: *Hum parvarish-e lauh-o qalam karte rahenge, Jo dil pe guzarti hai, raqam karte rahenge* (We will continue to nurture the legacy of paper and pen, What our hearts endure, we will continue to record). Akhtar is conscious that in the contemporary social context the writer's space for expression is limited, his agency curtailed. In one place, he writes:

Jaane kaisa daur hai jis meiñ ye jur'at bhi mushkil hai
Din ho agar to likhooñ use din, raat agar ho, raat likhooñ

I wonder what kind of an age this is, where even this much courage is tough to muster
That if I see it is day, I write it as day, that when it is night, I call it night

It is not that Akhtar has relinquished his right to speak his mind. But even if he chooses to do that, his audience's mind is fixed on other things. The upper classes are not inclined to listen to analysis or deep thoughts. Their attention is elsewhere, its span limited. The poet's frustration comes through again in the following lines:

Chaar lafzoñ meiñ kaho, jo bhi kaho
Us ko kab fursat, sune faryaad sab
Talkhiyaañ kaise na ho ash'aar meiñ
Hum pe jo guzri, hameñ hai yaad sab

Whatever you have to say, say it in four words
The ruler has no time for every complaint
How can bitterness not inflect my verses?
I remember all that I have ever endured

In these verses Akhtar appears to be indicting even his audience, which demands pithy and easily consumable sentiments and has no time for complexities in *sukhan*. Living in an era where Urdu poetry has become a cultural commodity, where ghazals have become products for superficial and pretentious enjoyment and where the complexities of the tongue are beyond the reach of most, the sacrifice of poetic sensibility at the altar of an insensitive marketplace grates on Akhtar. In an amazing poem, his vituperation is palpable:

Shahr ke dukaandaaro, kaarobaar-e ulfat meiñ
Sood kya ziyaañ kya hai, tum na jaan paaoge
...
Jaanta hooñ maiñ tum ko zaukh-e shaayari bhi hai
Shakhsiyat sajaane meiñ ek ye maahiri bhi hai
Phir bhi harf chunte ho, sirf lafz sunte ho
In ke darmiyaañ kya hai, tum na jaan paaoge

Merchants of the city, in the business of love
You will never understand what counts as profit, what as loss
...
I know that you have a taste for poetry
That you cultivate this skill to adorn yourself
But you just pluck syllables, listen merely to words
You will never understand that which lies between them

As anyone who has read progressive Urdu poetry knows, the word 'merchant' is used in this genre as a particularly derogatory epithet. Akhtar deploys it deliberately and accuses his addressee of being an exploiter of words, sentiments and expression. The hollow appreciation of poetry, all too common these days, is harshly condemned. The implicit commentary here is that those who are consumed by materialistic concerns and are focused on profiteering are incapable of understanding the true sentiment of poetry. Words for these patrons of the arts remain merely words; the real meaning (that which lies in between the words) is beyond their reach.

Akhtar's trademark cynicism is not limited to the establishment or to those who occupy exalted and privileged positions in the system. In his world, even human relations become transactional and pragmatic. In 'Aao, Aur Na Socho' (Come, Do Not Think Any Further), he negotiates a relationship with a 'beloved' that acknowledges the inherent falseness of accepted ideas about love, romance, and fidelity, but cannily suggests that they pretend to play the game by these rules for as long as it remains mutually entertaining.

Tum meri aankhoñ meiñ aankheñ d̲aal ke dekho
Phir maiñ tum se
Saari jhoot̲i qasmeñ khaaooñ
Phir tum voh saari jhoot̲i baateñ dohraao
Jo sab ko achchi lagti hai …

Jitne din ye mel rahega
Dekho, achcha khel rahega
Aur
Kabhi dil bhar jaaye to
Kah dena tum
Beet gaya milne ka mausam

Aao
Aur na socho
Soch ke kya paaoge

Look deep into my eyes
And I will make to you
All those false promises
And you can repeat to me those falsehoods
That everyone wants to hear …

As long this intimacy lasts
It will be an enjoyable game
And
When you have had your fill
You can tell me
That the season of togetherness has passed

Come
Do not think any more
For what is gained by thinking?

In a world where everything is commodified, where one often gets what one wants through deceit and self-deception, there is no space for the expectation of an untainted love. Akhtar seems inclined to give voice to a time in which expressions of passion and romance have become little more than empty eloquence and where sacrifice and commitment are no longer valued. The pursuit of love becomes a game to be played and the pleasures of a relationship are transient and temporal. Those who seek truth and awareness are destined to fail. As he says:

Aagahi se mili hai tanhaai
Aa meri jaan, mujh ko dhoka de

Awareness has brought me loneliness
Come, my love, please deceive me

The New Romantic

As we have already seen, Akhtar's attitude to love is considerably different from that of his predecessors. For classical poets love was a deep, intense, formulaic emotion bordering on conceit. For the Progressives love was often a ground that joined the lovers in struggle, as in Kaifi's *Uṯh meri jaan mere saath hi chalna hai tujhe* (Rise, my love, that we must walk together). At other times, it was an emotion that had to be sacrificed in order to achieve a greater goal, as in Faiz's *Mujh se pahli si mohabbat meri mahboob na maang* (Beloved, do not ask me for that old love anymore). Akhtar's attitude to love is markedly different, and at times, almost cavalier. Love is sometimes a futile and empty passion, to be dispensed with before getting on with the more immediate task of living. For example, we have this two liner that is dismissive of the central tropes of love poetry like *ishq* (passionate love), *vasl* (the union of lovers) and *hijr* (separation):

Lo dekh lo, ye ishq hai, ye vasl hai, ye hijr
Ab lauṯ chaleñ aao, bahut kaam paḏa hai

All right, look: this is Love, here is Union, and this is Separation
Now let us return, shall we? There is a lot of work to be done.

Love, when it does come about, is not everlasting. But its loss does not break the lover. Unlike the tragic Majnoon, he does not spend his life sifting the sands in search of his Laila. Akhtar mourns his lost love in rather matter-of-fact terms that remind one of an early Sahir:

Mohabbat mar gayi, mujh ko bhi g̲h̲am hai
Mere achche dinoñ ki aashna thi

Love has died, I too am sad
It was my friend in happier times

This is not to say that the poet does not suffer the pain of love's loss; the act of forgetting is not all that easily accomplished. In his poem 'Dushvaari' (Dilemma), the protagonist wants to erase his memories so that he may move on with his life. But he is powerless to do so for his wretched heart not only remembers all that ever happened, but also that which could not, that which had been left unsaid:

Maiñ bhool jaaooñ tumheñ
Ab yahi munaasib hai
Magar bhulaana bhi chaahooñ to kis taraah bhooloоñ
Ke tum to phir bhi haqeeqat ho

Koi khwaab nahiñ
Yahaañ to dil ka ye aalam hai, kya kahooñ
Kambakht!
Bhula na paaya ye voh silsila
Jo tha hi nahiñ
Voh ik khayaal
Jo aawaaz tak gaya hi nahiñ
Voh ek baat
Jo maiñ kah nahiñ saka tum se
Voh ek rabt
Jo hum meiñ kabhi raha hi nahiñ
Mujhe hai yaad voh sab
Jo kabhi hua hi nahiñ

I should forget you
Yes, that is prudent
But how can I do that, even if I want to?
You are after all a reality
Not a mere dream
Here, the condition of my heart is so unfortunate
(Wretched heart!)
That it has been unable to forget the chain of events
That never took place
That one thought
Which was never voiced
That one conversation
I couldn't have with you
That one connection
Which we never had
I remember everything
That never happened

Akhtar is an unconventional romantic. His engagement with love is very realistic in its expressions and explorations of ambiguities, vicissitudes, and (tragic) ironies. His protagonist often seems to be wistful about a past love that could not reach fruition, a love that casts its shadows on the present, forever looming over his current relationship:

Paas aake bhi faasle kyooñ haiñ
Raaz kya hai? Samajh meiñ yooñ aaya
Us ko bhi yaad hai ko'i ab bhi
Maiñ bhi tum ko bhula nahiñ paaya

Why the distances even in togetherness?
The secret unfurls thus
She also remembers an old love
And I too, haven't succeeded in forgetting you

The lovers of Akhtar's poems inhabit the twilight zone between bitter prior experiences and uncertain shared futures, in a present that is marked by a variety of very real emotions, including petty ones like jealousy and possessiveness:

Laakh ho hum meiñ pyaar ki baateñ
Ye lad̲aai hamesha chalti hai
Us ke ik dost se maiñ jalta hooñ
Meri ek dost se voh jalti hai

We may share a million words of love
But one fight is ongoing
She is jealous of one of my friends
And I am jealous of one of hers

Sometimes relationships end, but the memories of intimacies remain, only to resurface when the ex-lovers come together. In a moving poem called 'Aasaar-e Qadeema' (Ancient Remnants), Akhtar describes one such moment, comparing the failed relationship and the reminiscences it evokes to an archaeological find of an ancient ruined city whose glorious past can now only be discerned through the broken artefacts that litter its dug-up landscape:

Ek patthar ki adhoori moorat
Chand taambe ke puraane sikke

Kaali chaandi ke ajab se zevar
Aur ka'ee kaanse ke toote bartan
Ek sahra meiñ mile
Zer-e zameeñ
Log kahte haiñ ke sadiyoñ pahle
Aaj sahra hai jahaañ
Vahiñ ek shahr hua karta tha
Aur mujh ko ye khayaal aata hai
Kisi taqreeb
Kisi mahfil meiñ
Saamna tujh se mera aaj bhi ho jaata hai
Ek lamhe ko
Bas ik pal ke liye
Jism ki aanch
Uchat-ti si nazar
Surkh bindiya ki damak
Sarsaraahat tere malboos ki
Baaloñ ki mehak
Bekhayaali meiñ kabhi
Lams ka nanha sa phool
Aur phir door tak vahi sahra
Vahi sahra ke jahaañ
Kabhi ik shahr hua karta tha

A shattered stone statue
Some old copper coins
Strange ornaments of blackened silver
Several broken bronze vessels
Were unearthed
In a desert
And people say that centuries ago
Here where there is only a desert
A city was once settled
And a thought strikes me:
Even today, at a party
A gathering
When I come face to face with you
For one second
Just for one moment
The warmth of your body

The fleeting chance meeting of our eyes
The shine of your red *bindiya*
The rustle of your clothes
The fragrance of your hair
And sometimes, unintentionally
A tiny flower of touch
And then again, that unending desert
That desert where once
A city had flourished

What is striking in Akhtar's 'love poetry' is that his characters are mature individuals whose romanticism is always already undercut by a sense of realism. The lover of an earlier brand of Urdu poetry who paces the streets of his beloved that variously entices him, charms him, seduces him and ultimately breaks his heart is gone. Akhtar's poems are populated with lovers whose love can be fleeting, transactional or tragically enduring. If there is any common ground with the tradition of Urdu poetry, it is this: there are no happy endings.

The New Agnostic

Akhtar, like the Progressives before him, is very dismissive of religious orthodoxy and indeed of religion itself. He interrogates Faith for its role in constricting human agency, its divisiveness, its false panaceas and its horrific companion – sectarian violence. The staple stocks-in-trade of the progressive critique of religion are to be found in his work, but again, they are tinged by a certain tentativeness or a tongue-in-cheek humility:

Qaatil bhi, maqtool bhi donoñ naam khuda ka lete the
Koi khuda tha, to voh kahaañ tha, meri kya auqaat, likhooñ?

The murderer and the victim were both invoking the name of God

> If there was a God, where was He? But who am I to write about that?

In 'Waqt', a metaphysical ode to Time, Akhtar uses a very modernist imagery to question the omnipresence of God, pondering the possibility that time and space extend into a zone where there is no Supreme Being:

To har tasavvur ki had ke baahar
Magar kahiñ par
Yaqeenan aisa koi khala hai
Ke jis ko
In kahkashaaoñ ki ungliyoñ ne
Ab tak chhua nahiñ hai
Khala
Jahaañ kuch hua nahiñ hai
Khala
Ke jis ne kisi se bhi 'kun' suna nahiñ hai
Jahaañ kahiñ par khuda nahiñ hai
Vahaañ
Koi waqt bhi na hoga

Beyond the reach of all imagination
But somewhere
There must certainly be a space
That has not
Been touched by the fingers of the expanding galaxies
A space
Where nothing has yet occurred
A space
Where no one has heard the command of creation[81]
Where there is no God
There
Time too, will not exist

The antagonism of the Progressives towards religion was exacerbated by their distress at the violence fomented in the name of faith, particularly during and after the moment of

Independence. Akhtar's India, though far removed from the time of the Partition, still struggles with this demon. Communal riots now punctuate the calendar with metronomic frequency; they are planned, ritualistic and often predictable. Akhtar's poems on religious violence are infused with this contemporary sensitivity often accompanied by a quiet resignation. In 'Fasaad Se Pahle' (Before the Riot), he startlingly evokes the terror of a populace awaiting an inevitable riot with bated breath:

Aaj
Ye shahr ik sahme hue bachche ki taraah
Apni parchhaai se bhi ḏarta hai
Jantari dekho
Mujhe lagta hai
Aaj tyohaar koi hai shaayad

Today
This city, like a frightened child
Fears its own shadow
Check the calendar
I have a feeling
That today might be the day of a festival

The subtle invocation of *tyohaar* (festival) speaks volumes, for it is a reminder of the fact that processions brought out in the name of religion are often the source of the spark that sets off the conflagration.

Akhtar's treatment of the aftermath of a riot is also unique and reflects a deep sense of loss that demands the mourning of more than mutilated bodies and burnt homes. In a follow-up poem 'Fasaad Ke Baad' (After the Riot), he describes a heartbreaking conversation between the deep silence after the riot and its devastated landscape. The silence understands the need to grieve for the dead, but suggests that there may be another loss to mourn first: the loss suffered by those who came to pillage and loot, the loss of the precious wealth of centuries of culture.

Gahre sannaate ne apne manzar se yooñ baat ki
Sun le ujdi dukaañ
Ai sulagte makaañ
Toote thele
Tumhiñ bas nahiñ ho akele
Yahaañ aur bhi haiñ
Jo ghaarat hue haiñ
Hum in ka bhi maatam karenge
Magar pahle un ko to ro leñ
Ke jo lootne aaye the
Aur khud lut gaye
Kya luta
Uski un ko khabar hi nahiñ
Kam-nazar haiñ
Ke sadiyoñ ki tahzeeb par
Un bichaaroñ ki koi nazar hi nahiñ

The deep silence spoke thus to the landscape
'Listen, destroyed shop
Smouldering house
Broken cart
You are not the only victims here.
There are others too
Who have also been victimized
We will mourn them as well
But let us first weep for those
Who came to plunder
But were themselves looted
What was lost
They have no idea
They are shortsighted
For they do not even notice
The ruins of a culture centuries old.'

To Akhtar, religion is one of the major divisive forces in society, much like war, politics and caste hatred. In a poem written about a 'Darinda' (Beast), he compares human beings with animals, suggesting that the former have far surpassed the latter in terms of producing divides and enacting cruelty:

Mazhab na jang ney siyaasat, jaane na zaat paat ko bhi
Apni darindagi ke aage, hai kis shumaar meiñ darinda

It knows neither religion, war nor politics, and no caste hierarchies either
How can the beast compare to us in our bestial cruelty?

The New Realist

Unlike the heroic protagonists that populated the poetry of the Progressives who wrote in an earlier era and inhabited a different structure of feeling, Akhtar's subjects have often succumbed to the pressures of a society that demands acquiescence above all else. We have few of the troubadours that populated Sahir's poetry, the revolutionaries of Kaifi's and Majrooh's defiant verse, the uncompromised prisoners of Faiz's *zindaan* or the angry proletariat of Majaz's streets. Akhtar's subjects fight a different battle against a different world, in which dreams are destined to be shattered by Life:

Mareez-e khwaab ko ab to shafa hai
Magar duniya badi kadvi dava thi

The dream-afflicted have finally been cured
But Life proved to be bitter medicine.

The world demands its pound of flesh and the protagonists have little choice but to acquiesce. The best they can hope for are a few stolen moments to call their own:

Mere kuch pal mujh ko de do, baaqi saare din logo
Tum jaisa jaisa kahte ho, sab vaisa vaisa hoga

Let me have a few moments of my own, O people; the rest of my days
I will do exactly what you want me to.

Sometimes a defiant warrior does brave the forces arrayed against him and takes on the world, but eventually he is doomed to stand alone, awaiting his inevitable destruction. In 'Shikast' (Defeat), Akhtar develops the story of a warrior-hero, who after conquering many lands finally faces defeat. He stands alone on a dark hill, waiting for the victorious enemy forces who are coming to kill him, while behind him lies the charred remains of the boat that he had set on fire himself to prevent any retreat on his part. The lesson here is that the victories of one's past do not guarantee future victories, for:

Magar thi khwaaboñ ke lashkar meiñ kis ko itni khabar
Har ek qisse ka ek ekhtemaam hota hai
Hazaar likh le koi fat'ha zarre zarre par
Magar shikast ka bhi ek muqaam hota hai

Little did the army of dreams realize
That every story has an end
One may inscribe 'Victory' on a thousand places
But 'Defeat' has its own place too

The invocation of the *khwaabon ka lashkar* (the army of dreams) suggests that Akhtar might be speaking about a war of ideas, where a principled and uncompromising position is doomed to defeat.

A close reading of *Tarkash* makes clear that Akhtar is enamoured with the concept of the *khwaab* (dream), much in the same way that Faiz was captivated by the idea of the *qafas* (cage). The difference is that while the prisoner in Faiz's imagery is forever defiant, Akhtar's hero is forced to peddle even his dreams. In 'Jurm Aur Saza' (Crime and Punishment), a plaintiff addresses the judge who is prosecuting him for the crime of withholding some of his dreams despite having entered into a Faustian pact with society:

Mujh ko iqraar
Ke maiñ ne ek din
Khud ko neelam kiya
Aur raazi-ba raza
Sar-e bazaar sar-e aam kiya
Mujh ko qeemat bhi bahut khoob mili thi lekin
Maiñ ne saude meiñ khayaanat kar li
Yaani
Kuch khwaab bachaakar rakkhe

I admit
That one day
I auctioned myself
And voluntarily
Made myself available to the market
I was well compensated too, but
I was dishonest.
That is,
I kept a few dreams for myself

The 'dishonesty' is discovered, for dreams cannot be concealed. The judge hears the case and passes a judgement: the accused will have to give up his dreams, his flights of fancy, the songs flowing in his veins, his soaring soul, his voice, his memories, his feelings and thoughts, his every moment. The judge however is not yet done. For these are merely meant as recompense to the one who had bought the plaintiff. The punishment is worse; the accused will not be allowed to die.

The concept of *zeest-e be-amaañ* (a life without mercy) occurs several times in Akhtar's poetry. Akhtar's world is intransigent and uncompromising. The power structures are entrenched and victory is near impossible. The poet's heroes still struggle and sometimes sacrifice themselves for their ideals. However, unlike the martyr figure in the poems of his progressive predecessors whose sacrifice was public and epiphanic, Akhtar's rebel recognizes that his death may be unsung, its mark limited, its gains incremental:

Maiñ qatl to ho gaya tumhaari gali meiñ, lekin
Mere lahu se tumhaari deewaar gal rahi hai

True, I was murdered in your street
But my blood is now corroding your walls

The martyrs in the poems of the Progressives walked with dignity to the gallows, secure in the knowledge that their death heralded the revolution. However, in an era where sacrifice has been rendered inconsequential, Akhtar is often drawn to despair:

Jeevan jeevan hum ne jag meiñ khel yahi hote dekha
Dheere dheere jeeti duniya, dheere dheere haare log
Neki ek din kaam aayegi, hum ko kya samjhaate ho
Hum ne bebas marte dekhe kaise pyaare pyaare log

In generation after generation, we have seen the same game played
That the world eventually won, and the people were gradually defeated
'Goodness will one day be rewarded', don't try to convince me of this
For I have seen many beautiful people die helplessly

And yet, Akhtar's protagonists speak truth to power, laying

bare the hypocrisies and the soullessness of those who choose the path of compromise:

Vasl ka sukooñ kya hai, hijr ka junooñ kya hai
Husn ka fusooñ kya hai, ishq ke darooñ kya hai
Tum mareez-e daanaa'i maslehat ke shaidaa'i
Raah-e gumrahaañ kya hai tum na jaan paaoge

What is the tranquility of Union, and what the madness of Separation?
What are the enchantments of Beauty, and what the secrets of Love?
You who are afflicted by Wisdom, who are a slave to Compromise
What is the path of the Iconoclasts? You will never understand

Javed Akhtar's poetry reconfigures the fervent romanticism of the PWA poets into a troubled realism, but one that continues to defiantly tilt away at the windmills of his dystopic world. He provides proof that the rumours of the death of socially responsible Urdu poetry are greatly exaggerated. If one may be permitted a blasphemous theism, thank God!

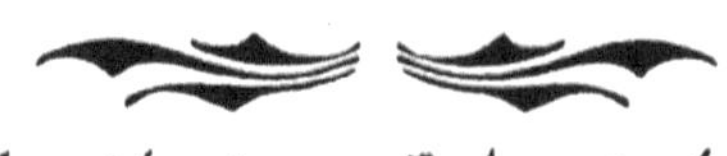

یہی جنوں کا یہی طوق و دار کا موسم
یہی ہے جبر، یہی اختیار کا موسم

پاؤں سرجو میں ابھی رام نے دھوئے بھی نہ تھے
کہ نظر آئے وہاں خون کے گہرے دھبے
پاؤں دھوئے بِنا سرجو کے کنارے سے اُٹھے
رام یہ کہتے ہوئے اپنے دُوارے سے اُٹھے
راجدھانی کی فضا آئی نہیں راس مجھے
چھ دِسمبر کو مِلا دوسرا بنواس مجھے

فلک نے دیکھ لیا اور زمیں بھی مان گئی
کسی کی آئی سواری کسی کی جان گئی

کچھ نہیں تو کم سے کم خوابِ سحر دیکھا تو ہے
جِس طرف دیکھا نہ تھا اب تک اُدھر دیکھا تو ہے

تقدیر کا شکوہ بے معنی جینا ہے تجھے منظور نہیں
آپ اپنا مقدّر بن نہ سکے اتنا تو کوئی مجبور نہیں
سُنتے ہیں کہ کانٹوں سے گُل تک ہیں راہ میں لاکھوں ویرانے
کہتا ہے مگر یہ عزمِ جُنوں صحرا سے گلستاں دُور نہیں

یہ ہم گنہگار عورتیں ہیں
جو اہلِ جُبّہ کی تمکنت سے
نہ رُعب کھائیں
نہ جان بیچیں
نہ سر جُھکائیں
نہ ہاتھ جوڑیں

یہ ہم گنہگار عورتیں ہیں
کہ جن کے جسموں کی فصل بیچیں
وہ سرفراز ٹھہریں
نیابتِ امتیاز ٹھہریں
وہ داورِ اہلِ ساز ٹھہریں

یہ ہم گنہگار عورتیں ہیں
کہ سچ کا پرچم اُٹھا کے نکلیں
تو جھوٹ سے شاہراہیں اَٹی ملے ہیں
ہر ایک دہلیز پہ سزاؤں کی داستانیں رکھی ملے ہیں
جو بول سکتی تھیں وہ زبانیں کٹی ملے ہیں

10

NEW STANDARD BEARERS OF PROGRESSIVE URDU POETRY

The Feminist Poets[82]

Anyone who is familiar with the field of Urdu poetry will readily recognize and acknowledge that it is extremely gendered. This gendering works at two levels. First, most of the poets are men; virtuosity in verse is still considered to be a male purview and women poets, even well-known ones, continue to be marginalized. Second, the predominant themes and metaphors of this genre assume the poet-as-male (and consequently the reader-as-male) and revolve around the themes of the beauty of the beloved, the plight of the lover and the pains of unrequited love. Women feature mostly as an abstraction and as the object of the male protagonist's desire[83]. As Rukhsana Ahmad points out in her introduction to *Beyond Belief* (the first collection of feminist poetry published in Pakistan), '(t)he bulk of published Urdu poetry is still love poetry bound in the old traditional idioms and conceits'[84]. These 'conceits' include the male poet as the embodiment of agency and the woman as a mere object, represented as 'a feckless beloved, who was endowed with heavenly beauty ... fair of face, doe-eyed, dark-haired, tall, willowy, for whom the poet was willing to die but who vacillated from indifference, shyness and modesty to wanton willfulness and cruelty[85].'

The PWA poets, notwithstanding their commitment to social change and egalitarianism were, for the most part, inheritors of this legacy of Urdu poetry as well as its purveyors. In their work, a woman was frequently seen as an exemplification of beauty and a repository of purity. She was often depicted as a weak victim of oppressive structures who depended on men to save and protect her and on their generosity of spirit and sense of righteousness to rescue her from her plight. A representative example of this attitude can be found in Sahir's poem 'Chakle' (Brothels) in which he, while painting a picture of the horror of the flesh trade and sex work, offers the following plea:

> *Madad chaahti hai ye Havva ki beti*
> *Yashodha ki hum-jins, Raadha ki beti*
> *Payambar ki ummat, Zulaikha ki beti*
> *Sanaakhaan-e taqdees-e Mashriq kahaañ haiñ?*
>
> Asking for help is this daughter of Eve
> She who shares Yashodha's gender, this daughter of Radha
> This member of the Prophets' congregation, this daughter of Zulaikha
> Where are they, those who sing paeans to the culture of the East?

In their role as social reformers, the Progressives did, at times, take issue against the oppression of women and sought to highlight their condition. Speaking against the institution of the veil in his poem 'Purdaah Aur Ismat' (The Veil and Honour), Majaz offers the following commentary:

Jo zaahir na ho, voh lataafat nahiñ hai
Jo pinhañ rahe, voh sadaaqat nahiñ hai
Ye fitrat nahiñ hai, mashiyyat nahiñ hai
Koi aur sha'y hai, ye ismat nahiñ hai

That which is not visible cannot be Exquisite
That which remains hidden cannot be the Truth
This is not Nature, nor is it Destiny
Whatever else it is, this is not Virtue

There are also the occasional moments when the progressive poet sees women as potential rebels and agents who have a role to play in the public space and in social transformation. In a poem 'Naujavaan Khaatoon Se' (To the Young Woman), Majaz writes:

Hijaab-e fitna parvar ab utha leti to achcha tha
Tu khud apne husn ko purdaah bana leti to achcha tha

Ye tera zard rukh, ye khushk lab, ye vahm, ye vahshat
Tu apne sar se ye baadal hata leti to achcha tha

Tere maathe pe ye aanchal bahut hi khoob hai lekin
Tu is aanchal se ek parcham bana leti to achcha tha

It would be better if you shrugged off this wicked veil
It would be better if you used your beauty to cover yourself

Your pale countenance, your dry lips, your anxiety, your fear
It would be better if you drove away these clouds from over your head

This scarf that covers you is beautiful indeed
It would be better if you converted it into a banner of revolt

While Majaz's poems take a position against the sequestering of women behind the veil, it is important to note that their tone tends to be patronizing for they are essentially exhortations by the male poet to women. Perhaps the poem by a male progressive poet that comes closest to representing a woman as a subject in her own right is 'Aurat' (Woman) by Kaifi Azmi:

Qadr ab tak teri tareekh ne jaani hi nahiñ
Tujh meiñ sholay bhi haiñ, bas ashk-fishaani hi nahiñ
Tu haqeeqat bhi hai, dilchasp kahaani hi nahiñ
Teri hasti bhi hai ek cheez, javaani hi nahiñ
Apni tareekh ka unvaan badalna hai tujhe
Uth meri jaan, mere saath hi chalna hai tujhe

Tod kar rasm ke but, band-e khadaamat se nikal
Zo'f-e ishra't se nikal, vahm-e nazaakat se nikal
Nafs ke kheenche hue halqa-e azmat se nikal
Qaid ban jaaye mohabbat, to mohabbat se nikal
Raah ka khaar hi kya, gul bhi kuchalna hai tujhe
Uth meri jaan, mere saath hi chalna hai tujhe

Zindagi jahd meiñ hai, sabr ke qaabu meiñ nahiñ
Nabz-e hasti ka lahu kaampte aansu meiñ nahiñ
Udne khulne meiñ hai nikhat, kham-e gesu meiñ nahiñ
Jannat ek aur hai, jo mard ke pahlu meiñ nahiñ
Us ki aazaad ravish par hi machalna hai tujhe
Uth meri jaan, mere saath hi chalna hai tujhe

The past hasn't recognized your worth
You are capable of producing flames, not just tears
You are Reality, not merely an interesting tale
Your Being is more than your mere Youth
You will have to rewrite the theme of your History
Arise my love, that we can walk together

Destroy the idols of Custom, break the shackles of Tradition
Free yourself from the enfeeblement of Pleasure, the false ideas of Delicacy
Step out from the confining circle of Femininity drawn around you

> And if Love becomes a prison, then reject the constraints of Love
> You will have to crush not just the thorns, but the flowers in your path too
> Arise my love, let us walk together
>
> Life lies in Struggle, not in the clutches of Forbearance
> The pulse of Existence is not nurtured by trembling tears
> Fragrance lies in flight and bloom, not in curling tresses
> There is another heaven that lies beyond a Man's protection
> Come, dance in the exuberance of its Freedom
> Arise my love, that we must walk together

Kaifi's poem is radical in the way it positions a woman as a fellow companion, in its exhortation that women break free from the confines of tradition and custom, but particularly in its insistence that women not only crush the 'thorns' of their path but also its 'flowers' (delicacy, elegance, femininity, grace, and even love) that serve as mechanisms of limitation and control. Where it falls somewhat short is that while Kaifi is establishing the position of his female companion as a comrade, he demands that she shed her accoutrements of femininity in order for her to 'accompany' him on his quest. Nor does Kaifi manage to fully reject the conventional characterization of women in the dominant discourse of the time, for the woman of his poem has the capacity to produce flames 'in addition to' the ability to shed tears; her existence is 'more than' her beauty and youth.

Notwithstanding a few scattered examples of such engagements with patriarchy, none of the PWA poets ever wrote in a manner that unambiguously assumed women's independent power, subjecthood and agency. For this to happen in the field of Urdu poetry, we had to wait for the works of the feminist poets from Pakistan, particularly Kishwar Naheed and Fehmida Riyaz. In order to understand and appreciate their work, it is important to place it in the context of the material and social conditions in Pakistan within which it was written.

The political, social and cultural milieu of Pakistan in the 1980s was defined by General Zia-ul-Haq's Islamization programme, and its attendant attack on women's rights. Zia's misogynist policies were an articulation of the anxieties of class and gender felt by middle-class men during this period who resented what they saw as the increasing presence of women in the public sphere and feared the repercussions this might have in the private sphere of the family. It is perhaps a testimony to the force of these anxieties that the state's blatantly sexist policies and the far-reaching changes they forged within Pakistani society and culture did not inform the work of progressive male poets in any significant way (perhaps the one exception was Habib Jalib, the only one who participated in the famous 12 February 1983 demonstration organized by the women's movement against the 'Law of Evidence'). This burden was left for feminist poets to bear.

The challenge posed by these feminist poets to the establishment worked at different levels: first, they were women poets writing in what was an overwhelmingly male literary milieu; second, they were feminists raising their voice against an increasingly hostile and misogynist social and cultural context; and third, they were producing work that effectively subverted existing, accepted conventions of poetic form and content. The poetry of these feminists was not confined to women's issues; they were fierce critics of the reactionary political, social and cultural changes taking place in Pakistani society. However, given that the brunt of the state's retrogressive Islamization policies along with the changes they wrought in other aspects of Pakistani life was borne by women (and minorities), most of their poetry did overwhelmingly address 'women's issues' such as the 'Zina Ordinance' (which included punishments such as stoning adulterers – both male and female – to death, and which tried rape victims under charges of *zina*, or illegitimate sex).

Not all women poets of the time chose to challenge the prescribed literary forms or themes, nor was all women's 'progressive' poetry (that which worked to subvert the patriarchal establishment) of one piece. Progressive poetry written by women ranged from the work of Parveen Shakir and Ada'a Jafri – whose poetry was less explicitly political insofar as it did not address explicitly 'political' issues, and who tended to use conventional poetic forms such as the ghazal (and in the case of Jafri, some of its standard expressions as well) – to that of poets such as Kishwar Naheed and Fehmida Riyaz, whose writings were stridently feminist in their tone and subject matter. However, given the male-dominated nature of the Urdu literary establishment, the very fact of a woman writing ghazals was itself subversive since it inverted the implicit convention that women were the objects rather than the subjects, or agents, of romance and desire. Feminist poets had to deal with a significant backlash, including criticism from the largely male status quo, for their 'loose morality' and their 'masculinity'[86], and were frequently subjected to the threat of violence from the state and individuals[87].

Since women were at the vanguard of the movement against Zia's martial-law government and its policies, it is not surprising that they were also the most political and prominent writers/poets/artists of the time. As Kishwar Naheed points out in her well-known poem, 'Hum Gunahgaar Auratеñ' (We Sinful Women):

Ye hum gunahgaar auratеñ haiñ
Jo ahl-e jabba ki tamkinat se
Na ro'b khaayeñ
Na jaan becheñ
Na sar jhukaayeñ
Na haath jodeñ
Ye hum gunahgaar auratеñ haiñ
Ke jin ke jismoñ ki fasl becheñ jo log
Voh sarfaraaz thahreñ
Nayaabat-e imtiyaaz thahreñ
Voh daavar-e ahl-e saaz thahreñ

Ye hum gunahgaar auratеñ haiñ
Ke sach ka parcham utha ke nikleñ
To jhoot se shaah-raaheñ ati mile haiñ
Har ek dahleez pe sazaaoñ ki daastaaneñ rakhi mile haiñ
Jo bol sakti theeñ voh zubaaneñ kati mile haiñ

It is we sinful women
Who are not intimidated
By the magnificence of those who wear robes
Who don't sell their souls
Don't bow their heads
Don't fold their hands in supplication
We are the sinful ones
While those who sell the harvest of our bodies
Are exalted
Considered worthy of distinction
Become gods of the material world

It is we sinful women
Who, when we emerge carrying aloft the flag of truth
Find highways strewn with lies
Find tales of punishment placed at every doorstep
Find tongues which could have spoken, severed

Besides being a harsh indictment of those who sold out to the establishment, these words also directly subvert the dominant stereotypes of women as weak and ineffectual and their accompanying ideas about 'femininity'. The phrase 'we sinful women', repeated like a chant throughout the poem, functions as a slap in the face of the religious orthodoxy and the state, referring as it does to the Zina Ordinance which uses the crutch of Islam to hold women responsible for all sex crimes.

Fehmida Riyaz's poem 'Chaadar Aur Chaardiwaari' (The Veil and the Four Walls of Home) was another explicit example of the way feminists used poetry as a medium of dissent against the Zia regime and as a critique of the hypocrisy of the religious orthodoxy. The poem derives its title from the name of the campaign started by Zia's Islamic Ideology Council, which was part of the general move to restrict women's participation in society to the domestic sphere. The poem is worth quoting in its entirety:

Huzoor, maiñ is siyaah chaadar ka kya karoongi?
Ye aap mujh ko kyooñ bakhshte haiñ, basad inaayat!

Na sog meiñ hooñ ke is ko odhooñ
Gham-o-alam khalq ko dikhaooñ
Na rog hooñ maiñ ke is ki taareekiyoñ meiñ khaft se doob jaaooñ
Na maiñ gunahgaar hooñ na mujrim
Ke is siyaahi ki mohr apni jabeeñ pe har haal meiñ lagaooñ
Agar na gustaakh mujh ko samjheñ

Agar maiñ jaañ ki amaan paaooñ
To dast-basta karooñ guzaarish
Ke banda-parvar!
Huzoor ke hujra-e mo'attar meiñ ek laasha pada hua hai
Na jaane kab ka gala sada hai
Ye aap se rahm chaahta hai
Huzoor itna karam to keeje
Siyaah chaadar mujhe na deeje
Siyaah chaadar se apne hujre ki bekafan laash dhaamp deeje
Ke is se phooti hai jo 'ufoonat
Voh kooche kooche meiñ haampti hai

Voh sar patakti hai chaukhatoñ par
Barahnagi apni dhaankti hai
Suneñ zara dil-kharaash cheekheñ
Bana rahi haiñ ajab hiyole

Jo chaadaron meiñ bhi haiñ barahna
Ye kaun haiñ? Jaante to honge
Huzoor pehchaante to honge!
Ye laundiyaañ haiñ!
Ke yarghamaali halaal shab bhar raheñ –
Dam-e subha darbadar haiñ
Ye baandiyaañ haiñ!

Huzoor ke natfa-e mubarek ke nasb-e virsa se mo'tabar haiñ

Ye bibiyaañ haiñ!
Ke zaujagi ka khiraaj dene
Qataar andar qataarbaari ki muntazar haiñ

Ye bacchiyaañ haiñ!
Ke jin ke sar pe phira jo hazrat ka dast-e shafqat
To kam-sini ke lahu se resh-e saped rangeen ho gayi hai
Huzoor ke hujla-e mo'attar meiñ zindagi khoon ro gayi hai

Pada hua hai jahaañ ye laasha
Taveel sadiyoñ se qatl-e insaaniyat ka ye khooñ chukaañ tamaasha
Ab is tamaashe ko khatm keeje
Huzoor ab is ko dhaamp deeje!
Siyaah chaadar to ban chuki hai meri nahiñ aap ki zaroorat

Ke is zameeñ par vujood mera nahiñ faqat ek nishaan-e shahvat
Hayaat ki shaah-raah par jagmaga rahi hai meri zahaanat
Zameeñ ke rukh par jo hai paseena to jhilmilaati hai meri mehnat
Ye chaar deewaariyaañ, ye chaadar, gali sadi laash ko mubarek
Khuli fizaaoñ meiñ baadbaañ khol kar badhega mera safeena
Maiñ Aadam-e nau ki humsafar hooñ
Ke jis ne jeeti meri bharosa bhari rifaaqat!

Sire! What will I do with this black *chaadar*
Why do you bless me with it?

I am neither in mourning that I should wear it
To announce my grief to the world
Nor am I a disease, that I should drown, humiliated, in its darkness
I am neither sinner nor criminal
That I should set its black seal
On my forehead under all circumstances

If you will pardon my impertinence
If I have reassurance of my life[88]
Then will I entreat you with folded hands
O Benevolent One!
In Sire's fragrant chambers lies a corpse
Who knows how long it has been rotting there
It asks for your pity
Sire, be kind enough
Give me not this black shawl
Use it instead to cover that shroudless corpse in your chambers
Because the stench that has burst forth from it
Goes panting through the alleys –
Bangs its head against the doorframes
Attempts to cover its nakedness
Listen to the heartrending shrieks
Which raise strange spectres

They who remain naked despite their *chaadars*
Who are they? You must know them
Sire, you must recognize them
They are the concubines!
The hostages who remain legitimate through the night
But come morning, are sent forth to wander, homeless
They are the handmaidens

More reliable than the half-share of inheritance promised your precious sperm

These are the honourable wives!
Who await their turn in long queues
To pay their conjugal dues

These are the young girls!
When Sire's affectionate hand descended upon their heads
Their innocent blood stained your white beard red
In Sire's fragrant chambers life has shed tears of blood

Where this corpse lies
This, for long centuries the bloody spectacle of humanity's murder
End this spectacle now
Sire, cover it up
The black *chaadar* has become your necessity, not mine

My existence on this earth is not as a mere symbol of lust
My intelligence gleams brightly on the highway of life
The sweat that shines on the brow of the earth is but my hard work
The corpse is welcome to this chaadar and these four walls
My ship will move full-sail in the open wind
I am the companion of the new Adam
Who has won my confident comradeship

In this powerful poem, Riyaz, by rejecting the *chaadar* being offered to her by the self-styled keepers of people's conscience, also rejects the Islamists' construction of her as a sexual object that is required by the law to be veiled and sequestered within the four walls of the home. She subjects these powers to biting sarcasm by repeatedly addressing them with mock honorifics such as 'huzoor', and a series of formulaic phrases such as *jaan ki amaan paaooñ*, *dast-basta karooñ guzaarish*, and *banda-parvar*. Since she is not in mourning, nor a sinner or criminal she argues with mock innocence, that she does not understand why she is being offered the black shawl (or, by implication, the seclusion of the *chaardiwaari*). The rest of the poem lists the crimes against humanity which her addressee is guilty of, particularly the (sexual) exploitation of women through the institutions of concubinage and marriage, an exploitation that often begins at a very young age. The poem ends with her concluding that it is he, not she, who needs the black shawl so that he may cover his own hypocrisy and shame. Although Riyaz never mentions Islam directly, it is the absent referent in her text, because it is under the *chaadar* (cover/cloak) of Islam that women have been subjugated for 'long centuries'. The 'spectres' of all these female victims who carry the stench of death are the skeletons in the Islamist's closet to which Riyaz 'respectfully' draws his, and our, attention.

The last stanza of the poem is worth noting, for in direct contrast to the depiction of women in Urdu poetry, Riyaz counterposes her own reading of women against the traditional as well as Islamist ideal of 'womanhood' and proposes a new female subject – an intelligent, sentient being (as opposed to object of desire and symbol of lust), a worker whose 'sweat shines on the brow of the earth', a quintessentially modern subject whose 'ship will move full-sail in the open wind'. The relationship between men and women is also redefined as one of comradeship between equals; this kind of comradeship is only possible, however, with a radically reinvented and redefined man – an Adam who is capable of winning her confidence and is thus worthy of her[89].

In her poem, Riyaz lampoons the normative Islamist discourse of a patriarchal and paternalistic relationship between women and men and rejects the notion of a woman as an obedient wife who revels in her role as the 'light of the home' and one who is supported by a husband who has unquestioned authority over her in all matters. The idea of an equal and companionate relationship with a man is thus a radical proposition, especially when accompanied by implications of a life of unfettered freedom expressed through the trope of the sailing ship, deliberately counterposed to the *chaardiwaari*. It is also worth noting that Riyaz's use of words like *laasha* (corpse), *gala sada* (rotten), and *natfa* (sperm) – words not normally used in poetry – along with the explicit references to sex and depravity provide another layer of subversiveness in terms of both form and content.

Yet another poem by Riyaz, titled 'Aqleema', goes thus:

Aqleema
Jo Haabeel aur Qaabeel ki maajaa'i hai
Maajaa'i
Magar mukhtalif
Mukhtalif beech meiñ raanoñ ke
Aur pistaanoñ ki ubhaar meiñ
Aur apne pet ke andar
Aur kokh meiñ
In sab ki qismat kyooñ hai
Ik farba bhed ke bachhe ki qurbaani

Aqleema
The sister of Abel and Cain
Sister
But different
Different between her thighs
And in the swell of her breasts
And inside her stomach
And in her womb
Why is it the fate of all these body parts
To be sacrificed like a fattened goat?

The explicit references to the female body are Riyaz's reminder to us that the patriarchal society objectifies its women and treats them as sacrificial lambs, destined to be butchered and consumed. The poem goes on to draw attention to the fact that Aqleema has a mind too, one that is rendered invisible by the patriarchal system, not merely to human beings, but also to God himself, who has chosen to reveal his Word to the world through male prophets alone.

Voh apne badan ki qaidi
Tapti hui dhoop meiñ jalte
Tele par khadi hui hai
Pathhar par naqsh bani hai
Is naqsh ko ghaur se dekho
Lambi raanoñ se oopar
Ubhre pistaanoñ se oopar
Pecheeda kokh se oopar
Aqleema ka sar bhi hai
Allah kabhi Aqleema se kalaam bhi kare
Aur kuch poochhe!

Imprisoned by her body
She stands atop a burning hill
Like an etching on a stone
Look at this etching carefully
Above her long legs
Above her breast-swell
Above her contorted womb
Aqleema has a head
Let God address Aqleema too sometime
And ask her something!

The deconstruction of the normative ideals of womanhood and femininity was a recurring theme in the work of the feminist poets, who deployed a radically different aesthetic both in the choice of their themes and their language in order to challenge existing standards of public discourse and poetry. 'Boodhi Ma' (Old Mother), by the contemporary Punjabi poet Gulnar, is an address to an old woman who has been repressed by patriarchal structures of power and control throughout her life and is a defiant call to all women to reject the roles imposed on them by societal and religious norms. It is interesting to note the unselfconscious use of the English word 'symbol' in the poem, another flouting of the conventions of Urdu poetry and its formal diction. This deployment of everyday speech in a literary piece is testimony to the fact that the Urdu for these poets is a living language:

Aaj tumhaari aankhoñ meiñ aansoo kyooñ haiñ?
...
Tum kyooñ udaas ho?
Tum ne to bete jane the
...
Haai ma, tumhaara muqaddar
Bachpan baap ki ghulaami, ladakpan bhaa'i ki ghulaami
Javaani shauhar ki ghulaami aur
Budhaapa betoñ ki ghulaami meiñ basar hua
Magar tumhaare to qadmoñ tale jannat hai
Phir poh maagh ki zaalim sardi meiñ
Tumhaare paaooñ barahna kyooñ haiñ?
Tum to ghar ki malika ho
Phir tumhaara thikaana ye dhool ka dher kyooñ hai?
Tum ne to saat betoñ ko apne pistaanoñ ki
Garmi se gabroo banaaya hai
Phir tumhaare vujood meiñ pyaas kyooñ hai?
Tumhaara vujood bhook ka symbol *kyooñ ban gaya hai?*
Boodhi ma meri taraf in nazroñ se kyooñ dekh rahi ho?
Maiñ ne voh but tod diye haiñ
Kohna ghulaami ki in rivaayaat se maiñ ne
Khud ko aazaad kar liya hai
Maiñ is khush-fahmi se nikal aayi hooñ
Ke mere qadmoñ tale jannat hai
Maiñ ne apne pairoñ meiñ chamde ke mazboot joote pahen liye haiñ
Maiñ ne apne haath se jhadoo chhod diye haiñ
Maiñ ne apne haath meiñ kitaab-o-qalam thaam liya hai
Maiñ ne apne sar se baap, bhaa'i, shauhar aur bete ki dee hui
Ghulaami ki chaadar ko noch giraaya hai
Aur apne sar par apni zaat ki rida odh lee hai
Maiñ ne apni aankhoñ se sharm ki patti utaar phenki hai
Aur sheeshe ki ainak aankhoñ par chadha lee hai
Taake maiñ duniya ko apni nazar se dekh sakooñ

Old Mother
Why are you teary-eyed today?

> ...
> Why are you sad?
> You, who have given birth to sons?
> ...
> Oh, Mother, your fate!
> Your childhood spent in bondage to your father
> Your adolescence under the control of your brother
> Your youth in bondage to your husband
> And your old age in your sons' servitude
> But doesn't Heaven lie beneath your feet?!
> Then why, in the cruel cold of winter
> Are your feet bare?
> But you are the Queen of the home!
> Then why is this pile of dust your abode?
> You are the one who gave life to seven sons
> The milk of your breasts gave them strength
> Then why is your body thirsty?
> Why has your Being become the symbol of hunger?
> Old Mother, why do you look at me this way?
> I have broken the idols
> And, from the traditions of base servitude
> Freed myself
> I have broken free of the false belief
> That Heaven lies beneath my feet
> I have put strong leather shoes on my feet
> I have thrown away the broom
> And instead hold the pen and the book firmly in my hands
> From my head I have yanked off the veil of bondage
> Granted by my father, brother, husband, son
> And I have covered myself with the mantle of my own selfhood
> I have thrown off the blindfold of shame from my eyes
> And put on glass spectacles
> So that I can see the world through my own eyes

In the Islamist rhetoric, women are idealized as mothers beneath whose feet lies Heaven, and as good wives who are the *ghar ki rani/malika* or the 'queens' of the domestic realm. Gulnar critiques these ideals by inserting the figure of a woman who, despite having adhered to all the conventions and expectations of the good woman in her *avatars* as daughter, sister, wife and mother of 'seven sons', is nevertheless left shelterless and uncared for. In contrast, Gulnar offers a protagonist who is the Islamists' nemesis: modern, enlightened, educated and unwilling to accept the roles assigned to her by mainstream society in general and religious orthodoxy in particular. She is sensible and hard-nosed (a far cry from the whimsical beloved of mainstream Urdu poetry), wears leather shoes, adopts 'spectacles' to see the world clearly through her own eyes, and has rejected the realm of abject domesticity for the world of letters and the realm of intellect. And unlike the protagonist of Riyaz's poem, Gulnar's woman does not appear to need a (male) companion in her quest for self-actualization.

***

While the feminist poets focused considerably on the condition of women in Pakistani society, they also articulated a comprehensive critique of their contemporary social conditions. Poems such as Kishwar Naheed's 'Sard Mulkoñ Ke Aaqaaoñ Ke Naam' (To the Lords of the Cold Nations) offers a commentary on Eurocentrism, while 'Censorship' and 'Section 144[90]' challenges the state's repressive policies. Fehmida Riyaz's 'Kotvaal Baitha Hai' (The Police Chief is Waiting) and 'Khaana-Talaashi' (The Search) describes her interrogation and the search of her home by the police. Ishrat Afreen's 'Rihaa'i' (Release) is a poem that talks about how the fight for liberation from 'the mountains of dead traditions, blind faith, oppressive hatreds' (*Pahaad murda rivaayatoñ ke, pahaad andhi aqeedatoñ ke, pahaad zaalim adaavatoñ ke*) is an obligation owed to the next generation, while Neelma Sarwar's 'Chor' (The Thief) reflects on the cruel disparities of wealth in society.

In a similar vein, Fehmida Riyaz's long prose-poem 'Kya Tum Poora Chaand Na Dekhoge?' (Will You Not See the Full Moon?) uses the moon as a metaphor for truth, while deploying colloquial terminology to criticize conspicuous consumption and ridicule the subservience of the Pakistani society to the petrodollars of the Saudi kingdom. Here are a few excerpts:

Kya maiñ ise roz-e raushan kahooñ
Ke tapte aasmaan par cheel ne chakkar kaata hai
Aur shaah-raahoñ ke jaal meiñ
Traffic ka zakhmi darinda ghurraane laga
Baazaaroñ meiñ
Baraamadi aashiya ki shahvat aankheñ malti hui bedaar ho rahi haiñ
Quvvat-e khareed!
Kotwaal ki moonh-chadhi faahisha
Dekho kaise dandanaati phir rahi hai
Maili, sookhi maaeñ
Koode ke dher meiñ haddiyaañ dhoond rahi haiñ
Bilbilaate bacchoñ ko
Khaamosh kar dene ke liye

Shahroñ ke behurmat jismoñ par
Plazoñ aur mashinoñ ke phode nikal rahe haiñ
Kaale dhan ki faisla-kun jeet ke jhande gaadte
Kal ke akhbaaroñ meiñ in ke ishtihaar dekh leta
Tumhaari muflisi par qahqaha lagaata hua
Tum apna sar takraao – balke kaat kar phaink do
Apni maqtool aarzuoñ ke qabristaanoñ meiñ
Hum tumhaari khopdiyoñ se ek minaar chunenge
Aur is ka koi chalta hua sa naam rakhenge
'Gulzaar-e Mustafa'
'Haaza min fazl-e rabbi'
Ya aisa hi koi garma garam naam
Kyoonke kaarobaar garam hai
Kyoonkar garam hai ye kaarobaar?
...
Ye ek bhayaanak raaz hai

Jo sab jaante haiñ aur koi nahiñ bataata

...

Hum insaan ko pees kar bauna bana rahe haiñ
Ehya al-shaikh, hamaare kaarnaame ki daad deejiye
Bakhshish! Ya akhi!
Aap ke muqaddas petrodollar ki qasam!

Should I call this the day of enlightenment and hope?
When the kite circles the burning sky
And in the web of highways
The traffic begins to growl like a wounded animal
In the market place
The Lust for imported goods awakes and rubs her eyes
Purchasing Power!
The interrogator's favourite whore
See how shamelessly she moves around
While dirty, dried-up mothers
Scavenge for bones in garbage heaps
To silence their sobbing children

On the molested bodies of cities
Mansions and shopping plazas have begun to erupt
Like boils
Declaring the decisive victory of the black market
You can see their advertisements in tomorrow's paper
Scoffing at your poverty:
You can beat your head against the wall, in fact, cut it off and throw it away
Into the graveyard of your murdered desires
We'll make a minaret of your skulls
And give it some trendy name
Like 'The Garden of the Prophet'
Or 'This is the Benevolence of God'
Or some other piping hot name
Because business is brisk
Why is this business flourishing?

...

It is a horrible secret
Which everyone knows but none mentions

...
We are grinding humans to produce dwarves
O Sheikh, praise our achievements!
Alms! O Brother!
I swear by your hallowed petrodollar

Understanding that the Islamization project was a 'culturalist evasion'[91] of the real issues facing Pakistan, Riyaz uses her poem to highlight the concerns of the people at large who live under conditions of starvation and depredation while the city panders to the desires of the elite. The poem is replete with gothic representation and a pastiche of strange and ominous images such as the kites circling a burning sky, the city as web or a trap and the pathological and almost sexual lust for imported commodities which awakens the 'whore of purchasing power'. This stark reference to the increasing commodity fetishism of the wealthy classes and the symbols of this fetish (the shopping plazas, the mansions) are described as boils on the molested body of the city, just as conspicuous consumption is a sore on the diseased body-politic of the nation-state.

The satirical allusions to the influence of petrodollars and the throwaway Arabic phrases are references to the Pakistani state's proclivity to look towards Saudi Arabia for affirmation in the political, economic and even cultural spheres, the increasing use of Arabic words on Pakistan Television, the introduction of Arabic as a compulsory subject in public schools and the Arabization of Urdu itself, all of which were a result of the Zia regime's effort to move ever-further away from an Indo-Islamic culture which was shared with India and towards an 'Islamic' identity defined by Arabic elements. The onward march of capital and the obscene culture of consumption it engenders are depicted through the superimposition of sexuality, depravity, lustfulness and disease in a way that highlights the indifference of the system to the poor and the dispossessed. Fehmida Riyaz's theme throughout her long poem is that Islamization is simply a ruse with which the rulers defuse dissent and construct consent while dividing the nation sharply between those who have economic and political power and those who do not.

***

The arrival of the feminist poets in the realm of Urdu poetry signalled the beginning of a new brand of progressivism, one that took on the establishment in ways that were radical and powerful. These poets – Kishwar Naheed, Fehmida Riyaz, Ishrat Afreen, Saeeda Gazdar, Neelma Sarwar, Sara Shagufta, Zehra Nigaah, Gulnar and others – transformed not merely the themes of Urdu poetry, but also its language and its grammar. As Rukhsana Ahmad writes, these poets represent 'that strand of the progressive tradition in Urdu poetry which had in the early forties so powerfully contributed to the freedom movement.[92]' They, more than anyone else in the contemporary period, are the true inheritors of the tradition of progressive poetry, its champions, and its trailblazers. A very short poem by Ishrat Afreen titled 'Intisaab' (Dedication) sums up the contribution of the feminist poets to literature quite well:

Mera qad
Mere baap se ooncha nikla
Aur meri ma jeet gayi

My height
Surpassed that of my father
And thus, my mother won

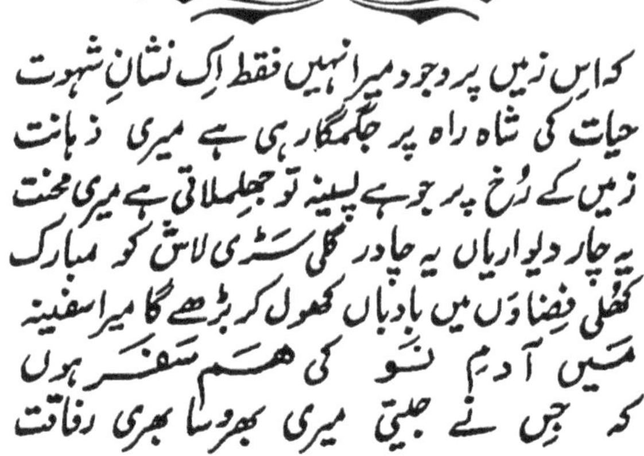

کہ اس زمیں پر وجود میرا نہیں فقط اک نشانِ شہوت
حیات کی شاہ راہ پر جگمگا رہی ہے میری ذہانت
زمیں کے رُخ پر جو ہے پسینہ تو جھلملاتی ہے میری محنت
یہ چار دیواریاں یہ چادر گلی سڑی لاش کو مبارک
کھلی فضاؤں میں بادباں کھول کر بڑھے گا میرا سفینہ
میں آدمِ نَو کی ہم سفر ہوں
کہ جس نے جیتی میری بھروسا بھری رفاقت

وہ اپنے بدن کی قیدی
تپتی ہوئی دھوپ میں جلتے
ٹیلے پر کھڑی ہوئی ہے
پتھر پر نقش بنی ہے
اس نقش کو غور سے دیکھو
لمبی رانوں سے اُوپر
اُبھری پستانوں سے اُوپر
پیچیدہ کوکھ سے اُوپر
عقیلہ کا سر بھی ہے
اللہ کبھی عقیلہ سے بھی کلام کرے
اور کچھ پوچھے

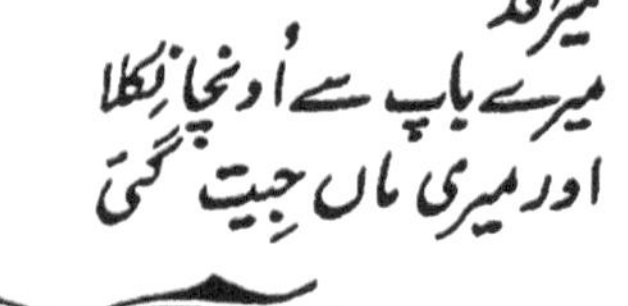

میرا قد
میرے باپ سے اُونچا نکلا
اور میری ماں جیت گئی

ماٹی سے ہم لعل نکالیں موتی لائیں جل سے
جو کچھ اِس دنیا میں بنا ہے بنا ہمارے بل سے
کب تک محنت کے پیروں میں دولت کی زنجیریں
ہاتھ بڑھا کر چھین لو اپنے سپنوں کی تصویریں
ساتھی ہاتھ بڑھانا

یہ محلوں یہ تختوں یہ تاجوں کی دُنیا
یہ اِنساں کے دشمن سماجوں کی دُنیا
یہ دَولت کے بھُوکے رواجوں کی دُنیا
یہ دُنیا اگر مِل بھی جائے تو کیا ہے

ذرا مُلک کے رہبروں کو بُلاؤ
یہ کوُچے، یہ گلیاں، یہ منظر دِکھاؤ
جِنہیں ناز ہے ہند پر اُن کو لاؤ
جِنہیں ناز ہے ہند پر وہ کہاں ہیں

چین و عرب ہمارا ہندوستاں ہمارا
رہنے کو گھر نہیں ہے سارا جہاں ہمارا
جِتنی بھی بلڈنگیں ہیں سیٹھوں نے بانٹ لی ہیں
فٹ پاتھ بمبئی کے ہیں آشیاں ہمارا

11
A REQUIEM ... AND A CELEBRATION

Yahi junooñ ka yahi tauq-o daar ka mausam
Yahi hai jabr, yahi ikhtiyaar ka mausam

This is the season of passion, this the season of the chain and noose
This is the season of repression, this too the season of resistance.

– Faiz Ahmad Faiz

The news on 10 May 2002 was heartbreaking. Kaifi Azmi, the stalwart of Azamgarh, was no more. Kaifi's death brought home the fact that the time of a generation of socialist Urdu poets had finally come to an end. We had bid farewell to Majrooh Sultanpuri in 2000 and to Ali Sardar Jafri in 2001. Sahir, Faiz, Makhdoom, Majaz, Josh, Firaq, Jan Nisar ... it seemed like eons since they had left. And on a hot May evening, as people trooped into the Constitution House in New Delhi for a final condolence meeting, the mood was sombre. Kaifi's famous words, 'I was born in Enslaved India, lived most of my life in Free India, and will die in Socialist India' were echoed by dozens of speakers at the meeting and later reproduced in a thousand obituaries. But even as the eulogies for Kaifi poured in from all over the world, our mind's eye was focused on Gujarat, where Kaifi's 'Saanp' (Snake) of communalism had devoured hundreds of innocents, burnt whole neighbourhoods to the ground and destroyed places of worship and tombs, including that of the seventeenth century poet Wali Deccani-Gujrati, who had written the following couplet on the eternal durability of literature:

Rah-e mazmoon-e taaza band nahiñ
Ta qayaamat khula hai baab-e sukhan

The path of new themes is not closed
The door of language remains open till doomsday

The despondent mourners at Kaifi's funeral must have wondered: Kaifi had certainly not died in an egalitarian India, but was it in an India that had forsaken even the basic principles he had taken for granted? Had the doors of Wali's *sukhan* closed prematurely? Had Kaifi's vision, his life and his labour been in vain? Those were hard days for the proponents of secularism, an ideal that had been so dear to the Progressives' heart. And while the fate of 'secularism' was tragic, it was far better than that of 'socialism', a term that had been viewed with increasing suspicion for several years. The dominance of a new capitalist order across the world, the collapse of identities and the consequent Balkanization of nations and communities, the suppression of peoples' movements and the withering away of the dream of a just world had taken its toll.

Towards the end of their time, the last of the Progressives continued to write about social conditions, but their poetry often tended to be dystopic. The destruction of the Babri

Masjid on 6 December 1992 had signalled the arrival of a new age in Indian politics. Kaifi Azmi expressed his anguish in a *nazm* titled 'Doosra Banvaas' (Second Exile) in the following words:

Paaoñ Sarju meiñ abhi Raam ne dhoye bhi na the
Ke nazar aaye vahaañ khoon ke gahre dhabbe
Paaoñ dhoye bina Sarju ke kinaare se uthe
Raam ye kahte hue apne dwaare se uthe
Raajdhaani ki fiza aayi nahiñ raas mujhe
Cheh Disambar ko mila doosra banvaas mujhe

Hardly had Ram dipped his feet in the Sarayu
When he noticed dark bloodstains on the banks
Leaving the river without washing his feet
Ram began his resigned journey yet again,
'The climate of my capital has been vitiated
On the 6th of December, I was exiled yet again'

Ali Sardar Jafri, the diehard nationalist[93], expressed his disillusionment with the promise of nationalism[94] in the following words:

Suna hai bandobast ab sab ba andaaz-e digar honge
Sitam hoga muhaafiz, shahr be-deewaar-o dar honge
Sazaaeñ begunaahoñ ko milengi begunaahi ki
Ke fard-e jurm se mujrim ke munsif bekhabar honge
Falak tharra uthega jhoote maatam ki sadaaoñ se
Kafan pehnaaenge jallaad, qaatil nauhagar honge
Yateemoñ aur bevaaoñ ke baazoo baandhe jaayenge
Shaheedaan-e wafa ke khooñ bhare naize pe sar honge
Jo ye taabeer hogi Hind ke dereena khwaaboñ ki
To phir Hindostaañ hoga, na us ke deedavar honge

We hear that governance now will have a different cadence
Tyranny will now be the protector; cities will be without walls or doors
Innocence will now be a punishable crime

Judges will profess ignorance of criminal deeds
The sky will tremble with the cry of counterfeit grief
Executioners will be in charge of funerals, killers will organize mourning
Orphans and widows will find their hands and feet bound
The heads of martyrs of the faith will be held aloft on spears[95]
If this be the realization of India's ancient dreams
Then soon, there will neither be India, nor any of its connoisseurs

***

The PWA continues to survive in pockets all over the country and is occasionally in the news for its activism. The 'Abhyudaya Rachayitala Sangham' (Progressive Writers' Association) remains active in Andhra Pradesh and the 'Janvaadi Lekhak Sangh' maintains the PWA legacy in North India. PWA chapters in Tamil Nadu and Kerala still remain open. In Pakistan, despite being banned since 1951, the PWA is very much a part of the popular discourse and the contemporary feminist poets have infused a new life into progressive Urdu poetry.

However, the death of Sardar Jafri and Kaifi Azmi perhaps draws a curtain on that glorious period in Urdu literature when the poetry of resistance dominated cultural production. The formal movement that started in a Chinese restaurant in London in 1935 and found its first voice in Lucknow in 1936 is now over. The stalwarts who gave that special cadence to the poetry of the Independence movement, who embraced an international ethos, who celebrated modernism and repudiated capitalism, who wrote songs that were sung on streets, who brought about a revolution in the form of the Urdu poem while espousing the cause of content – their era needs to be bid adieu. They were quixotic dreamers, courageous combatants and fearless champions of justice. And while they may not have lived to see the fulfilment of their vision, at least they tried to leave the world a better place than they found it.

***

The thirtieth anniversary of the Progressive Writers' Association, held in New Delhi in 1966, turned out to be the PWA's last hurrah. The season of resistance that the movement had brought about in the field of Urdu literature was coming to an end.

Over a thousand writers from across the world were to hear the final address of the General Secretary of the PWA, Krishen Chander, who in a poignant moment summed up his feelings. 'Ours was no air-conditioned movement,' he said. 'Our stories were written in dingy rooms and dirty huts; our poems were born in processions and workers' meetings; our songs in police lock-ups. When I took over his office, I asked the then General Secretary, Ram Bilas Sharma for the funds of the association. He gave me a pencil. We had no funds, no files, no office, no dictaphone. And yet, with nothing in hand but a pencil, we wrote the most glorious chapter in the cultural renaissance of our people.'

While the PWA had a complex and checkered history and while its landscape was strewn with missteps, infighting, rivalries and inconsistencies, it is perhaps proper to end this book with a celebration. For no matter what else may be said about it, the Progressive Writers' Movement offered us a vision – provisional, fluctuating, tentative, yet powerful – of a utopia that was centred around the notions of egalitarianism and social justice. This unique and remarkable movement reminded us that cultural spaces are vital terrains of engagement. The poets who so freely offered us a lyrical and compelling manifesto of action have us in their debt. As Ghalib once said:

Surma-e muft-nazar hooñ, meri qeemat ye hai
Ke rahe chasm-e khareedaar pe ehsaañ mera

I am the kohl that adorns, and my only price is this
That the eyes of my patron remain indebted to me

So here, in no particular order, is a partial (and necessarily incomplete) repayment in the form of some acknowledgements, offered not merely in the spirit of gratitude, for that would be a weak recompense, but of solidarity with the spirit of resistance and revolution the progressive poets engendered:

To Josh, for his passion and his fervour. To the poet whose spirit is embodied in this story we once heard about his time in Hyderabad. One day, the ruling *nizam* was passing through a street accompanied by his sizeable entourage. In accordance with the custom, all traffic was halted while the *nizam* went by. It so happened that a commoner was being rushed to a hospital. Since royal comfort, no matter how trivial, could not be compromised, the guards refused to let anyone through till the *nizam* had safely departed. But by then, it was too late. The leisurely procession had claimed its victim. Josh, the *shaayar-e inquilaab*, stormily wrote:

Falak ne dekh liya aur zameeñ bhi maan gayi
Kisi ki aayi savaari, kisi ki jaan gayi

The sky bore witness, the earth too cried
Someone passed in splendour, someone else died

To Majaz for his iconoclasm, for his passion, for his anger, for his palpable angst at the conditions of his times, for his vision of a better world:

Kuch nahiñ to kam se kam khwaab-e sahar dekha to hai
Jis taraf dekha na tha ab tak, udhar dekha to hai

At the very least, we dreamed of a fresh dawn
At the very least, we imagined something new

To Ali Sardar Jafri for his steadfastness to the cause, for his principled positions and for this personal moment on May Day, 2000: Jafri had penned a poignant poem about the break-up of the Soviet Union which went *Alvida ai surkh parcham, surkh parcham alvida* (Farewell O Red Flag, Red Flag, farewell). When we asked him to recite it for us a few years later he refused, claiming that it was a dirge written for the moment that signalled the commencement of a unipolar world dominated by capitalist interests, and therefore demanded mourning. However, not wanting to disappoint us, he did narrate the poem, replacing the word *alvida* (farewell) with *marhaba* (bravo), converting it (in his words) from a *marsiya* (a lament) to a *qaseeda* (an ode): *Marhaba ai surkh parcham, surkh parcham marhaba.*

To Sahir, for his commitment to the movement, for bringing a progressive edge to Hindi film music, for writing the finest and the most moving anti-war poem ever, 'Parchaaiyaan' (Shadows), in which the protagonist whose love had been sacrificed at the altar of an earlier battle does not wish the same fate for the generations that are to follow.

Aur aaj jab in pedoñ ke tale
Phir do saaye lahraaye hain
Phir do dil milne aaye haiñ
Phir maut ki aandhi uth-ti hai
Phir jang ke baadal chaaye haiñ

Maiñ soch raha hooñ in ka bhi
Apni hi taraah anjaam na ho
In ka bhi junooñ naakaam na ho
In ke bhi muqaddar meiñ likkhi
Ek khoon meiñ lithdi shaam na ho

And today, when under those same trees
Two other shadows rendezvous
Two other hearts meet
The storms of death gather again
The clouds of war obscure the sky

May they not meet the same fate as ours
May their passion too not prove fruitless
May the futures of these two lovers
Not be inscribed on a bloodied horizon

To Kaifi, for his 'Aavaara Sajde', for his *Sarmaaya*, for his optimistic insistence that he would die in an egalitarian India.

Door se beevi ne chilla ke kaha
Tel mahnga bhi hai, milta bhi nahiñ
Kyooñ diye itne jala rakkhe haiñ
Apne ghar meiñ na jharoka na munder
Taakh sapnoñ ke saja rakkhe haiñ

Aaya ghusse ka ek aisa jhonka
Bujh gaye saare diye
Haañ, magar ek diya naam hai jis ka ummeed
Jhilmilaata hi chala jaata hai

From afar, my wife cried out
Oil is expensive, nor is it easily available
Why then do you light all these lamps?
Our homes, with neither windows nor ledges
Have no room for these shelves filled with dreams

A gust of angry wind blew
Extinguishing all lamps
All? No, one among them called Hope
Continues to flicker away

To Majrooh, for transforming the ghazal in which the *gham-e dauraañ* (the sorrow of life) found as much prominence as the *gham-e jaanaañ* (the sorrow of the heart), for defying convention by giving the once-pathetic protagonist of the ghazal a new pride and a new hope:

Taqdeer ka shikva be-maani, jeena hi tujhe manzoor nahiñ
Aap apna muqaddar ban na sake, itna to koi majboor nahiñ

Sunte haiñ ke kaanṯe se gul tak, haiñ raah meiñ laakhoñ veeraane
Kahta hai magar ye azm-e junooñ, sahra se gulistaañ door nahiñ

Don't blame Fate, for it is you who has no desire for Life
You are unable to write your own destiny? Surely, no one is that helpless

We are repeatedly told that the path from the thorn to the rose is strewn with desolation
Yet, the power of my passion insists that the garden is round the corner from the desert

To Faiz, for everything he ever wrote, for insisting that the path to the gallows was as glorious as the path to the lover's house, for words that provide comfort, offer inspiration and generate faith:

Qafas hai bas meiñ tumhaare, tumhaare bas meiñ nahiñ
Chaman meiñ aatish-e gul ke nikhaar ka mausam

Bala se hum ne na dekha to aur dekhenge
Furogh-e gulshan-o saut-e hazaar ka mausam

The cage may be in your power, but you do not control
The season of the flowering of the bright rose

And so what if we do not see it? For the ones following us will witness
The brightness of the garden, the singing of the nightingale

To Makhdoom Mohiuddin (the *aashiq-e mazdoor*), Salaam Machlishahri, Habib Jalib, Firaq Gorakhpuri, Safdar Mir and scores of others whose verses sustained the progressive spirit of the movement. To Sulaimaan Khateeb and Sarwar Danda for writing Deccani verse that was both side-splittingly funny and sharply political. To Ahmad Faraz, Fehmida Riyaz, Kishwar Naheed, Hasan Kamal, Munawar Rana, Gauhar Raza and others who keep the progressive sentiment alive and vibrant. To Javed Akhtar for carrying the legacy of those who went before him, for his *tarkash* full of sharp arrows, for the depth of his film lyrics. We acknowledge these poets for the role they played in the anti-colonial struggle and the freedom movement, for giving voice to resistance and rebellion against structures of oppression, for their solidarity with peoples' movements all over the world and also for the role they will continue to play in shaping things to come and for inspiring this generation of activists with their words that still strike a hundred chords in one's heart. Their vision of a just society remains incomplete, but their aspirations continue to live on.

Dekh raftaar-e inquilaab, Firaaq
Kitni aahista aur kitni tez

Behold the pace of revolution, Firaq
How slow, and how swift

Let us end this book then with a note on Kaifi Azmi, the last of the stalwarts who defined the Progressive Movement in Urdu poetry. The span of Kaifi's lifetime contains the story of a language and its engagement with the history of a nation. Kaifi left the world with the twin ideals of the Progressives – socialism and secularism – in a state of *inteshaar* (dispersion, confusion, anxiety). But even in the darkest moments, his bitter-sweet words remind us of the still-awaited fulfilment of the progressive poets' dream:

Kabhi jamood, kabhi sirf inteshaar sa hai
Jahaañ ko apni tabaahi ka intezaar sa hai
Tamaam jism haiñ bedaar, fikr khwaabeeda
Dimaagh pichhle zamaane ki yaadgaar sa hai
Hui to kaise bayaabaañ meiñ aake shaam hui
Ke jo mazaar yahaañ hai, mere mazaar sa hai
Koi to sood chukaaye, koi to zimma le
Us inquilaab ka jo aaj tak udhaar sa hai

At times inert, at times chaotic
The world awaits its own destruction
Bodies awake, thoughts drowsy
The mind, a reflection of the dead past
The sun sets in a strange wilderness
Around a tomb that looks strikingly like my own
Someone pay the price, someone take responsibility
For the revolution that is still owed to us

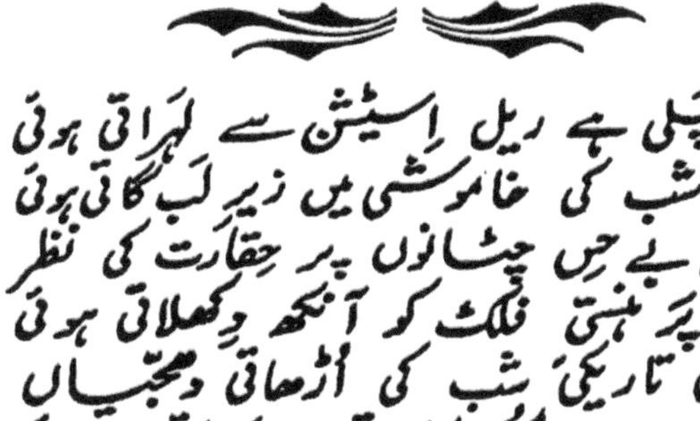

پھر چلی ہے ریل اِسٹیشن سے لہراتی ہوئی
نیم شب کی خاموشی میں زیرِ لب گاتی ہوئی
ڈالتی بے حِس چٹانوں پر حقارت کی نظر
کوہ پر ہنستی فلک کو آنکھ دِکھلاتی ہوئی
دامنِ تاریکیٔ شب کی اُڑھاتی دھجیاں
قصرِ ظلمت پر مسلسل تیر برساتی ہوئی
زد میں کوئی چیز آجائے تو اس کو پیس کر
ارتقائے زندگی کے راز بتلاتی ہوئی
الغرض بڑھتی چلی جاتی ہے بے خوف و خطر
شاعرِ آتش نفس کا خون کھولاتی ہوئی

تیری باتوں سے پڑی جاتی ہے کانوں میں خراش
کفر و ایماں کفر و ایماں تا کُجا خاموش باش

بن گیا قصر تو پہرے پہ کوئی بیٹھ گیا
سو رہے خاک پہ ہم شورشِ تعمیر لیے
اپنی نس نس میں لیے محنتِ پیہم کی تھکن
بند آنکھوں میں اِسی قصر کی تصویر لیے
دِن پگھلتا ہے اسی طرح سروں پر اب بھی
رات آنکھوں میں کھٹکتی ہے سیاہ تیر لیے
آج کی رات بہت گرم ہوا چلتی ہے
آج کی رات نہ فٹ پاتھ پہ نیند آئے گی
سب اُٹھو میں بھی اُٹھوں تم بھی اُٹھو تم بھی اُٹھو
کوئی کھڑکی اِسی دیوار میں کھل جائے گی

دِل نا اُمید تو نہیں ناکام ہی تو ہے
لمبی ہے غم کی شام مگر شام ہی تو ہے

مَیں زِندگی کا ساتھ نبھاتا چلا گیا
ہر فِکر کو دھوئیں میں اُڑاتا چلا گیا

جیبیں ہیں اپنی خالی کیوں دیتا ورنہ گالی
وہ سنتری ہمارا وہ پاسباں ہمارا

ہم محنت کش اِس دُنیا سے جب اپنا حِصّہ مانگیں گے
اِک باغ نہیں اِک کھیت نہیں ہم ساری دنیا مانگیں گے

کئی یادوں کے چہرے نئے ہیں کئی قصّے پُرانے ہیں
تری سَو داستانیں ہیں تیرے کتنے فسانے ہیں
مگر اِک وہ کہانی ہے جو اب مجھ کو ستاتی ہے
زِندگی آ رہا ہوں مَیں

میری ہاتھوں کی گرمی سے پگھل جائیں گی زنجیریں
میرے قدموں کی آہٹ سے بدل جائیں گی تقدیریں
اُمیدوں کے دِیے لے کر یہ سب تیرے لیے لے کر
زندگی آ رہا ہوں مَیں

میں پل دو پل کا شاعر ہوں
پل دو پل مری کہانی ہے
پل دو پل میری ہستی ہے
پل دو پل مری جوانی ہے

فٹ پاتھوں کے ہم رہنے والے
راتوں نے پالا ہم وہ اُجالے
آکاش سر پے پیروں تلے ہے دُور تک یہ زمیں
اور تو اپنا کوئی نہیں اور تو اپنا کوئی نہیں

بچپن میں کھیلے غم سے زر دھن گھروں کے بیٹے
پھولوں کی سیج نہیں کانٹوں پہ ہم ہیں لیٹے
دُکھ میں رہے سو غم سہے دِل یہ کہے
روٹی جہاں ہے سورگ اپنا وہیں
اور تو اپنا کوئی نہیں اور تو اپنا کوئی نہیں

میں ہر اک پل کا شاعر ہوں
ہر اک پل میری کہانی ہے
ہر اک پل میری ہستی ہے
ہر اک پل میری جوانی ہے

دل ناامید تو نہیں ناکام ہی تو ہے
لمبی ہے غم کی شام مگر شام ہی تو ہے

میں زندگی کا ساتھ نبھاتا چلا گیا
ہر فکر کو دھوئیں میں اُڑاتا چلا گیا

جیبیں ہیں اپنی خالی کیوں دیتا ورنہ گالی
وہ سنتری ہمارا وہ پاسباں ہمارا

ہم محنت کش اس دُنیا سے جب اپنا حصہ مانگیں گے
اک باغ نہیں اک کھیت نہیں ہم ساری دنیا مانگیں گے

کئی یادوں کے چہرے ہیں کئی قصے پُرانے ہیں
تری سو داستانیں ہیں تیرے کتنے فسانے ہیں
مگر اک وہ کہانی ہے جو اب مجھ کو ستاتی ہے
زندگی آرہا ہوں میں

میری ہاتھوں کی گرمی سے پگھل جائیں گی زنجیریں
میرے قدموں کی آہٹ سے بدل جائیں گی تقدیریں
اُمیدوں کے دیے لے کر یہ سب تیرے لیے لے کر
زندگی آرہا ہوں میں

ENDNOTES

1 Our account of the formation and the history of the Progressive Writers' Association has drawn from a variety of sources, foremost among them being Carlo Coppola's magisterial 1975 dissertation (Carlo Coppola, 1975, *Urdu Poetry, 1935-1970: The Progressive Episode*. Unpublished doctoral dissertation, University of Chicago). In addition, see Ali Sardar Jafri, 1959, *Taraqqi Pasand Adab*, Aligarh: Anjuman-e Taraqqi-e Urdu; Sajjad Zaheer, 1959, *Raushnai*, New Delhi: Azad Kitaab Ghar; Ali Sardar Jafri, 1984, *Taraqqi Pasand Tehrik ki Nisf Sadi,* New Delhi: Delhi University Press; Amar Amiri, 1991, *Taraqqi Pasand Adab: Ek Tanqeedi Jaayeza,* Calcutta: Osmania Book Depot; Ralph Russell, 1999, 'Leadership in the All-India Progressive Writers' Movement, 1935-1947,' in Ralph Russell, *How Not to Write the History of Urdu Literature and Other Essays on Urdu and Islam,* New Delhi: Oxford University Press, pp. 69-93. Russell's essay was originally published in 1977.

2 Carlo Coppola, *ibid*, p. 76.

3 'Nirala' was an enthusiastic supporter of the movement, a staunch opponent of the caste system and an advocate of solidarity among various caste and religious groups; his poem 'Kukurmutta' (Mushroom) exemplifies these sentiments in a very economical fashion:

Khaansaama, baavarchi aur chobdaar
Sipahi, saees, bhishti, ghudsavaar
Tamjan vaale kuch desi kahaar

Naaee, dhobi, teli, tamboli, kumhaar
Feelwaan, oontwaan, gadeewaan
Ek khaasa Hindu-Muslim khaandaan

Chefs, cooks and doormen
Foot soldiers, stable-hands, water-carriers, horsemen
Bearing their equipment, some native palanquin-bearers
Barbers, washermen, oilers, betel-sellers, potters
Elephant-mahouts, camel-riders, cart-drivers
What a full Hindu-Muslim family.

4 See Ali Sardar Jafri, *op. cit.*, pp. 40-42.

5 Reprinted in *Bisvin Sadi Mein Jan Kala,* edited by Jan Natya Manch, New Delhi, 2000, pp. 74-88.

6 Except perhaps its predecessors Sir Sayyid/Hali/Azad.

7 Henceforth, we use the term Progressives as a shorthand to refer to the Urdu poets of this tradition.

8 *In the Mirror of Urdu: Recompositions of Nation and Community 1947-1965* by Aijaz Ahmad, Indian Institute of Advanced Study, Simla, p. 28.

9 As Aijaz Ahmad (*ibid*, p. 11) puts it 'the bulk of the writers of Urdu at the time of the Partition constituted, regardless of religious or regional origin, an identifiable social group, that is, a community with a dense and shared structure of feeling, which lasted far beyond the Partition itself, despite the massive demographic dislocations in the ensuing years; that a secularist belief in the composite culture of Hindus and Muslims in India was the predominant ideological position in this community.'

10 Although formally issued during the conference establishing the All Pakistan Progressive Writers' Association, the manifesto of the APPWA had already been 'in effect' since the change in the line of the CPI after its 1948 Congress. The new, more militant party-line, called the Ranadive doctrine after the new Secretary General of the CPI, officially declared the end of the strategy of the United Front. The peasant struggles in Telangana and elsewhere, and their brutal suppression by the new 'socialist' government of post-colonial India, had resulted in the changed strategy as well as the changed analysis of the Indian national bourgeoisie and its political leadership represented by Nehru and Sardar Vallabhbhai Patel. The new line was a shift from the old United Front line of anti-imperialism to one

of anti-capitalism and anti-feudalism, the two poles around which communist strategy in the colonial and post-colonial countries has historically revolved.

11 As the secretary of APPWA, Ahmad Nadeem Qasmi argued in a report on these years to the association, and as many Pakistani communists have variously admitted, the new strategy was one of Left adventurism, and was based on a misconception that Pakistan was now a capitalist state, and that the communist movement in India and Pakistan had entered a new stage – one of militant revolution. Ranadive admitted this in his self-criticism before the CPI in 1950 when he was replaced as the General Secretary.

12 See, for instance, the issue titled *People's Art in the Twentieth Century: Theory and Practice* brought out by the Jan Natya Manch, July 1999-September 2000; *On Whose Side Are You, Masters of Culture,* 1987, Progressive Publishers; 'Questions of Culture' by Antonio Gramsci, in *Selections from Cultural Writings*, 1985, Lawrence and Wishart.

13 Speakers at the Conference for the Reform of Urdu Literature and Poets who put together a collection titled *Madaava* (edited by Furqat Kakorwi) deployed satire and parodies to critique, among other things, the free verse employed by the progressive writers, their quotidian themes, and their use of unconventional tropes.

14 p. 67.

15 Sonagachi is the red-light district of Calcutta, Chowringee, its wealthy neighbourhood.

16 This thought was given voice by C.M. Naim at a conference presentation.

17 Many of the poems quoted in this book, including this one, are fragments of longer poems. We have tried to use representative verses that minimize losses in narrative continuity.

18 The iconic betrayer in Indian history, who sided with the British in the battle of Plassey in 1757, the site of the East India Company's first military triumph, which formally inaugurated colonial rule in India. Clive defeated Nawab Siraj-ud-daulah, who is referred to as 'Siraj' in the same line of the poem.

19 Maharani Lakshmi Bai of Jhansi fought the British in India's first battle of independence in 1857, and was killed in the conflict.

20 After the 1857 revolt was suppressed, Bahadur Shah Zafar, the last Mughal king, was exiled to Burma.

21 Tipu Sultan, who was the ruler of Mysore, in the late eighteenth

century, fought a series of battles with the British before being killed in the battle of Srirangapatna in 1799.

22 The heads of Bahadur Shah Zafar's two sons were reportedly presented to him on a tray during his exile in Burma.

23 *Savera*, Lahore, No. 4, p. 4, 1947.

24 *1948 Ka She'ri Adab*, *Savera*, Lahore, No. 5 and No. 6, 1948.

25 The date when India constituted itself as a republic.

26 Ali Sardar Jafri, *op. cit.*, pp. 17-22.

27 See, for instance, Faiz's translation of 'A Letter from Prison' (*Zindaan Se Ek Khat*) in Faiz, 1981, *Sham-e Shehr-e Yaaraañ*, Lahore: Karwan Press, p. 109.

28 Carlo Coppola, *op. cit.*, p. 641.

29 The reference here is to the United Nations.

30 This couplet is 'borrowed' from a poem by the Persian classical poet, Hafiz.

31 The 'night of the wretched' refers to the night that followed the martyrdom of Imam Husain at Karbala in 61 AH. This event is often used as a metaphor for idealism, personal courage and great grief.

32 A battle in Islamic history known for heavy casualties.

33 For a comprehensive and empathic treatment of the representation of the Palestinian struggle in Urdu poetry, see Shahab Ahmed, 1998, 'The Poetics of Solidarity: Palestine in Modern Urdu Poetry,' *Alif*, 18, pp. 29-64.

34 Marshall Berman, 1987, *All That is Solid Melts into Air: The Experience of Modernity,* Hammondsworth: Penguin, p. 311.

35 Referring, no doubt, to other markers of progress, such as hydroelectric dams and nuclear power.

36 Of course, it is important to note that it is not just any random 'foreign' achievement which is so appropriated; it is a Soviet one.

37 See Altaf Husain Hali, 1948, *Muqaddama-e Sher-o Shaa'iri* (Ed. Rafiq Hasan). Allahabad: Rai Sahib Lala Ram Dayal Agarwal. For a more detailed discussion on Hali's *Muqaddama,* see Carlo Coppola, 1975, pp. 4-12.

38 See, for example, the treatment of the PWA in Ralph Russell, 1992, *The Pursuit of Urdu Literature,* London: Zed Books, pp. 34-48.

39 For a detailed discussion of this trend, see Harbans Mukhia, 1999, 'The Celebration of Failure as Dissent in Urdu *Ghazal*', *Modern Asian Studies*, 33:4, pp. 861-881.

40 Chengiz Khan and Nadir Shah are notorious in Indian history as raiders and despoilers of local wealth.

41 A gathering of kings in Hindu mythology. Serves here as a metaphor for an assembly of the elite.

42 Eeshwar being one of the ways Hindus refer to God; Allah is the Muslims' name for God.

43 Yves Thoraval, 2000, *The Cinemas of India* (1896-2000), New Delhi: MacMillan, p. 55.

44 Nasreen Munni Kabir, 1999, *Talking Films: Conversations on Hindi Cinema with Javed Akhtar*, New Delhi: Oxford University Press, p. 51.

45 *ibid* p. 51.

46 As an aside, it is interesting to note that Hindi film comedians often chose to take on Christian names such as Johnny Walker, Polson, Charlie, Johnny Lever; but that is another story.

47 Yogendra Malik, 1988, 'Socialist Realism and Hindi Novels' in *Marxist Influences and South Asian Literature*, edited by Carlo Coppola, New Delhi: Chanakya Publications, p. 115.

48 See Yogendra Malik, *ibid*, p. 115 and Mukul Kesavan, 1994, 'Urdu, Awadh and the Tawaif: The Islamicate Roots of Indian Cinema', in *Forging Identities* edited by Zoya Hasan, New Delhi: Kali for Women, pp 244-257. Kesavan also talks about the influence of Hindi literary stalwarts such as Bharatendu Harishchandra, Pramath Nath Mitra and Thibo Babu in the role Hindi writers played in the domain of popular culture.

49 See the entry on Guru Dutt in Ashish Rajadhyaksha and Paul Willemen, 1994, *Encyclopaedia of Indian Cinema*, New Delhi: Oxford University Press, p. 93.

50 Quoted in Yves Thoraval, *op. cit.*, p. 50.

51 Peter Manuel, 1993, *Cassette Culture: Popular Music and Technology in North India,* New Delhi: Oxford University Press.

52 The instructions given to these lyricists included ones like 'write this verse without using the "m" sound' since saying anything with "m" in it required the lips to come together and would interfere with the lip-synch of the song'.

53 In Nasreen Munni Kabir, *op. cit.*, p. 123. This logic presumably leads Akhtar (in our opinion, an outstanding lyricist) to write songs like: *Aap kitne sweet kitne nek ho; Birthday ka jaise koi cake ho* (You are so sweet and virtuous; Just like a birthday cake). Sweet, OK. But a virtuous cake?!

54 Manuel, *op.cit*, p. 9.

55 See, for example, Jyotindra Das Gupta, 1970, *Language, Conflict and*

National Development: Group Politics and National Language Policy in India, Berkeley: University of California Press.

56 Mushirul Hasan, 1997, *Legacy of a Divided Nation: Indian Muslims Since Independence*, New Delhi: Oxford University Press. Hasan also recalls Mohsinul Mulk's poignant verse that symbolized Urdu's plight, *Chal saath, ke hasrat dil-e mahroom se nikle, Aashiq ka janaaza hai, zara dhoom se nikle* (Walk along, that the defeated heart may fulfil its [last] desire, After all, it is a lover's corpse, give it a flamboyant burial), p. 160.

57 One of the best sources is probably Christopher R. King, 1994, *One Language, Two Scripts: The Hindi Movement of the Nineteenth Century,* New Delhi: Oxford University Press.

58 Aijaz Ahmed, 1996, 'In the Mirror of Urdu: Recompositions of Nation and Community 1947-65'. In *Lineages of the Present*, New Delhi: Tulika, pp. 205-208.

59 For example, Sadhvi Rithambara uses words like *naarebaazi*, *naam-o nishaañ*, *lalkaar, shaitaan, dushman*, etc. routinely in her speeches, while her poetry is littered with words that would conventionally be seen as Urdu.

60 While we use Urdu in the fashion that is commonly accepted, we subscribe to the view that the linguistic distinctions between Hindi and Urdu are arbitrary.

61 An interesting instance of this is offered by Javed Akhtar, who says that Majrooh Sultanpuri was the poet who first used the term *sanam* (literally: idol) to refer to a beloved. Now, it is a staple form of addressing a lover in Hindi film songs.

62 For purposes of economy, we have only included a single sample for each poet. For a more comprehensive listing, see *http://www.cs.wisc.edu /~navin/india/songs/.*

63 See the searchable database of Hindi film songs at *http://www.cs.wisc.edu /~navin/india/songs/,* where it is possible to retrieve the songs by lyricist. An interesting exercise would be to compare the 300+ lyricists found at this site with another very detailed database available at *http://www.urdupoetry.com.* This website maintained by Nita Awatramani cites around 350 poets, and at least 100 names are common across both these databases, yet another piece of empirical evidence of the depth of relationship between Urdu poetry and Hindi cinema.

64 For a brief history of the linkage between the PWA and Indian cinema, see Ashish Rajadhyaksha and Paul Wilemen, 1998, *op. cit.*, p. 180.

65 This song is adapted from Kaifi's poem 'Andeshe' (Premonitions).

66 While this ghazal has traditionally been attributed to Zafar, Javed Akhtar

informs us that this was actually written by his grandfather Muzter Khairabadi. See Nasreen Munni Kabir, 2005, *Talking Songs: Javed Akhtar in Conversation with Nasreen Munni Kabir*, New Delhi: Oxford University Press, p. 36.

67 In a lighter vein, Kaifi Azmi once compared this practice to digging a grave ahead of time and demanding a corpse of the right dimension!

68 Even Ghalib was not beyond such sycophancy. In the last ghazal of his *divaan,* he makes obsequious references to a financial patron, *Diya hai khalq ko bhi ta use nazar na lage, bana hai aish Tajammul Husain Khaañ ke liye* (God has bestowed riches on the world to protect him from envy, Otherwise, all wealth was meant for Tajammul Husain Khan).

69 The ghazal is structured relatively strictly and is made up of five to twenty autonomous couplets. Each line of the ghazal has an identical meter and rhythm. The couplets follow a rhyme scheme that goes aa, ba, ca, da, etc. The first two lines and the second line of every other couplet typically have a common end-rhyme called the *radeef* which is preceded by the rhyming *qaafiya*. As an example, here are two couplets from a ghazal written by Hasrat Mohani and used in the film *Nikaah* (Marriage, 1981):

Chupke chupke raat din aansoo bahaana yaad hai
Hum ko ab tak aashiqi ka voh zamaana yaad hai
Khainch lena voh mera parde ka kona daf'atan
Aur dupatte meiñ tera voh moonh chhupaana yaad hai

Those nights and days of tear shedding, I still remember
Yes, that era of intense loving, I still remember
Me suddenly pulling away the curtain between us
And you behind your *dupatta* hiding, I still remember.

The *radeef* in this ghazal is the phrase 'yaad hai' which is found at the end of the first two lines and is repeated at the end of every second line of the succeeding couplets. The rhyming *qaafiyas* are *bahaana, zamaana* and *chhupaana.*

70 Akhtar Husain Raipuri, a socialist literary critic, had written a landmark essay in 1935 titled 'Adab Aur Zindagi' (Literature and Life) in which he had criticized the format of ghazal for being nothing more than the plaything of the rich and the indolent. The Progressives endorsed this view.

71 Peter Manuel, *op. cit.*, pp. 131-152. Also see an instructive table in the same book on pp. 297-298, that lists examples of songs in the 1980s and early 1990s based on Western tunes.

72 The song is very similar in rhyme and meter to an older communist organizing song that includes the line *Hum har ek desh ke jhande pe ek laal sitaara maangenge* (On every country's flag, we will demand a red star).

73 See, for instance, his commentary in Nasreen Munni Kabir, 1999, *op. cit.*.

74 The poet's nom de plume, usually inserted in the last verse of a ghazal as a mark of authorship. Most poets become known by their *takhallus* such as Kaifi (Athar Hussain Rizvi), Firaq (Raghupati Sahai), Sahar (Mahendar Singh Bedi), etc.

75 Sahir's conflicted relationship with Pakistan is reflected in the following ironic verse: *Chalo us kufr ke ghar se salaamat aa gaye lekin; Khuda ki mamlekat meiñ sokhta khaanoñ pe kya guzri* (Thank God we arrived safe from the land of infidels; But in God's own kingdom, what happened to the broken-hearted?).

76 Carlo Coppola, *op. cit.*, p. 611.

77 *Ibid*, p. 40-41.

78 Nikolai Bukharin, 1934, 'Poetry, Poetics, and the Problems of Poetry in the USSR.' *http://www.marxists.org/archive/bukharin/works/1934/poetry/1.htm*

79 Christopher Caudwell, 1955, *Illusion and Reality: A Study of the Sources of Poetry*. New York: International Publishers, p. 68.

80 George Thomson, 1945, *Studies in Ancient Greek Society*. New York: International Publishers, p 27.

81 This refers to the Quranic verse about creation (Maryam: 35), where it is said of God: '... he merely says to it 'Be' and it is.' 'Kun' translates to 'be' in Arabic.

82 We are grateful to our friends, particularly Saadia Toor (who should, in all honesty, be listed here as a co-author), for their help with this chapter. We also want to point out that feminist poetry and an analysis of these works has a vibrant history in Pakistan. See, for instance, Neelam Hussain, Samiya Mumtaz, and Rubina Saigol (eds.), 1997, *Engendering the Nation State, Volumes I and II*, Lahore: Simorgh Publications; and Jawaria Khalid and Samina Rahman (ed.), 1995, *Apni Nigaah: Auraton Ki Likhi Takhleeqaat Aur Tanqeedi Jayeza*, Lahore: ASR Publications.

83 Admittedly, some might dispute this claim, citing the example of the ghazal in which both the lover and the beloved are referred to in male terms. However, the themes of these poems and the actions of

its protagonists, particularly in the context of the times, leave us with little doubt about the gender of the subjects/objects of the poet's voice.

84 Rukhsana Ahmad (editor and translator), 1990, *Beyond Belief*, Lahore: ASR Publications, p. iii.

85 *ibid*, p. ii.

86 The charge of masculinity was most often thrown at Kishwar Naheed because of her blunt personality and her even more blunt poetry.

87 Both Fehmida Riyaz and Kishwar Naheed were targeted repeatedly by the state. Fourteen cases of sedition were filed against the magazine edited by Fehmida Riyaz, one of which carried the death sentence. Riyaz had to go into exile to India along with her family. Naheed was constantly harassed in her job as a civil servant and frequently threatened. Cases were filed against her as well. Clearly, both were seen as threats to the state.

88 A standard way of beginning an address to the prince or emperor.

89 This poem can be interestingly juxtaposed against Ishrat Afreen's 'Adhoore Aadmi se Guftagu' (Dialogue with an Incomplete Man) in which the poet declares:

Maiñ tumheñ apna idraak-o-ehsaas kis taraah dooñ?
Fikr ke is safar meiñ tumheñ saath kiss taraah looñ?

How can I share my thoughts and feelings with you?
How can I take you along on this journey of the intellect?

Despite his 'artistic skills ... stature ... personality', the man being addressed by Afreen is seen by her as no more mature than a callow boy see:

Sirf ek ladke ho tum
Jo ke roti hui ladkiyoñ
Ya udaanoñ se mahroom zakhmi-badan titliyoñ
Saahil se bandhi kishtiyoñ
Fakhtaon ke toote paroñ meiñ sisakti hui lazzat-aazaarioñ meiñ panaaheñ talaashe
Jo khilandari si khwahish ke peeche lapakte hue,
Apne aadarsh bhi tod de

You are a mere boy

Who is attracted to
Weeping girls
Wounded and flightless butterflies
Boats anchored at the shore
And who seeks sanctuary in the simpering pleasures found in the broken wings of a dove
Who for the sake of immature desires
Will sacrifice his principles

90 Section 144 in the Penal Code is used to restrict assembly of people in public spaces, a common law deployed to prevent public gatherings and therefore, pre-empt dissent.

91 Samir Amin's term.

92 Rukhsana Ahmad, *op. cit.*, p. iv.

93 Jafri's commitment to the nation-state, was formally articulated in his address to the 1936 PWA convention. His speech titled 'On the Formation of the Hindustani Nation and the Problem of its National Language' is available in Sudhi Pradhan (Ed.), 1985, *Marxist Cultural Movement in India: Chronicles and Documents (Vol. III)*, Calcutta: Pustak Bipani, pp. 156-214.7.

94 This poem is obviously inspired by a ghazal by Mirza Ghalib, which begins *Gulshan meiñ bandobast ba rang-e digar hai aaj* (The arrangement in the garden is different today).

95 The imagery is derived from Karbala, when the martyred Imam Husain's head was paraded impaled on a spear, and his family imprisoned.

www.ingramcontent.com/pod-product-compliance
Ingram Content Group UK Ltd.
Pitfield, Milton Keynes, MK11 3LW, UK
UKHW041631190726
13854UKWH00006B/2418

9 788186 939260